**Halfway Houses:
Community-
Centered
Correction and
Treatment**

Halfway Houses: Community-Centered Correction and Treatment

Oliver J. Keller, Jr.
Florida Division of Youth Services

Benedict S. Alper
Boston College

Heath Lexington Books
D. C. Heath and Company
Lexington, Massachusetts

Library of Congress Number: 72-116684

To Our Daughters, Alison, Louisa and Fredrika and "the community" of their future . . .

Contents

Foreword

It is difficult to train an aviator in a submarine. He can learn theory, one can discuss aeronautical and navigational problems with him; if funds and space allow he may even be provided with a simulated trainer; but, sooner or later, if he is to fly, he must try and retry his wings aloft, preferably guided and assisted. So it is with the prison and the reformatory as training grounds for responsible community life.

To the extent that we pursue rehabilitative purposes in our institutions for criminals and young offenders we require graduated release procedures: working-out, halfway houses, sheltered hostels, group homes. "Halfway" is an essential concept of enlightened corrections.

We talk of rehabilitation, but that word is a misnomer. Those who come to the correctional system usually need *habilitation* rather than *rehabilitation*. Their social setting and their personal development were antipathetic to, and inadequate for, a conforming and productive life, long before they were convicted. It is a task larger than readapting the convicted offender; it requires perception of the chasm between the institution and the subculture in which, typically, the offender has lived and to which he will return. Bridges must be built between the institution and the community.

The President's Commission on Law Enforcement and the Administration of Justice was thus both practical and hardheaded in its stress on Community Based Corrections as a central technique of bringing efficiency and decency into our present squalid, overcrowded and inadequately funded penal systems, local, state and federal. It is an important method of reducing recidivism. No one knows precisely the contribution that crimes committed by those we have previously convicted and sentenced makes to the total incidence of crime, but it is agreed that it is no insubstantial part. Each increment of adapting the convicted offender to a crime-free life helps to reduce crime, and the fear of crime, that now adversely condition the quality of life for us all, particularly in our cities.

The halfway house and the community treatment center function not only as release procedures. Equally, they serve as alternatives to institutional commitment. Further, as yet less frequently realized, they should be used as alternatives to the institutional recommitment of certain paroled prisoners and young offenders. They are then halfway-back houses; halfway-in houses; and, if the phrase be forgiven, *out*houses.

Keller's and Alper's book, drawing together practice and theory on correctional halfway houses and community treatment centers, will contribute to more effective community protection. Further, to the reader's relief, it avoids that convoluted jargon that baroquely decorates much penological literature. It speaks with direct force to professional and social concerns.

The Center for Studies in Criminal Justice of the University of Chicago supported the data-gathering on which this book is based. We were fortunate in obtaining two such practical scholars, such thoughtful practitioners, as Keller and Alper to the task. It is a privilege for us to be associated with what will be an important contribution to correctional practice.

Norval Morris

Julius Kreeger Professor of
Law and Criminology
Director, Center for Studies in
Criminal Justice,
University of Chicago Law School

Preface

This book is the product of the collaboration of two persons who share a common view of the correctional field: both its failures and its areas of hopeful accomplishment. We met in the course of our separate pursuits of more effective ways of treating offenders, thereafter joining forces in seeking out what might be considered to be the best programs to be found anywhere in the United States. We here pool our findings and our convictions for those who share with us the resolve that newer and more humane, as well as more effective treatment methods, for the offenders in our society must and can be found.

While the young and youthful offender is the main focus of this presentation, we are aware, as will be the reader, that much of what is contained within has immediate and direct application to the adult offender as well.

The rate of failure from our fixed institutions for young and old offenders has remained more constant through the years than any other index upon which we rely — cost of living, Dow-Jones, or the annual precipitation of rain. An average of the recidivism rates reported by the most reliable researchers runs consistently in a range from one-half to two-thirds. No other facility created by our society for dealing with any other area of social pathology which showed such a consistently high rate of failure could so long endure. Yet, year after year — century after century, one might say at this point — we permit the huge, impersonal, heavily guarded penitentiaries, prisons, and reformatories of this nation to grind out 98% of their inmates back into society, knowing that most of those so released will be back in custody before many months have passed.

As proof that our society refuses to heed the lesson taught by this high failure rate, we continue to proliferate such institutions, whose only difference is their modernity of gadgetry and electronic controls, and in the enormity of their cost. Current building costs now run in the vicinity of $20,000 to $25,000 per inmate cell. At prevailing interest rates, this means an annual carrying cost for capital building expenditure of something over $1500 a year per inmate, just for interest on the bonds issued. Added to this are per capita costs which currently threaten to run as high as $10,000 per year in certain public institutions for children. These institutions and these costs derive from the widely held and seldom questioned premise that the maximum or medium security needs of a small number of convicted offenders shall be permitted to dictate the conditions under which the great majority of offenders, who require no such rigid controls, shall be held. If every patient received in a hospital were to be treated as a dangerously contagious case requiring tight quarantine controls, this would constitute a parallel — though admittedly exaggerated — to our attitudes toward inmates of our penal and reform stations.

Most of these institutions are too large. Most of their inmates are held under overlong sentences. Most of the programs designed for their treatment are ineffective. None of them can afford the expensive individualized therapy which the condition of many of their charges warrants. Most of these charges are released into the community in full awareness that their first ninety days of freedom are the most precarious. Seldom is anything done to provide the supportive care at this stage which can help them to deal constructively with this period of danger and to reintegrate them into society.

It is our contention that new approaches are needed desperately at this time to cope with what appears to be — despite all the criticism that can be made of the statistics upon which such a conclusion is based — a greater burden of criminal behavior than any other society has ever before experienced. Unless we are to find ourselves swamped under this burden, we must boldly seek out and resolutely adopt measure for coping with it, measures which must be beyond anything this country has ever before attempted.

At the same time we raise the alarm, we aim to present two suggested remedies, both based on our observations — as reported in these pages — and on our common viewpoint toward those observations.

The first is that as criminal activity originates in the community, the community has some responsibility for dealing with it. Hence the idea of the community residential center. Regarding this we submit a wide range of ongoing examples.

The second is that the subculture in which most delinquents and criminals dwell and make their way is impervious to the exhortations of the correctional "establishment" and proof against any but the most extensive — and expensive — psychotherapeutic thrust. It is within that subculture, within the peer group, within the orbit of the gang values from outside the institution which constitutes itself within, that a way can be found to break the hold of the subculture and free the individual, through self awareness, through understanding and through self-motivated redirection, to enter upon a way of life which is basically more acceptable both to himself and to society. This approach is through what is come to be known as guided group interaction, a technique now more than twenty-five years old, which is finally come into its own.

Since Adam and Eve were hurled from the Garden, both to atone their transgressions and to find salvation through the sweat of their brows, mundane judges and their colleagues in the correctional field have been caught up in the same dilemma. We incarcerate to punish, to redress a wrong, at the same time hoping against hope that some one, some method, will somehow get across to the offender that only in his correction and rehabilitation will he be able to make his way back to constructive membership in society. Caught between these opposing philosophies, it is no wonder that the great majority of released offenders fall back into criminal activity as the only way of life which is, at least, consistent with their outlook, needs and resources.

At this writing, in the State of Florida, a program is under way to integrate all the services for delinquent children in institutions, foster homes, halfway houses and on parole, within one unified approach: the provision of guided group interaction services for these children. This is the first instance, to our knowledge, where an entire state system has accepted and attempted to put into practice a consistent approach toward all the children committed to it by the courts. By the time this book is published, some tentative and preliminary results of this attempt may be available. Meanwhile, the reader is invited to read what follows against the knowledge that what is said here is being applied in practice, that what is described and commented on here is not one more tome to take its place alongside the miles of researches and reports on the problem of antisocial conduct and convicted offenders. Here is both a description of a hopeful new "ferment in the field" as Professor Daniel Glaser of Rutgers University has called it, and a blueprint for those legislators, administrators and concerned citizens who realize that the time is growing very short in America for finding more effective ways of dealing with this problem.

For our times are marked by a growing realization that many of the problems for which we have traditionally sought direction and support from government — at all levels — may have to find the solution ultimately in these very communities where the inadequacies of present dealing are most keenly felt. The education of our children, the safety of our neighborhoods, the equitable and democratic resolution of the crises in housing and urban living are increasingly the concern and the immediate object of citizen awareness and action. Crime as the paramount domestic problem confounding our nation is not, and need not be — as we attempt to point out in these pages — beyond the pale of effective community action, through the rehabilitation of offenders, and ultimately, as a result, the prevention of further antisocial behavior.

This book originated as a report prepared for the Ford Foundation, which funded an inquiry into community-based correctional programs. Through the resources of the Center for Studies of Criminal Justice of the University of Chicago Law School, contacts were initiated with all the states, as well as with Great Britain, Australia, Denmark, and Canada.

During the two-year period of this study, answers to questionnaires were received from forty states. The authors also made personal visits to eighty-one halfway houses, group foster homes, "urban homes," apartment complexes, special day care centers, for both probationers and parolees, residential and nonresidential, in twenty-two states. This field material was supplemented by countless interviews at the federal, state and local levels, with correctional administrators, social agencies, clinics, courts and probation services, parole boards, universities and research institutes. The resulting mass of information was then critically appraised by the two coauthors whose professional life has been spent in the field of crime and delinquency, with special reference to children and young people.

To those who made this venture possible: the Ford Foundation for its financial support and for the encouragement and guidance of Dr. Robert W. Chandler, our sincere thanks. To Norval Morris, of the University of Chicago Law School, our gratitude for his initiation of this project, his wise counsel, and his kindness and patience during the throes through which any project, having merit, must pass. The Center secretary, Anna Reuter, was a constant and capable reliance, editorial as well as secretarial. Our appreciative thanks are extended to Joseph C. Basta and Jerry F. Boren, sociology students at Boston College, who competently assisted in the preparation of footnotes and index, and to Sandra Reitman for indefatigable secretarial aid.

It is no small part of our satisfaction in presenting these findings and conclusions for the consideration of other interested persons, that out of this joint concern and common pursuit has come a deep and abiding friendship between us.

Oliver J. Keller, Jr.
Benedict S. Alper

**Halfway Houses:
Community-
Centered
Correction and
Treatment**

By Way of Introduction

1   . . . In Retrospect

The Bloody Past

Present interest in halfway houses and other community measures as a humane approach to the treatment of delinquents and criminals is of relatively recent origin. If the history of mankind has been one of intolerance and cruelty toward the nonconformist, it has been nothing less than savage toward the antisocial and the criminal.

Dickens referred to his native land in the later 1700's and early 1800's as "one of the most bloody-minded countries on the earth,"[1] a place where the public was invited to view not only hangings, but also whipping, burning, disemboweling, and dismembering.[2] In that same period in England, the total number of offenses for which the death penalty could be prescribed was 222.[3] Of every ten criminals hanged, nine were under twenty-one, many of them no older than nine or ten years of age.[4] Persons arrested for lesser offenses were thrown into verminous jails in which were commingled adults and children, males and females, the debtor and the felon, the convicted along with persons awaiting trial.

American Efforts

English and Continental reformers were at work during this same period to ameliorate such conditions, but it is heartening to recall that some of the earliest successes also appeared in the United States. Many of the first arrivals from Europe had come here to escape brutality and injustice. It is worthy of note that Dr. Benjamin Rush of Philadelphia, who pioneered in improving the lot of both the "lunatic" and the criminal, was also a signer of the Declaration of Independence. Just before the turn of the nineteenth century, the Quakers established Philadelphia's Walnut Street Jail — the forerunner of the modern penitentiary.[5] Here, for the first time, were confined persons who had committed serious crimes against both persons and property. Solitary confinement and hard labor now replaced the death sentence. New York shortly followed with a new institution at Auburn.[6] Here silence was the rule, whether in solitary confinement at night or in congregate work during the day in the prison shops.

By 1842, when Dickens visited the United States, he wrote: "In an American prison or house of correction, I found it difficult to persuade myself that I was really in jail — a place of ignominious punishment and endurance."[7]

While the United States then, for a time, pioneered in adult penal treatment, it lagged with respect to child offenders. In Rome as early as 1703, Pope

Clement XI had established an institution to separate delinquent boys from adult criminals.[8] Known as the Hospice of San Michele and advanced for its time, it nevertheless sanctioned flogging and isolation in tiny cells. Not until 1825 was the first institution for delinquent children established in New York City,[9] followed soon after by Boston and Philadelphia.

American Emphasis on Large Institutions

American penology has a history of seeming dedication to large institutions. At a time when Great Britain was creating many small "approved schools," for children in trouble with the law, Massachusetts established the first public reform school in the United States in 1847, with far greater population capacity, thereby setting a precedent for similar institutions which were to follow.[10]

The same penchant for bigness is found in the construction of reformatories for offenders in their late teens and early twenties, which appeared in the 1870's. Utilizing the "points" system which had been originated by Alexander Maconchie, first in Ireland and later in Australia, the first reformatory was established at Elmira, New York, in 1876, and by 1900 twelve states had followed. If an inmate advanced in accordance with a graduated scale of conforming behavior, he could move from one grade to the next, even leaving the institution prior to expiration of his maximum sentence. Rehabilitation and reformation were to replace penitence and expiation with academic and vocational training helping to pave the road to freedom.[11]

Growing Concern for Children

The establishment of separate schools for younger offenders paralleled other nineteenth century concerns for children, as exemplified by compulsory public education, shelters for the dependent and neglected, and restrictions on child labor. In 1899 the first juvenile court was created in Cook County, Chicago followed, within a relatively short period of time, by the child guidance clinic as a diagnostic and therapeutic adjunct to the court.

Concern for emotionally disturbed children has grown with the increase in delinquency which has marked the past quarter century. Shortly after World War II, a number of investigations brought to light brutal conditions and obvious mismanagement in our public schools for committed delinquents. Albert Deutsch, a newspaperman, wrote of the savage beatings, the use of high-pressure water hoses, and other humiliating and degrading forms of cruelty. Critics called attention to the overcrowding of state training schools which housed populations so heterogeneous as to make effective treatment impossible.[12] Sophisticated delinquents, truants and runaways, mental defectives and children on the verge of psychosis[13] were all treated alike with a dosage of extreme regimentation and an overemphasis on discipline. Crowded dormitories, lack of privacy and diversions, conduced inevitably to homosexuality. Inadequate salaries failed to attract trained clinicians or "cottage parents" from any but the lowest socioeducational levels. While some of these parents attempted to deal warmly with their charges, others reacted rigidly and brutally to any infraction of institution rules.[14]

Long periods of institutional confinement wreak a destructive influence on the self-concepts of persons condemned to such patterns of humility toward staff members. The traditional custodial setting literally strips its inmates of their personal possessions and, with it, their self-pride and their identity. Ill-fitting prison-made clothing and uniforms are but the first in a "series of abasements, degradations, humiliations, and profanations of self."[15] Additional indignities, such as numbers stenciled on uniforms and shaved heads, develop the inmate's hatred not only toward institution authority but ultimately for society at large. Many prison and training school work programs are monotonously designed only to kill time. While useful in helping maintain the institution, they hardly prepare the offender for later employment in the community.[16] Good work habits cannot be instilled in a short four-hour work day. Nor can the pushing of a broom around a cell-house floor pass as "upgrading job skills" even when these are euphemistically described as ". . . training boys in the care of floors, walls, lights, and windows, regulation of light and heat, and other ventilation problems."[17] As awareness grew of the harmful monotony and abnormality of such large institutions, demand grew for other, if untried, methods of dealing with offenders.[18]

Parallels with the Mental Health Field

Two hundred years ago, both the criminal and the insane were equally the butt of public ridicule and official torment.[19] One hundred years ago, our states were erecting huge institutions for both groups — located away from the city, as if to solve crime and "insanity" by banishing its victims — both the deranged and the delinquent. Today, with increasing knowledge in the behavioral sciences, we are beginning to learn that the offender and the mental patient do not, in confinement, learn to adjust to the society of free men except in false and slavish ways, but rather they adapt to the subcultures within their particular institution, and that the longer they remain in such artificial situations, the more difficult it is for them to conduct their lives successfully when they are again on the outside.[20] Mental health associations are educating the public to the desirability of community treatment of mentally disturbed persons with the result that a wide variety of community stations are being established in local neighborhoods whose aim is both to ease the patient's transition back into the community, and to prevent his removal from his home, in the first place.

Halfway House Antecedents

The precise origins of halfway houses for youthful offenders are not entirely clear. One of the first such efforts in behalf of delinquent children — in Great Britain — bears an astonishing resemblance to present-day halfway houses. In the eighteenth century, the Philanthropic Society of London, appalled by the numbers of children who lived by begging and stealing, organized in 1788 three small cottages for such children who had been picked up in the streets. Craftsmen and their wives who lived in the cottages, each with a dozen children, taught them gardening, tailoring and shoemaking. Children nevertheless continued to be thrown into jail long after this pioneer effort. By the mid-nineteenth century, a large number of agencies provided shelter, particularly those places named after Dr. Barnardo the great British philanthropist who alone opened 112 homes during his lifetime.[21]

In our own country, community concern for the welfare of prisoners was expressed early in the development of the penitentiaries. These came into being one hundred and fifty years ago at the time that capital punishment for most offenses was largely abandoned. An important part of the thinking which underlay these early penal stations with their emphasis on solitary confinement, hard labor and repentance, included the provision of ministering services from citizens who lived outside the walls and who came into the institution to work with individual prisoners. While we, today, may look with some amusement upon such steps to lift the moral level of the convicts of that day, this should not detract from appreciation of the fact that they nevertheless represented an early attempt to bring some representation of community concern into the isolated life of the penitentiary.

Meanwhile, the idea of some kind of shelter for ex-prisoners within the community had long been known. Jean Valjean was neither the first nor the last ex-convict to find on the outside a sympathetic roof, a meal and a warm bed. That such basic provisions did not fully solve the problem is not to disparage the early efforts of those, chiefly under religious auspices, who sought to mitigate the lot of the newly released prisoner. These early shelters can be said to have borne within them the earliest seeds of the movement known today under a multiplicity of names as the community center.

Thereafter it was a logical development that probation should come into being as an expression within the community itself of the early ministering to individuals confined within walls. In time this innovation came to be widely accepted, while concomitantly in another area of social concern — the mentally ill — residence within the community began to supplement the custody given in insane asylums, as they were called, in many countries.

To the Low Countries, to Switzerland and to England goes the credit for being the first to settle persons with mental disturbances within homes — usually in small rural neighborhoods. This development can be found as early as 1870, and by 1910 it was an accepted procedure in many European countries.

Countries other than our own have been readier to think in terms of open facilities for offenders. Many releasees from European prisons can turn for help to small, homelike centers, often privately financed and with a staff consisting only of a director and his wife. Such halfway homes provide the former prisoner with a place where he can eat and sleep, but may offer little in the way of treatment.[22] Europe's "probation hostels" provide an alternative to incarceration for convicted offenders supervised in the community. As in the homes for parolees, these usually serve only a small number of men at one time.

Massachusetts, New York and Pennsylvania pioneered in the halfway house field, as they had in the development of prisons and probation. In the early 1820's, a Massachusetts Commission had urged the establishment of what would now be called halfway houses.[23] The difficulties confronting men released from prison were even then recognized as largely the result of the social stigma of imprisonment, and the related difficulty of finding employment. Some forty years after the Commission's recommendation, a halfway house for women released from institutions did open in Boston, in 1864, and operated there for about twenty years.[24] A group of Quakers in New York City in 1845, despite public indifference and hostility, opened a halfway house which has managed to survive to this day as the Isaac T. Hopper Home.[25] Another pioneering effort established in 1889 in Philadelphia — the House of Industry — continues to receive parolees from Pennsylvania prisons.[26]

In the late 1890's, the same charitable concern prompted the establishment of a temporary shelter for ex-convicts in New York City despite opposition by the American Prison Association that proliferation of such places would perpetuate "prison stigma" and create a "permanent class of undesirable citizens."[27]

This view was not shared by Maud Booth, who, with her husband, co-leader of the Volunteers of America, in September of 1896, quietly rented a large building in the Washington Heights section of Manhattan.[28] When its purpose was know, it became an object of such attention by the police that Mrs. Booth appealed for help directly to Theodore Roosevelt. Most of the first residents were from Sing Sing. Two years later this agency moved to Long Island. Known as Hope Hall, it was described as comfortably furnished, boasting a piano, phonograph and well-stocked library.

In 1903 a second Hope Hall opened in Chicago, and eventually, additional halfway houses, under the same auspices were to be found in San Francisco; New Orleans; Fort Dodge, Iowa; Columbus, Ohio; Waco, Texas; and Hampton, Florida. Parole authorities increasingly argued against them on the grounds that such association of former prisoners was forbidden by regulations. Several Hope Halls lasted for only a short time, others functioned for many years, but ultimately they all ceased operation.[29] While they lasted, however, they provided temporary shelter in pleasant surroundings quite different from overnight missions, for thousands of released prisoners. Maud Booth has never received the full measure of appreciation which her pioneering efforts merit.

Foster homes for neglected and homeless children in urban slums first appeared in Massachusetts in the 1850's. For the next twenty years, the New York Children's Society sent thousands of such children to other states.[30] While most of them fitted the description of "neglected and dependent" children, many others had also committed petty violations of the law. Since little interest was expressed in how these children were treated by their foster parents, it is not surprising to learn that hundreds of them were the objects of attempted proselytism and were otherwise exploited as unpaid servants and laborers. Yet this is the forerunner of the foster home placement idea, which has been a great reliance as a substitute for the reform school and the orphanage.

While little activity can be discovered during the 1920's and the depression years, a mission-type home known as "The Parting of the Ways" came into existence in 1932 in Pittsburgh to provide shelter for ex-offenders.[31] The Salvation Army and the Volunteers of America have over the years provided for prisoners in the dormitories they maintain for homeless men, and other "mission" agencies make temporary lodging available to ex-offenders. Not until the 1950's, when Dismas House, St. Leonard's House, and 308 West Residence appeared, however, do we see the beginnings of what is today a national halfway house movement for the care of offenders, child or adult.[32]

Summary

Corrections in America has developed at unequal rates, even though in some respects, and at some period our country has pioneered in many novel, even revolutionary schemes. Philadelphia's Walnut Street Jail was the first move away from the death penalty for major crimes. The Elmira reformatory shifted the emphasis toward rehabilitation, and away from punishment. The juvenile court was created to assure that children would be dealt with in other than adult criminal fashion. In contrast to the European experience of smaller, more open facilities, however, Americans have consistently tended to overlarge, security-oriented institutions removed from population centers. This is as true, historically, for the mentally retarded and disturbed as for the sentenced offender, child or adult.

Although early, sporadic, instances of halfway houses are found in the United States, it was not until the close of the nineteenth century, with the spread of Hope Halls, that any sizable number of prisoners were assisted. Curiously enough, it was parole, itself a forward-looking development, which played a part in the discontinuance of these first halfway houses. Not until the 1950's, with the growing dissatisfaction at high recidivism rates, combined with a new awareness of the problems facing the released prisoner, did halfway houses again appear in any number.

Even more recent are such places for delinquent children. Although enlightened treatment of problem children within the community are found in the Philanthropic Society of London in the eighteenth century, such early examples are rare indeed. When foster homes were initiated for dependent and delinquent children in the nineteenth and the first half of the twentieth centuries, stipends, if any, were extremely meager and little was done to supervise the quality of care provided by persons acting as foster parents. What we know today as the community treatment idea, residential or nonresidential, for persons halfway-in or halfway-out of the institution, for probationers and parolees, for children and adults, is largely the product of the last twenty years.[33] Its growth has eclipsed its historical antecedents; its spread confounds its sponsors no less than its opponents; by current view it bids fair to become the most memorable development in penology in the second half of the twentieth century.[34]

2

The "Halfway House" Idea

Originality and Diversity

As the term is used throughout this book, *halfway house* refers to any relatively small facility, either residential or nonresidential, usually located in or close by a city or town. Persons involved in the programs of such places participate in the daily life of the open community, either working, or going to school "outside." Devoid of the customary security provisions, a halfway house may be publicly or privately supported, be psychotherapeutically oriented or reality-based, derive from religious or secular auspices. Persons who live under its comparatively free conditions are expected to undergo a group experience of limited duration. The halfway house stands — literally — halfway between the community and the institution, and may serve persons who are released from an institution, as well as those received directly from a court.

Changing Attitudes toward Corrections

Present interest in this type of community-based facility arises from several sources, most important of which are public concern over spiraling crime rates, combined with a growing dissatisfaction with the demonstrated ineffectiveness of present methods of dealing with offenders. Pressure of another sort comes from the pertinent professions and the findings of sociology and the behavioral sciences. Humanitarian and utilitarian interests combine to urge rehabilitation, rather than punishment. The conviction grows that unless society is prepared to acknowledge and support a rising cyclical pattern of criminality, followed by arrest, trial, imprisonment and parole, some effective and positive action must be taken to help reintegrate the object of that cycle back into the community.

The halfway house represents only one positive action. There is a rising recognition that as crime, similar to other expressions of social pathology, originates in the community, responsibility both for preventing and correcting criminal behavior must originate there as well. Funds from state and federal sources as well as from foundations are becoming available for antipoverty programs, for innovative school experiments, and for community efforts against racism, citizen apathy and civic decay. Recent court decisions articulate increased concern for the rights of the accused, and the guarantee of the civil rights and liberties amendments to the federal Constitution. Within a very few state correctional systems, there is a move to substitute a diversity of treatment methods for individualized types of offenders in place of mass handling. With the realization that the maximum security needs of a few offenders should not dictate the custodial level for most, the federal government as well as state and local jurisdictions are applying work-release procedures to permit inmates to work at jobs in the free community during the day, returning to custody at night. The question which comes easily to mind does not so readily find an adequate reply: if offenders can be released from custody for a part of the day — to work or to attend school as normal citizens — what value is served by confining them at night and on weekends in secure, custodial stations? The answer may well be found in future years as the public becomes less reluctant to permit the "convict" who works in free association during the day, to sleep and live next door under equally "free" conditions.

Although halfway houses may serve wide varieties of offenders, they are basically of only two distinct types: the "halfway-in," and the "halfway-out." The halfway-in house generally serves the younger offenders — those under a court order of probation, or others who may have failed on probation and are considered worthy of another opportunity to remain in the community — still under supervision. A few of these community halfway-in houses are nonresidential — permitting their participants to continue to live at home, but requiring attendance at programs in the house for the major part of each weekday.

Opinion differs widely as to the persons to be accommodated in these houses. While the primary concern here is with the youthful offender, precise age brackets are by no means uniform. Many places which receive 17-and 18-year-olds also accommodate persons up to age 80. Some serve populations both delinquent and nondelinquent. Most halfway houses provide short-term programs; others — especially those for younger offenders — may keep them in residence for two years or longer.

By far the better known, the halfway-out facility is designed to assist persons who are ready to leave an institution and who are deemed to be in need of further help in readjusting to society. An apt parallel may be drawn between this process in the life of a convicted offender and the decompression chamber through which the deep-sea diver passes in order to adjust gradually to sea level pressures before being permitted to surface completely. Placement in the halfway-out house can be a condition of parole or a comparatively brief, community-based experience prior to release on parole. In some instances it serves as a place to which persons who may be doing poorly on parole can repair in lieu of returning to the traditional secure custodial institution.

No single definition can possibly fit or describe the wide range of places and facilities which are called — or which call themselves — halfway houses. There is a scarcity of descriptive material in the literature, and writers on the subject are frequently in disagreement as to how best to define the concept. As of this writing, no single comprehensive picture could possibly encompass the hundreds of stations which serve offenders "halfway" between the institution and the free society. The third annual meeting of the International Halfway House Association in spring, 1967, failed to arrive at any agreement with regard either to the official name for the organization, or the type of facilities entitled to belong to it. At this point it is perhaps accurate to say that a new "art" in the area of corrections is in process of development, that innovation and diversity are perhaps the only characteristics which all these places have in common.

For example, a small population is an essential characteristic of the halfway house idea and is found almost universally. Some houses accommodate as few as 10 or 12 boys or men, yet others may have facilities for 25 or 30, while the pioneer Dismas House, one of the best-known halfway houses in the United States, has accommodations for 60 men, although it is seldom fully occupied.

Most authorities maintain that a population of approximately twenty is close to ideal, permitting "informal and close interaction" among the residents.[1] Practice reveals many exceptions, however. For example, where halfway house rooms are scattered throughout a YMCA building, each boy is permitted to follow his own program of education or employment and residents of such a "house" may have little occasion to interact with one another. Some centers actively discourage their residents from associating with one another on the outside. In halfway houses of the boarding house or "mission" type, the residents often prefer to "do their own time," which results in little close association with fellow residents. Intensity of interaction between the persons whom it serves cannot be listed as a standard characteristic of all halfway houses.

Location offers a wide range of choice, as well. While some are conventional in appearance, others are private houses, converted motels, YMCA's, remodeled schools, an Odd Fellows Hall, the premises of a former parish house or mission annex, a beach club, or nursing home. Refurbished apartments may provide quarters in large middle-class buildings or in small flats in tenement areas. Some authorities advocate locations on institution grounds. Such residences may grant greater freedom and provide greater personal warmth than do others whose physical location and appearance more closely fit the halfway house stereotype.

Nor does uniformity of opinion exist with respect to group-care foster homes. A spokesman for the State of Wisconsin, while disclaiming the existence there of a halfway house program, nevertheless described his state supported group foster home service to children as "halfway" between institutions and the home community.[2] Foster homes caring for as many as eight children may well qualify as halfway house facilities, however differently they may describe themselves.

Halfway houses are found in rural settings as well as in small towns and metropolitan areas. They may be located in slum and skid row areas, in commercial or transitional areas, in working class neighborhoods, or in middle class suburbs. Behind the front door, the interiors vary greatly. Some resemble middle class, private homes, others have the appearance of a casual fraternity house, while still others pride themselves on polished floors and the placement of beds with strict military precision.

Some halfway houses designedly strive to create a family atmosphere, with substitute parents, while others are as institutional in appearance as in their staff arrangements. Of twenty-eight youth-serving residential centers responding to a recent questionnaire, ten had no employees living on the premises: in some places no adult staff members are on duty during the night.[3]

While operating generally at a lower per capita cost than do state correctional institutions, many halfway houses — both federal centers and state facilities — report the opposite to be the case. Some halfway houses which "operate on a shoestring," admit that they offer little more than room and board; others boast a wide range of services. Some halfway house programs emphasize the development of work skills and vocational guidance. Others, especially of the halfway-in variety, stress the influence of behavior and attitudes as their chief concern, with individual and group counseling services and individual psychotherapy.

Staff requirements and qualifications range from highly trained professionals to ex-convicts, as well as volunteers from the community. Attitudes range from the authoritarian, which may be but slightly removed from that of many institutions, to tolerant acceptance by permissive and understanding friends.

Admission criteria are also widely diverse. Some centers exclude offenders who have committed certain acts or exhibit deviant tendencies: arson, sexual assault, crimes of violence, alcoholism, overt homosexuality, or narcotics usage. Still others impose no restrictions whatsoever on intake. Although agreement on the part of the prospective resident to enter the program is usually considered an essential element, some community-based residences receive individuals as the result of a court order, or as a precondition to their release on parole.

One feature common to most halfway houses is that they post no special sign or plaque that might identify their purpose, or otherwise make them distinguishable.[4] Yet, this too, is not universal: a few bear their names prominently on signs lettered by their proud residents.

Confusion about halfway houses is compounded by avoidance of the term by those houses which prefer to be known as "residential treatment centers" or "rehabilitation residences." It is impossible to compile one all inclusive directory of halfway houses, and judging by the variety and individuality of some of the more recently established places (to say nothing of the rapidity of their proliferation) it may not be possible to do so in the immediate future. Proponents of the halfway house movement do not view this as a disadvantage, however, stressing that its strength lies precisely in the area of experiment and innovation.

Parallel Developments

Developments in recent years designed to bridge the gap between the closed institution and the open community include honor farms, forestry camps, prerelease centers and work-release programs. Honor farms are usually located close to, or on the grounds of, existing prisons. Men are assigned to them who are considered better-than-average risks, with records which reveal little likelihood of further threat to life or property. Although guards are stationed, supervision on these farms is less intense than within the prison; many of the men are shortly due for parole consideration and judged as unlikely to run away.

Forestry camps for offenders without either walls or fences are likewise less restrictive than institutions. In some states they accommodate between twenty and fifty boys each. While community contacts are favored, some traces of institutional life remain, like the periodic "head counts" and "bedchecks."

Prerelease programs, largely out of federal prisons and reformatories, made their appearance in the late 1940's. Located in the correctional institution, the prerelease living unit aims to facilitate the move from institution controls to independent living. Here the prisoner has a choice of civilian clothes, lives in a room of his own, and is subjected to a minimum of supervision. He is expected to attend group discussions with prospective employers, union representatives, employment officials, and parole officers. He may also be permitted to leave the institution frequently: for an interview with a prospective employer, an athletic event or musical program, or a picnic with his family.

A number of correctional systems now permit some inmates to hold jobs in the community following the example initiated many years ago by the state correctional service of Wisconsin. Under the precedent set by the so-called "Huber" law, large numbers of federal prisoners are currently enrolled in these programs, traveling by public transportation to their jobs each workday morning and returning at night to the institution. Advisory committees of citizens screen the applicants for work release programs, in order to exclude men with records which might make them ineligible for outside placement.

While these developments parallel many of the features of the halfway house and are likewise indicative of a rapidly changing lay and professional attitude toward offenders, they will not receive further attention here.

Summary

Considerable variety, even disparity, is found in the locations, treatment goals, staffing patterns, and the age and the person served by the halfway house. Its salient — and universal — feature is that it attempts to bridge the gap between the open society and the traditional institution. Community-based, absence of the stigma — and stigmata — of correctional facilities, it presents a new approach, reflective of a more enlightened public and professional attitude toward offenders. Its existence emphasizes the responsibility of the community for the phenomenon of crime which originates in the community. It accommodates both the parolee in need of assistance to find a job and a home, and the probationer whom the court prefers not to commit to an institution. Representing an enlightened innovation in American corrections, the halfway house, both "out" and "in," emphasizes the potential advantages inherent in community living. It has equal value to the offender who may be spared a prison sentence as for the parolee who faces his first few months of freedom[5] in society with a trepidation born of the overlong terms of imprisonment which so many offenders are subjected to.

From the abundance of material descriptive of halfway houses, and out of their infinite variety of approach and program, a core of basic elements characteristic of the halfway house concept can be extracted. First, halfway houses are organizationally related to corrections, either as a result of a court order or the administrative action of some public agency. Second, the halfway house idea necessarily connotes a group situation. Third, it is usually small in size, both absolutely as well as relative to the size of our overlarge penal stations. Fourth, contact with the free community is both its hallmark and its essence. Fifth, the trappings of the correctional institution — walls, fences, locked doors, uniformed guards, and weapons close at hand — are absent. Sixth, some rules and regulations, however minimal, assure order and give structure to the living situation. Last, despite varying lengths of time spent in a halfway house, the basic aim is to provide a short, intensive and transitional experience.

The Individual and the
Group Process

3 Treatment Approaches

General Comments

The common purpose of the halfway house — whether designed for the offender who might otherwise be committed to an institution, or to ease the return to society of one who has been — finds little agreement as to the manner in which its goals should be accomplished. Programs vary with individual directors even within a single state agency. "It became apparent," states a report on the halfway house concept in corrections, "that each particular program is practically an entity in itself, arrived at by people willing to experiment in a field where total confusion and ambiguity reign regarding concept and theory."[1]

Small halfway houses operating on low budgets aim at placing their treatment emphasis on the establishment of meaningful relationships between delinquents and the stable, trustworthy and "significant" adults who guide the program. No formal effort at treatment is attempted, such places preferring to regard their establishments as "homelike," where stress is laid on intimate contact between warm and nonjudgmental persons who serve as parent substitutes for their young charges. When the delinquent in such a setting once discovers that he can safely place confidence and trust in certain adults, he may then be considered ready to extend that attitude toward other adults in the outside world. This is generally the philosophy of most group-care homes. In an accepting environment, where a boy receives both love for himself and recognition for his achievements, he may find himself readier to accept support from other children, like himself, who are available for companionship and for exchange of mutual problems — and out of a common past. By such routes as this, even severely disturbed and aggressive children can be gradually led to accept socially approved standards.

Not all houses succeed in creating this family atmosphere, though they may be comfortably furnished, amply equipped and have adequate financial resources. Intimacy, flexibility and understanding of the warm, family stereotype are difficult to achieve. Overstaffing, even overprofessionalization, can result in formal scheduling of activities, in the obvious presence of such equipment as one-way mirrors, filing cabinets and recording equipment.

While there appears to be merit in having a mature, husband-and-wife team reside within a halfway house, equally effective programs are found where the staff members work an eight-hour day. The "Mom" and "Pop" house-parents who live in seem best suited for younger children, while more mature adolescents function well in, and may even prefer, relationships with staff which are more impersonal. Rapid turnover in adult leadership and consequent shifts in treatment philosophy are apt to be unsettling to children in residence, resulting in an atmosphere temporarily charged with tension.

Differing Probation and Parole Treatment Concepts

Some halfway houses for parolees are clear in their conception of their limited role, which is simply to offer the ex-prisoner the security of a place where he may eat and sleep, as well as some insulation from criminal associates and shelter from overzealous police.[2] In addition to providing this general support, such places also attempt to find employment for their residents, assist them with their family problems, and help reduce gradually the tensions attendant upon leaving long confinement for the freedom of an open society.

Other halfway houses designed for probationers deliberately avoid a "comfortable" climate, with staff members even making some effort to arouse anxiety. While the aim is not to foster unhappiness among their young charges, they do, in the words of one director, "want the pot to be boiling,"[3] or, in those of another, "It seems to me the aim is to create a degree of discomfort and uncertainty in order to foster self-examination." This discomfort is "both internal and external."[4] By avoiding too comfortable or homelike an environment, and by refusing to put staff demands and expectations in too specific terms, the aim is to create an atmosphere which will ultimately conduce to personality change.

In general, it may be said that those centers which offer an alternative to incarceration appear to be more concerned with fostering changes in delinquent behavior and attitudes than do those which serve persons released from an institution. These latter may proceed on the assumption that treatment should have taken place during the period of sentence. Parolees in such houses are encouraged to enroll in community-based training programs, are counseled regarding their social behavior and their approach to employers; are helped to fill out applications; advised as to the requirements for union affiliation or social security, and urged to discuss their conflicts and difficulties before changing jobs. One halfway house in California neatly sums up its objectives as the provision of: "recreation facilities, wholesome meals, and helpful advice for paroled young men who are looking for a job and a new start."[5]

The very opposite opinion is put forward by those who view their responsibilities as something more than merely assisting offenders during a period of transition. One of these writes:

I believe one of the biggest pitfalls a community-based program can fall into is that of assuming the "treatment job" has been taken care of in the institution. Experience has taught me that it is when individuals begin to work and interact with others in the free community that the same old problems begin to arise, and in my opinion it is a misnomer to assume that all the individual needs is room and board and assistance with getting a job.[6]

This belief finds endorsement from operators of probation halfway houses, particularly those under government auspices. In New York and New Jersey, for example, definite efforts are made to redirect the attitudes of delinquent children, who arrive from the court often outwardly passive or even cooperative, but harboring within themselves deep feelings of hostility and distrust. The halfway house must manage, within a few months, to restructure the deep-seated attitudes of such children, if commitment to an institution is to be avoided. When such boys

. . . first arrive, many of them are hostile, defiant, and rebellious. Others, while not defiant, are just as alienated, attempting to withdraw into themselves. Almost all these boys not only do not get along well with people, but they are also afraid of them. They are illprepared to face life. While in search of pleasure, and while totally concerned about themselves, they don't want to look at themselves realistically. Their hostility masks the real fear inside them. When boys first come here, they will tell you anything. They don't trust adults. They're afraid of being laughed at.[7]

Another description rounds out, in more detailed fashion, a profile of the same type of boy:

He is distrustful of everything — of his family, his peers, and authority. He has no confidence in adults, seeing them chiefly as "square Johns" or "lemons" who are trying to "mess over" him. He is fearful, often acting overly aggressive to prove himself to peers. Most of the time he is angry and hostile. In extrovert fashion, he may shout, swear, and fight. If an introvert, he may pout, refusing to say anything, or giving only short, smart answers. He is impulsive, expressing what he feels right then and there.

Despite overt expressions that he is great and good at everything he does, especially in the sexual area, he often reveals an extremely low self-concept. He generally lacks the confidence to change his ways, and whines, "I can't." Or, just the opposite is true, asserting with much braggadocio, "I can change whenever I get out, or whenever I get good and ready." Frustrated because he has been caught in some act that gives him status in his delinquent world, he feels hurt, believing the world owes him a living.

His family history often reveals disturbed associations, including divorce, separation, drinking, incest, crime or promiscuity on the part of his parents. Having learned the hard way to trust almost nobody, he considers himself a born loser. His total concern is for himself. Fearful of becoming involved with others, and then experiencing further hurt and rejection, he lacks concern for other people. Believing that his way is best, he resorts to rationalizing his behavior, and uses other persons as scapegoats. Revenge is an important part of his thinking, with much talk of getting back at persons who have presumably hurt him. He will set himself up for a "put down" by others, and then blame his own disparagement on the jealousy and hatred of such persons.

He has strong criminal tendencies, admiring delinquent ideas and attitudes. His eyes are quick to observe easy pickings, such as a car with keys in the ignition, and marks those individuals who can be easily cheated. He is convinced that might makes right, that the strongest are the best, and that the worst thing about stealing is to be caught. Lying or "conning," are second nature to the true delinquent.[8]

Formal Treatment Efforts

There appears to be greater uniformity in the claim put forward by most halfway centers that they offer "counseling" of one sort or another, than in the actual programs which they make available to their residents. Counseling may be of two general types — individual and group. A recent assessment of treatment programs in post-institutional halfway houses serving youthful offenders summarizes its findings as follows:

Group services have been one of the more common and important distinctions given in the literature comparing halfway houses with other types of small group living situations such as group foster homes; yet little information is given as to the specifics of group structure and dynamics.[9]

Ten out of eighteen respondents state that their model of group treatment is not patterned after any particular theorist, practitioner, or institution. With respect to this large number (about 55 per cent), we question the nature, quality, and effectiveness of such services.[10]

In the area of individual counseling, as with formal casework treatment, opinion is likewise extremely varied. A senior psychologist who deals with delinquents expresses his opposition to this one-to-one approach:

Individual psychotherapy has proved to be ineffective in the treatment of delinquency because most delinquent adolescents are unable to tolerate the anxiety liberated by psychotherapy. Furthermore, the adolescent resists assuming an overtly dependent role upon an adult and is fearful of closeness. Clinicians working in correctional institutions have turned increasingly to the use of group psychotherapy. However, it has proved necessary to modify the usual group therapy techniques to suit the needs and limitations of this unique population.[11]

After a six-year study of four hundred potentially delinquent girls in a vocational high school, researchers concluded that basic changes in character simply are not brought about through individual therapy.[12]

In contrast may be cited the results of a thoroughgoing experiment in California — known as PICO (Pilot Intensive Counseling Organization). This study exposed a group of delinquents in the custody of the Youth Authority to psychotherapy, on either an individual or a group basis in an attempt to determine which form was more efficacious.[13]

Success — as judged by how well the boy performed later in the community — depended upon whether or not, at time of his admission to the program, he had been "classified by clinical judgment as either amenable or nonamenable to treatment by individual counseling."[14] Of all the boys considered suitable for individual casework, those who received it did better on parole than those who were treated instead by group counseling. On the other hand, those not deemed suitable for individual casework, who were nevertheless subjected to it, reacted with a higher rate of failure than those who were exposed to group methods.[15]

The PICO experiment indicates that individual casework appears to be more effective for certain offenders than do group forms of treatment. "Probably each method has advantages for some subjects and not for others, and each method varies greatly on several dimensions, rather than being a uniform phenomenon. Furthermore, some combination of the two methods may well be optimum for most persons."[16]

In the conventional training school one-to-one contacts between boy and staff member are almost impossible to achieve with any effective frequency. Staff caseloads are so heavy that even those young people sufficiently troubled to require intensive attention rarely see a clinician more than one hour a week. Such brief encounters may permit the staff to arrive at a diagnosis but hardly to achieve the close relationships so important to the restructuring of basic attitudes, selfconcepts and values.

Though far smaller than the training school, the halfway house finds it equally difficult to provide intensive casework services, if only by reason of cost. The per capita annual cost in an eastern mental health center for children between the ages of 6 and 15 runs in the neighborhood of $10,000. Although originally individual therapy was undertaken with children here, many of whom were delinquent, therapy later shifted to a group basis.[17]

There is, of course, more to individual counseling than the formal "fifty-minute hour" of the psychoanalytic session. Offenders can be helped to establish meaningful "first friend" relationships with particular staff members.[18] What has been described as the "therapy of friendship," can be brought about in ways which would be impossible in the formal clinic setting:

I think it is pretty evident that the one-to-one classic casework interview is not effective with the majority of delinquents, but personnel of many community residential centers which use a group approach are now willing to admit that a certain degree of one-to-one relationship goes on, be it a discussion over a cup of coffee, a staff person and resident working together on some project, riding in a car or whatever the situation may be.[19]

Use of Groups

Group sessions help to ease tensions between staff and residents, and consequently to reduce administrative problems. Weekly group counseling sessions, coupled with some individual counseling, is characteristic of many halfway houses for parolees. Where a more intensive program of therapy is desired, group meetings may be held three to five times a week. The number considered desirable for a group session varies greatly. Some meetings are limited to five or six members, others include all the residents of the house, as many as ten or twenty persons. The optimum number is usually placed at ten.[20]

Some groups announce an agenda in advance, with separate meetings devoted to such topics as marriage, use of leisure time, installment buying, personal budgeting and hygiene. The group leader may, from week to week, be an employment specialist, a police or parole officer, or a representative from industry or labor. Some group leaders help their young people plan and carry out jointly agreed projects such as dances, parties or overnight trips.

Such discussions have value to their participants, even if they are not normally viewed as "treatment," which in its more formal sense relates to material in the areas of personal adjustment and motivation. Here the mutual interchange between members of a peer group, with many problems and antecedents in common, provides a motivation both for sharing their anxieties and for helping one another in working them out:

Today we can no longer speak of the individual alone, as we did at the beginning of our psychological knowledge early in the present century. A human being is not a separate entity in a capsule with only intrapsychic problems and dynamics. We are constantly interacting with our human environment, and continually changing in the process.[21]

Group techniques are more effective than individual efforts in a number of situations: "Certain people with behavior disorders seem to respond not at all to individual interviews, yet begin to involve themselves with others who show similar problems."[22] As members begin to speak of their own problems in the group, others are impelled to follow suit. In this process of mutual interchange, individual feelings of guilt diminish, with consequent improvement in concepts of self. "The experience seems to bring relief and is of value in that it helps to correct the feeling that one's problems are unique."[23]

The group process provides a setting where individuals can be pressured to face up to the truth of their actions and to examine their feelings more objectively than in the one-to-one counseling session, where criticism or comment may be resented.

This kind of interpretation often makes a different impression from that made by the therapist. It is not always more fully accepted and may at times arouse much hostility, but this again shows greater freedom of reaction than is possible toward the social worker who is nevertheless an outsider.[24]

In the one-to-one interview, the disturbed or hostile individual cannot escape clinical probing. But in the group, it is easier for him to skirt a distressful area, with the group leader helping to divert attention if he begins to sense extreme anxiety.

Involving Offenders in Group Sessions

Not all halfway houses schedule group meetings, nor are all its spokesmen equally enthusiastic about them. Some places report that their residents not only resist attending group meetings, but also refuse to become involved,[25] citing them as unpleasant reminders of similar meetings held within the institution.[26] The structure of some houses may possibly account for this attitude. Some men resent their residence in a halfway house; in some large places both staff and residents may advise newcomers against personal involvement with others within the house.[27] Furthermore, the length of stay within the halfway house may be so brief, and turnover of residents so rapid that no real group involvement is possible. Under such circumstances as these, informal contacts on an individual basis between residents and staff are all that can be hoped for.

The individual who conducts the meeting can easily determine its success or failure. A staff member, at worst, can be instrumental in the refusal of the group to become involved. For example, he may refuse to answer their questions, including such all-important ones as what they have to do to gain release.[28] Staff can discourage participants from openly expressing their feelings, or punish some discussants as a result of information brought to light during the sessions, or by implying that they are "sick." Instead of therapy, group discussion can become "a formal, ritualized dialogue between staff and residents,[29] especially if staff have not previously been persuaded of the value of group meetings.[30]

Deep group involvement can seldom take place without the release of a certain amount of tension, aggression and even explosiveness. "Deviance, and rebellious acting-out, in order to become grist for the mill, must first be seen in order to be understood. The group must deal with deviance and not supress its expression."[31] Some group leaders nevertheless prefer a smooth administrative course, and although they may arrange group meetings with scheduled frequency, they deliberately fend off any tendency among participants to deal frankly with one another with regard to basic personal or interpersonal problems.

Effective results can hardly develop from a group meeting which makes attendance compulsory.[32] Although a resident in a house for young probationers may know that participation in a group is directly related to his eventual release, he is under the compulsion to attend. This is a subtle way of communicating to him that he is assuming at least partial responsibility for any delay in the date of his discharge from the house.[33]

Three Basic Group Treatment Approaches

Many halfway houses employ some form of group therapy without much regard for the basic theory on which their methods are based. "Are the descriptions of the services the expressions of 'independent' thinking or simple descriptions of vague, token activities which gain status through accepted terminology, i.e., group service, group therapy, etc?"[34] Unequivocal statements about these techniques are impossible to make, for what passes for counseling in one setting may be called group psychotherapy in another. Differentiations can be made, however, as between such matters as frequency of meetings, depth of material discussed, staff training, and underlying theory.

Three different group approaches may be distinguished: group counseling, psychoanalytic group psychotherapy, and guided group interaction. Group counseling is the least demanding in frequency, depth and training required. The other two group approaches, by contrast, involve relatively frequent meetings which aim to probe rather deeply.

Several rules are common to all therapeutic group sessions: (l) participants are expected to talk with complete candor; (2) no physical violence against persons or property is tolerated; (3) no material divulged in the course of the session may be disclosed outside the group.

Where personal problems are under discussion, group leaders, in all three group approaches, tend to let the participants do most of the talking. Although the leader may appear to take an inactive part, such is not always the case in practice:

Although verbally inactive, the therapist is far from passively involved. He remains the most powerful person in the group, and, whether by mannerisms, expression, or simply his presence, gives direction, sets the tone, and remains a potent source of security. The point is that the therapist is sometimes most active (powerful) when apparently least involved.[35]

Group Counseling

Group counseling, usually limited to one or two sessions weekly, probes far less deeply than either group psychotherapy or guided group interaction. Largely supportive in nature, and confining discussion to problems as they arise — on the job, with police or parole officers and with staff — group counseling permits its participants to speak freely about the things that bother them. Administrators may learn about deficiencies in their programs, at the same time finding that free expression also reduces management problems. The fact that someone is willing to hear "their" side, helps to diminish anger and frustration; friction between staff and residents lessens, disciplinary problems decrease, and absconding becomes less frequent.

In group discussion, the participant begins to realize that others have problems similar to his own, that their suggestions may help him solve some of his difficulties, as well as make him aware that others are interested in him. As he, in his turn, attempts to assist others, he gains in confidence and self-respect, and begins — hesitantly at first — to behave in helpful, rather than hurtful fashion. As he struggles against his own negative behavior, he finds himself receiving not only staff approval, but also — and far more important — the approval of those whose opinions matter most to him: his peers.

Although professionally trained staff members may conduct the group sessions in some places, there are other houses where the discussions are conducted by persons who have received only the briefest instruction, or who have acquired their skill on the job. Those who tend to incline toward psychogenic views of delinquency hold that treatment should be entrusted only to professionals. Others who regard antisocial behavior as more largely sociogenic in origin are not so averse to the use of nonprofessional staff:

Group counseling . . . contains potentialities of a revolutionary character . . . Primarily the change is based upon the participation of the rank-and-file of employees in the program. Group counseling provides new treatment functions for correctional officers.[36]

Proposals have also been advanced for ex-offenders to be used to treat delinquents, because their experience may be helpful in convincing young people that there are modes of behavior alternative to their prior patterns of aggression, hostility and delinquency. Lack of professional training may be outweighed by the ex-offender's knowledge of the current argot. The parallels in their background and experience help to establish the rapport which is essential to allay fear or self-consciousness on the part of their young charges.

Guided Group Interaction and Psychoanalytic Group Therapy

The group approach in dealing with adolescents derives from certain theoretical premises, chiefly those of Adler, Fromm, and Horney: "Man is not only creative; he is also self-conscious. He knows what he wants and he strives consciously to reach his goals. The idea of unconscious motivation is not accorded much weight by these social-psychological theorists."[37]

The terms employed in the different group approaches make it difficult to differentiate clearly one method from another. What is "guided group interaction" in one part of the country may be called "group psychotherapy" in another, although for both the approach may be equally non-Freudian. Guided group interaction was first developed for delinquents at Highfields, New Jersey, in the 1950's. Stressing that interchange between people in a group can influence individual attitude and outlook, this approach "assumes that the delinquent will benefit from a social experience where, in concert with his peers and the leader, he can freely discuss, examine and understand the problems of living, without the threats that had been so common in his previous learning experience."[38] Guided group interaction is based on the view that delinquent adolescents are capable of realistically appraising their true life situations and of making reasonable decisions based on that appraisal.

Where this form of treatment is well established, visible group cultures are evident, with the participants developing a strong "we-feeling." New-found ease of verbal communication leads to increased independence, cooperation, commonality of interests and sharing of norms and values. When the discussants have been enabled to express their feelings honestly to one another over a period of time, mutual understanding and empathy, or group solidarity, emerges.

Traditional group psychotherapy has its own adherents. At the start of the original Highfields experiment, ". . . numerous small residential treatment institutions with a neo-Freudian or an orthopsychiatric orientation and a very high worker-to-child ratio have been established for delinquent and emotionally disturbed children, especially in the New York City area."[39]

While guided group interaction stresses the group as a distinct entity, group psychotherapy tends rather to emphasize the individual within the group situation. Guided groups confront their participants with the "here and now" of their behavior; group psychotherapy maintains that problems are best solved not by rational deduction, but rather through exploration of unconscious materials.[40] Traditional group psychotherapy holds that the patient must relive the traumatic episodes of earliest childhood, thereafter transferring the reexperienced emotions of love and hate to other group members, particularly the leader, with the result that the small group becomes a replica of the original family constellation.[41]

Guided group adherents emphasize the importance of developing mutual concern and esprit de corps, while the traditionalists hold that such a development is actually contratherapeutic. A key tenet of the guided group process requires its members to interact constantly; at work, meals, recreation, and during meetings.[42] The psychotherapeutic school holds a quite different view: that group participants should be discouraged from seeing one another outside of the therapy sessions.[43] Guided group exponents maintain that facing up to his shortcomings, within the confines of an understanding group, equips one to deal with situations which will arise later in the free community. Those who favor the psychoanalytic approach insist that deep, underlying problems cannot be mastered in this fashion and that the improvement in behavior claimed by supporters of guided groups represents temporary and largely superficial attitudinal changes.[44]

Essential differences are also found regarding group leadership. Most workers in guided group interaction maintain that an intelligent and sensitive person can be trained to be a competent leader within a matter of weeks or months. Few universities offer instruction in this method, which leaves persons interested in it no choice but to intern at a guided group center in order to develop competence. In contrast, group psychotherapy holds to the view that leaders should undergo years of training, even to inclusion of a medical degree and extensive clinical experience in individual psychotherapy.[45]

From the purely practical point of view, persons with these qualifications are simply not available for work with delinquents. Their numbers are insufficient and correctional budgets cannot possibly meet their salary expectations. From the theoretical viewpoint, questions arise as to the desirability of group leadership whose training has been along traditional psychoanalytic lines, because:

Their previous concentration on individual psychotherapy of a psychoanalytic type made it difficult for them to work freely at first in this psychotherapeutic technique. They tended to carry the attitudes and ideas they had accumulated in their individual psychotherapy experience into their work as group psychotherapists. Very frequently it was found that they were all treating the patients in the group as individuals and not utilizing the group and the group method in performing group psychotherapy . . ."[46]

From the social work field comes a concurrent view:

Much work with groups has been done and still is being done as if the person in charge were working individually with each member, but in the presence of others. This may be legitimate with extremely withdrawn mental patients, but in any other situation it is not helpful."[47]

A high degree of professional self-discipline is required to transfer training and experience gained in one-to-one situations over to effective working with persons in groups.

In contrast to the proponents of guided groups and other nontraditional group therapists, the neo-Freudians tend to regard any attempt at deep exploration of adolescent feelings as undesirable, and instead recommend less intensive forms of treatment, such as counseling or guidance, to deal largely with conscious material:[48]

The state of maturity and life experiences of adolescents makes them unfit for introspective plumbing of the unconscious. The surface nature of their incestuous and libidinal urges and their transferential antagonism to adults (and, therefore, to the therapist) militate against their entering into a relation and into their own psyche, as required by a true analytic therapy.[49]

From the sociologist interested in class relationships comes the observation that clinicians too often ascribe motives to patients which are based on their own middle-class perspectives, rather than on those of their patients. "Freudian terminology of motives are those of an upper bourgeois patriarchal group with strong sexual and individualistic orientation,"[50] and what is outside that middle-class experience is perforce labeled "sick." While the delinquent, may, in his own way, be responding to pressures of school failure, unemployment and delinquent companionship, the motives attributed to him by psychoanalytically trained clinicians may more clearly reflect their own outlook than the needs of their patients. "The motivational structures of individuals and the patterns of their purposes are relative to societal frames," and it is therefore unrealistic for persons of one socioeconomic level to impute to all others their own "vocabulary of motives."[51]

From certain schools of psychiatry comes a somewhat different attack on psychoanalysis as an effective therapeutic approach to delinquents. "Reality therapy," for example, holds that irresponsible and neurotic behavior is not due to unconscious conflicts, but is rather the result of — and the reaction to — current problems and immediate needs. In demonstrating to a delinquent that there are ways of expressing his behavioral needs other than through criminal activity, the group leader can more effectively influence antisocial attitudes, and emphasize the search for practical solutions to immediate problems.[52]

The truth may well be that the psychoanalytic and the group dynamic approaches are closer in practice than advocates of either would care to admit. It is manifest that "diversity of opinion and misunderstanding" characterizes the entire area of group treatment, the best solution being that "intensive psychoanalytic psychotherapy may be the method of choice for adult neurotics and character problems . . . while different levels of group therapy are urgently needed for other populations such as delinquents," resulting finally, in a "tendency toward a reapproachment of the two basic, complementary ideologies."[53]

There are apparently more similarities than differences between group psychotherapy and guided interaction than we heretofore have either recognized or have been willing to concede. Second, it seems reasonable to hypothesize that both the group psychotherapists and guided group enthusiasts emphasize differences in technique which may be more a matter of disciplinary faith than a reality. Third, the rigorous training and theoretical preparation insisted upon by most group psychotherapists may well be more related to their own vested interests than it is to competency or effectiveness. Fourth, "guided groups" insistence upon the opposite may well be a reaction formation.[54]

Present halfway house commitment to "reality" therapy and to nonprofessionally trained treatment personnel may also be an understandable reaction to the strong emphasis in past years on the necessity for mental health services for delinquents. All too often, the ineffectiveness of many correctional programs has been attributed to the lack of professionally trained personnel rather than to their basic treatment approaches. A clinical session of one half-hour once a week hardly constitutes treatment, when the bulk of the correctional staff are relegated largely to custodial functions with no commitment to — or responsibility for — the therapeutic process.

The search for easy panaceas often results in treatment plans that exist only on paper. Judges are empowered in one state to refer a delinquent child to a state mental hospital if two psychiatrists find him to be emotionally disturbed. Yet, "treatment" facilities in such hospitals may be as bad as, or worse than, those prevailing in the reform school.

Involving Parents

The life histories of many delinquent children indicate that serious family discord and disruption are closely associated with antisocial behavior. Finding himself in a female-dominated household where the father is seldom, if ever, home a boy from the lower social-economic classes, concerned about his maleness and seeking some model with whom to identify, frequently turns to the gang in search of an outlet for his need to be assertive, daring and independent.[55] Even when the parents are living together, the father's inability to hold other than a low-paying job may make him an object of the contempt of his children. The father's own awareness of his situation may be similarly expressed in aggressive, brutal behavior toward members of his family, or by retreat into alcoholism.[56]

In middle- and upper-income families other problems are directly associated with delinquency. The slum or ghetto family may view hatred of any authority, stealing, drunkenness, sexual promiscuity, and avoidance of school as standard behavior. The emotional difficulties of the upper-income child seem, equally directly, to be fostered by the family situation.[57] Like his slum peer, the middle-class delinquent may lack a masculine model, not because of the absence of a recognized father, but because the latter is often so frantically engaged in the race for affluence that he has little time for his family. If the mother shares the drive for upward social mobility, the child may feel himself oppressed by the material goods which he senses are more important to his parents than is he himself. A boy may be under terrific parental pressure to succeed, to perform excellently in his studies or in athletics.[58] Notable success in these areas may, in understandably perverse fashion, be viewed as a threat to the father's own self-importance. [59] Lack of satisfactory child-parent relationships may thereafter be expressed, particularly during adolescence, by vandalism, rebellion against adult authority, and parasuicidal behavior behind the wheel.

By the time such adolescent offenders have been arrested and appeared in court several times, communication between parents and child may simply fail to exist. If the latter is then sent off to a halfway house, his family is left in complete hopelessness as to their ability either to understand or to cope with him. Feeling themselves powerless to change the course of events, they may appear almost eager to dump their child on any agency willing to take him in. The halfway house staff will want at this point to try to reopen communication by helping the parents to understand the problems of their child and to realize that their plight is by no means unique. By bringing to these unhappy adults some understanding of the behavior of their children, they help foster feelings of mutual support and confidence.

These are some of the reasons the halfway house, particularly the nonresidential, attempts to draw fathers and mothers into program participation. Where the residential center is located in a rural area, transportation may present an obstacle to full parental involvement.

Such parental involvement is valuable both during the treatment period and following release. Despite the fact that halfway house placement is preferable to commitment to an institution, parents may nevertheless be suspicious and resentful. Lower-income parents may be no clearer in their understanding of program aims, and this is often compounded by anger that their sons are expected at the same time to work for meager wages of which they receive no part.

Parental understanding and cooperation is essential to the success of residential treatment, but it has even greater relevance to nonresidential centers. If a boy is to return each night to parents who disparage staff efforts, or insinuate that he is being duped by police or exploited by staff members, treatment may either be negated, or, at best, greatly prolonged. Parents can be a vital source of information regarding their child's behavior within the home and with his companions. They are able to observe his rate of progress within the program, and his eventual performance in the community once he has been released.

Enlisting the cooperation of parents may be countered by their open hostility to their child, their indifference or rejection, as instanced by failure to visit or correspond with him once he is in custody. Some nonresidential centers insist that any candidate for admission must have the agreement of at least one parent or "meaningful adult" before he will be permitted to participate in treatment.[60]

Various methods are employed to ensure parental participation in group sessions with other parents, including the imposition of a court order of contempt with possible punishment of a fine, or a year in jail, for failure to attend. Such measures may be questioned from a legal as well as an expedient point of view. Imposition of sanctions against the child may also be attempted, such as the denial of home visits to boys whose parents fail to cooperate. Most halfway house administrators express opposition to such practices, however.

Positive procedures are more likely to be effective in inducing parental participation, such as payment of bus fare, hiring a baby sitter or the provision of an evening meal. As the parents begin to sense that both they and their child are being helped, they come more willingly, even enthusiastically, and may begin to try to persuade other reluctant parents to take part in the group.[61]

Participation provides parents with an opportunity to socialize with others who have comparable life situations with the result that some who were previously disillusioned may suddenly realize that their very numbers give them strength. Acting as a group, they have been known to put pressure on municipal leaders to increase police protection, improve neighborhood services, or compel enforcement of ordinances prohibiting the sale of liquor or pornography to children.

Adolescent reactions to parental involvement are likely to be mixed. Some who disapprove of the idea cite as their objection that their parents would have little interest in attending. Other groups of youngsters who have derived benefit from their own peer meetings are likely to press for their parents to become involved. A not-infrequent result is that for the first time some children find themselves able to communicate with their parents.[62]

Various ways of involving parents in treatment have been devised.[63] In some programs the parents meet separately from their children, in the belief that they are better able to relate to one another and to discuss mutual problems.[64] Counselors in some houses hold conferences with individual families when this is considered desirable. Some therapeutically oriented centers make an effort to involve the entire family in treatment, and parents are expected to bring their other children with them to the sessions. They are also encouraged to take an interest in the details of their child's program, and even assist in some of the activities involving all the children in the center. Parents may be invited to observe the conduct of their child with staff and peers in special rooms equipped with a one-way mirror.[65] Families may be asked to come to the house for weekly meetings which engage the entire assemblage of boys, parents, and siblings. Younger children can be helpful by furnishing information to staff regarding an older brother's behavior, as well as indicating the general atmosphere at home.[66]

Group members may be induced to engage in roleplaying, with the resident playing the role of his father, while his father plays the part of the boy. Such activities can encourage family attendance and make for large and interesting meetings with the group's attention focused on one or more topics.[67]

Summary

No two halfway house directors would agree on what they mean by treatment, which in all instances is the expression of the philosophy of the individual director, who determines his program accordingly. Centers with small budgets make few formal efforts at treatment, and rely instead on the creation of a family-like situation and the establishment of healthy relationships between child and adult. In the more generously endowed center, where there may be a clearly formulated notion of treatment, the large number of staff, and the strictly professional approach may actually prevent the creation of a family living situation.

Some differences between the programs of those halfway houses which serve parolees and those which serve probationers are worthy of note. In the former, emphasis is placed on providing shelter, meals, recreational and social opportunities, job assistance, and an atmosphere of friendly acceptance. In the latter, staff are more likely to be concerned with changing the attitudes and values which motivate behavior. For delinquents who are customarily suspicious, hostile, and negative in their outlook toward themselves and the world, the treatment approach seems especially pertinent, although not readily achieved. By designedly creating an atmosphere of anxiety about inmate life styles, staff can themselves expect to experience uneasiness and tension on occasion.

Individual and group counseling is done by persons from a wide variety of backgrounds: teachers, custodial officers, psychologists, professionally trained clinicians as well as by ex-offenders. Few halfway houses can afford professional services of the one-to-one type on any frequency basis, with the result that much effective therapy takes place on an informal basis.

Programs of group counseling are characteristic of many houses where formal efforts at treatment are attempted. Group meetings on a weekly or semi-weekly basis are found to reduce tension, and ease administrative burdens. Often conducted by nonprofessionals, they can attempt to explore personal problems or deeply concealed feelings as well as help by bringing to the group members the realization that their difficulties are not unique, and that their own experiences can be helpful to others similarly troubled and situated.

Houses serving probationers often schedule group meetings with greater frequency and focus attention on the altering of attitudes through peer pressure. Such group treatment is known as guided group interaction. The term *group psychotherapy*, which may be employed in some centers, is seldom psychotherapy in the traditional sense.

An effective ongoing guided group interaction program can produce a strong group culture which helps guide its members to face realistically their life prospects and to demonstrate genuine concern for one another. Traditional psychotherapists emphasize the role of the unconscious and the irrational elements in the human psyche and therefore tend to resist any reliance on group dynamics. Group solidarity and mutual concern are thereby deemphasized. The practice of group psychotherapy tends to be restricted to persons with academic and medical training who are also experienced in conducting such sessions. Contending that adolescents are not ideal subjects for deep analysis, they prefer such terms as *guidance* or *counseling* as more accurate descriptions of therapeutic efforts with this age group.

Adequately trained therapists are not available in anywhere near sufficient numbers to meet the demands of correctional work. Proponents of the guided group approach therefore advocate the enlistment of intelligent and empathic leaders to carry on this therapy. The Freudian view may be regarded as representing the middle-class orientation of its practitioners, which does not always make them sympathetic to or skillful in dealing with, persons from lower economic levels.

Because delinquency is frequently the end result of severe family disorder, some halfway houses undertake to involve parents in treatment in an attempt to establish communication which has been faulty or nonexistent between them and their children. Some halfway houses do not accept children unless parents are themselves willing to get involved in treatment. Efforts to insure their attendance include persuasion, sanctions against their child, and even the threat of a court order.

Some houses which involve parents in group sessions also make provision to meet them privately. At others, parents may become participants in group discussions, sometimes including all their children. Once initial suspicion and resentment have been overcome, parents may find themselves deeply involved, and more effective in dealing with their children as a result of new insights gained within the group setting.

4

Dynamics of Group Interaction

Sociologists tend to agree that delinquency is largely a group phenomenon:

... the greater part of delinquent behavior is not that of individuals engaging in highly secretive deviations, but is a group phenomenon; habitual delinquents tend to look affectively both to their peers and to the norms of their system for meaning and orientation.[1]

Affiliation within a group is essential to all human beings, but it has particular, even crucial significance, for adolescents who, in their efforts to find independence and to loosen parental ties, characteristically band together in groups composed of their peers. In this transitional period in an adolescent's life, when anxiety is aroused by his difficulty in finding a suitable identity and a satisfactory life style, the peer group supplies needed support, and what it favors becomes the desideratum for its individual members. Concerned with their status in the eyes of their fellows, boys will take the most foolhardy of risks in order to win attention and recognition. Adolescent girls who are excluded from cliques considered popular and desirable, experience — and evidence — feelings of extreme rejection

Adolescent behavior is like that of other human beings, except that the distinctively rapid emotional, intellectual and biological changes which this age group experiences, emphasize their social needs more strongly than at any other period in the entire life span. It is as if, in order to appear finally on the adult scene as distinguishable individuals in their own right, they had first to serve in the ranks of persons in their own same chrysalid stages of development. If man can know himself only as he sees himself reflected in the behavior of others ("the looking glass self" — as Cooley has theorized,[2]) then the small, intimate group — one's family and companions and friends — is "fundamental in forming the social nature and ideals of the individual."[3]

When one examines the nature of the group life of most children who come before the juvenile court — their families, school classes and their gangs — the nature of their self-regard, based on the reflection which these groups mirror back to them, is understandably self-demeaning, even self-abasing, and finally even self-destructive. It were almost better, one is tempted to conjecture, that these young people should live apart rather than draw the sustenance of their self-regard from such sources as these, except that: "If there is one truth that modern psychology has established, it is that the isolated individual is sick."[4]

For the young delinquent, as for every other young person, the self "arises in the process of social experience."[5] One's relations to others cause the self to appear, and only through understanding what the "generalized other" expects of him, can the individual come to know, with any confidence, how to conduct himself.[6] Groups to which individuals belong, or would like to belong, are the totality of these generalized others, or "reference groups" which are the basic regulators of individual conduct:

Deliberately, intuitively, or unconsciously each person performs for some kind of audience; in the drama of life, as in the theater, conduct is oriented toward certain people whose judgment is deemed important.

A reference group is an audience, consisting of real or imaginary personifications, to whom certain values are imputed. It is an audience before whom a person tries to maintain or enhance his standing.[7]

Group Norms

Even when the relationships found in an assemblage of persons are so tenuous that it hardly constitutes a group in the true sociological sense, it may still exercise considerable influence over the individuals within it. Though without leadership, and composed of persons with only a transitory involvement, a group can construct norms of considerable strength. Two recent research efforts confirm this principle of group dynamics.

When individual subjects were placed in a completely dark room, into which a tiny beam of light was projected, through an optical illusion the immobile light appeared to move as the subjects stared at it. Thereafter, each individual reported his own account of the direction in which the light had moved, and its distance. When all the subjects were later gathered in a group, where each could present his individual estimate, a group judgment was found to replace prior individual opinions. Although fully as erroneous as had been the separate estimates, the group norm had thereafter considerable influence upon the subjects, who later interrogated individually about the movement of the light beam, tended to support the group norm, rather than their earlier original statements.[8]

The second research went even further, showing that many individuals will yield to a group norm, even though their own senses clearly reveal that they were in the right and the group was wrong. Of eight persons in an experimental group, only one was truly performing the assigned task of comparing and matching lines of varying lengths. The other seven, cooperating with the researchers, had all agreed to give a false response. Although one-fourth of the subjects rejected the group norm, one-third accepted it. Despite the evidence that they were right and the consensus of the other seven was wrong, these persons nevertheless accepted the group statement. When the group size was later reduced to only four, with one naïve subject and three "plants" who cooperated with the researchers, the same results obtained. Most of those who accepted the majority view were persons who lacked confidence in their own judgment; others, while knowing their own measurement to be accurate, could not tolerate the holding of an opinion which differed from that held by those around them.[9]

In both these experiments, the assemblages of subjects would hardly qualify as groups: The participants were brought together only for the experiment; there was no opportunity for other norms to develop; there was no leader. It may be validly argued that if individuals can be influenced so strongly by other persons with whom they have had only the most minimal contact, then members of a group who interact constantly and closely during a large part of their waking hours will be *a fortiori* considerably influenced.

Thrasher's early and classic study of juvenile gangs pointed to the importance of group opinion in maintaining control over individual members.[10] Whyte's later study of a street-corner gang clearly demonstrated that the very routine followed by the gang was closely associated with the control it exercised over its members who, at different hours of the day, knew where to find each of their fellows.[11] At least one psychiatrist has noted the power of the group in inducing conformity, that as the individual patient progresses in treatment he craves the affirmation of his peers far more than he does the approval of the therapist.[12]

If a group as tentative as a brief experimental gathering can quickly produce norms, then street-corner gang members in their constant day-to-day association can be assumed to be subject to norms of far greater intensity. If, as Thrasher indicates, routine contributes to group control,[13] the halfway house for such former members of gangs can satisfy this element. Although without formal controls or written rules, the residential halfway house imposes a routine of waking at the same time each morning, working as a group, eating together, and returning to the center each afternoon. The nightly group meetings soon establish their own protocol and, all in all, despite the informal atmosphere, there is a definite pattern to much of life within the halfway house.

For norms of the group to exercise strong control over its members, a relatively homogeneous group seems desirable. Sociology one hundred years ago noted that when people share common ideals and interests they become attracted to one another.[14] Most delinquent boys in guided group centers, black and white, come from slum neighborhoods, have experienced family disorganization, have broken the law, clashed with the police, spent time in detention centers, and in general have been rejected by the established educational, recreational, and religious institution of their community.

Manipulating Delinquent Ambivalence

Guided group centers attempt to change the attitudes and consequent behavior of such boys by manipulating the peer group so that it endorses, rather than opposes, acceptable standards. Here the program is not applied to a totally negative situation, for there is often ambivalence on the part of delinquents toward such standards, and though the particular reference group may support criminal norms, the members of it: "are aware of conventional structure and its expectations."[15] In the same vein, "Evidence from a variety of sources suggests that disadvantaged youngsters do not become alienated from the goals of the larger society."[16] A study on the use of marijuana concluded that moral compunctions against the drug lessen in effectiveness as smokers move more and more deeply into groups which rationalize its usage. In conventional groups, where they are "unable to explain away or ignore these conceptions, use will not occur at all."[17]

Many delinquents are torn to some degree by the disparity between conventional and criminal norms. As members of the total society, they are aware of approved goals and of the recognized means for attaining them, such as via education and employment.[18] When they accept the view that their personal circumstances rule out access to these goals through legitimate avenues, they seek and find support from others such as themselves in turning to criminal behavior for the power, pleasure and money which this can promise to provide.[19]

Homans and the Group Process

While all this is of value in understanding the dynamics of small groups, it does not explain precisely the dynamics of what takes place within the guided group interaction process as a means for effecting change in delinquent adolescents. In the words of one investigator of a variety of group studies: "Research has, on the whole, neglected matters of internal organization and process."[20]

Homans' studies of the characteristics universal to small group processes and his theory of group dynamics, based upon five separate studies, can be helpful in understanding the proceedings within the guided group. The results of his Western Electric group research of the early 1930's were later confirmed in four other quite different groups — a street corner gang, a South Sea island village, a small manufacturing plant, and a New England town, results which could be used in working "toward a sociological theory which will state, in convenient and compact form, the interconnected uniformities detected in the behavior of men in groups."[21]

Homans made his observations of a group in the Hawthorne Plant of the Western Electric Company, within a compartment known as the "Bank Wiring Observation Room." The company wanted to learn the causes of employee satisfaction and dissatisfaction and, to obtain this information, placed a small number of workers in this Room, where they could be inconspicuously observed for some months. Equipment was located within the Room in such a way that production would apparently be as efficient as possible and, in order to stimulate maximum output, extra wages were promised for high productivity.

In developing his theory of its dynamics, Homans defines the small group as a "number of persons who communicate with one another over a span of time, and who are few enough so that each person is able to communicate with all the others face to face."[22] It is, in short, a primary group such as described by Cooley, "characterized by intimate face-to-face associations and cooperation."[23] Furthermore, the small group has specific limits; in Homans' words: "Our definition of the group draws a line between the systems we shall study and their different environments ... Everything that is not part of the social system is part of the environment in which the system exists."[24]

The environment, in the case of the Bank Wiring Observation Room, consisted of the shop where the men worked, their positions within it, the machinery and tools at their disposal, as well as the total plant in which the Room was located. Homans refers to all these as the "physical" and "technical" aspects of the group environment. In addition, and likewise of significance, was the "social" aspect, encompassing a multitude of elements: management's organization plan, the wage system, the supervisors, other workers in the plant, and the men's families and associations away from work.[25]

In order to exist, a group must meet certain conditions of its environment. In the case of the Room, the most important demands related to the "social" aspect of the environment, consisting of the company's expectations that a certain volume of work be produced by the group within the Room, for, obviously, if these minimum standards were not attained, the men would be discharged and the group dissolved.

Human groups not only survive within their particular environment, but they also evolve: the men within the Room did not function merely as automatons who were meeting the necessary production quotas, but other events also took place in the course of working and talking together, quite apart from the immediate task at hand: the putting together of telephone equipment. Human groups, therefore, exist within a total social system, composed of two subsystems: the external system is conditioned by the group's total environment, but the internal system begins to develop as soon as the group members begin to work together.[26]

In both external and internal systems, four key factors are found to be characteristic of human groups everywhere: activity, interaction, sentiments, and norms.[27] As soon as the men were placed in the Room, the first two of the four factors of the external system became evident: certain jobs had to be performed (activity); some communication with one another was essential in the performance of their work (interaction). In the external system of the Room, both activity and interaction were largely determined by the company: they decided what the jobs would be and they located work stations within the Room to facilitate cooperative efforts between men performing particular jobs.

The other two factors of the external system were not so quickly discerned.

At the time the men were assigned to the Room, they had certain feelings about their jobs (sentiments). Some may have simply wanted to make money: others, conceivably, had pride in working for a highly regarded company. Into the Room they also brought certain standards of performance (norms), derived from past work experience, and representative not only of other workers in the same factory, but also of associates outside.

Inevitably, in human groups, the internal system arises from the external, with the same four factors: activity, interaction, sentiments and norms.[28] Where activity may have been the outstanding feature in the external system, sentiments play the chief role in the internal one. Although, as in the external system, all factors are in a state of mutual dependence (hence a system), the sentiments which the employees feel toward one another will affect the behavior of the group, which in turn, eventually influences the environment in which the group exists. One major reason the group is so difficult to study is because external and internal systems are interdependent, with interlocking parts and, in such a self-adjusting system, the precise line between what is cause and what is effect, disappears.[29]

In the Room, the external system permitted interaction between the men; as they worked together, they talked, resulting in the rise of the internal system. For the most part, working and talking together resulted in sentiments of friendship. Although the personalities of some men made them unpopular, the overall tone within the Room was one of friendliness. These positive sentiments resulted in activity and communication which had no direct relation to the men's jobs, and which were actually at odds with the company's plans. For the stronger became the "we-feeling" of the group within the Room, the less became their loyalty to those outside the group.[30]

Feelings of friendship among the group members were followed by the development of norms which were at odds with the goals of the company. Despite wage incentives for upping production, the men believed that increased output would result in layoffs, and even though some individuals would stand to profit from increased productivity, the consensus was that the group would not. Total production for the Room was determined by the group, with individuals responsive to what Olmstead calls "submission to group ideals."[31]

In summary, then, Homans' theory of the small group process is as follows: When a new group is formed, people come to it with certain previously determined sentiments and norms, including attitudes toward the job ahead of them, as well as the norms of other groups to which they may belong. In the course of working with others in the new group, they interact or communicate, and generally, but not always, this leads to liking. If such sentiments of friendship continue to develop, group members will tend to conduct activities beyond the original purpose for coming together. By and large, but within limits, the greater the interaction, the greater the liking; the more people enjoy one another, the greater the ensuing interaction and common activity. Out of the course of this circular pattern — with activity, interaction and sentiments all influencing one another — group norms will develop. If, however, interaction is marred by friction, resulting in indifference or dislike, the process will be quite the opposite: hostile sentiments will lead to lessened activity and interaction, with the consequent eventual dissolution of the group."[32]

Once a group has begun to function, internal and external systems become so mutually dependent upon one another that it is extremely difficult to separate them. The development of the internal from the external, or "build-up," can be seen when a new guided group interaction program goes into operation. The development of the internal system, with its emphasis on positive sentiments to replace previous antisocial values and attitudes, is understandably far more painful in the halfway house than in an industrial plant. The principal aspects in the environment surrounding a group are, according to Homans, three: "physical, technical and social, all of which are interrelated, and any one of which may be more important than the others for any particular group."[33]

When a residential guided group center is established, a delinquent boy is liable to find himself in the following physical situation: he has been brought together with a score or so of other boys in a building without any security features, and at least some distance from his immediate home neighborhood. He now finds himself forced to interact with perhaps half-a-dozen adult supervisors and some twenty new companions. He may find that he is to share a room with as many as three other boys. While isolated from his former associates, he knows that he is still close enough to a nearby community so that he is not completely cut off from it.

As in its physical aspect, the technical phase of the environment of the halfway house has been deliberately planned. A boy may be expected to work with his fellow residents at a nearby public institution, and to take part in ninety-minute group discussions on five nights each week. Although attendance may not be explicitly mandatory, the pressure is nevertheless there, because he soon comes to realize that his eventual release depends on his active participation.

The social aspect of his environment is to some extent the product of the adult authorities who have determined the number of boys and have devised an arbitrary wage program. A large segment of the social environment which has not been determined by the center administrators consists of the values and norms which the boy has brought with him from his family and peer groups on the outside.

The physical, technical and social aspects within this environment furnish the four key factors of the external system: activity, interaction, sentiment and norms. The work program, usually involving hard manual labor and the nightly discussion sessions occupy the active portion of the day, and together with the physical arrangements, compel the boys to interact constantly with one another and with the staff. The director will aim to manipulate these two factors in such a way as to influence actively the sentiments and norms of the residents.

With a totally new group, this is a formidable task. The boy's sentiments, as observed in the external system, are largely negative. His primary reason for having accepted placement here is because he regarded it as preferable to the reformatory. But whether openly or inwardly, he is still opposed to adult authority. With the exception of one or two other boys whom he may have known at home, he is hostile or indifferent toward the others. Inwardly resistive to the entire program, he now engages reluctantly in the daily work and the nightly group discussions. Although harboring feelings of hopelessness, despair, and self-hatred, he feels no genuine desire to change. Accustomed to being locked up, he is either puzzled by the lack of custody or views this as evidence that the halfway house is run by "suckers" who can be easily "conned."

His dominant norms are likely to be that the smart individual looks out for himself, and that the only truly reprehensible person is the stool pigeon who informs on his fellows to anyone in authority. When coupled with the delinquent sentiments described above, the norms of the external system may well bring disaster to the new guided group center. For if its residents can get away with it, they will lie to, steal from, threaten, abuse and injure one another, undermine the staff, and find ways of obtaining drugs and liquor from the outside.

In a halfway house for adolescent offenders, the external system may obviously not always succeed in producing the internal system desired by the adults in charge, with the result that whatever internal system emerges from the external, may be just as negative as any that exists in a custodial institution. If staff are frightened or unsuited to the task, or if they have merely transferred prison methods to the community setting, the negative attitudes of the inmates will be apparent. When these antisocial sentiments are transformed into activity that threatens the community, the halfway house has failed and may conceivably be forced to close.

While individual boys may feel some degree of friendship toward a few others in the group, such positive sentiments toward the whole group will not immediately prevail. Where staff efforts to involve the group members in common activity and constant interaction fail, the delinquent norms continue to prevail. Then the wide gulf characteristic of so many correctional institutions will appear, with adult staff opposed to the residents whose ideals and models remain those of the criminal or delinquent: "Social worlds differ considerably in their solidarity, and in the sense of identification felt by their participants. Probably the strongest sense of solidarity is to be found in the various subcommunities — the underworld, ethnic minorities . . ."[34]

The first few months of a new guided group center are therefore the critical ones. Overcoming strong commitments to criminal norms is a difficult task for staff, but certain powers are held by the adults: foremost of these is the authority to recommend transfer to the reformatory. Just as Western Electric could discharge those employees who failed to attain minimum production goals, so can the halfway house staff return to court those boys whose behavior and attitudes have become intolerable.

Even when the new staff has not yet had time to develop confidence and competence, they can keep returning delinquents to court until a small nucleus for the creation of a positive group finally remains, for some boys' reluctance to be placed behind bars exceeds their reluctance to change. Once this nucleus comes into being, the possibility for the development of a positive group culture has greatly increased. Constant vigilance is now required lest negative influences cause socially acceptable norms to revert to delinquent norms.

Fear of commitment to a reformatory, while a major motivating factor, is not the only incentive for a boy to relinquish criminal norms. Every newcomer is bound to bring some positive sentiments with him to the center, and if staff are quick to capitalize on these, the desired group culture may emerge more rapidly and without the need for threats. At least three such positive sentiments are found. The first of these is curiosity. Although outwardly contemptuous at the lack of rules and regulations, the new arrival is often both puzzled and intrigued by the unwonted freedom.[35] Second, most delinquents are fully aware of what are acceptable standards, even though they are ambivalent about them, and if this ambivalence is utilized, the boys may begin to move away from antisocial norms. The third incentive is the response which human beings make to the manifestation by others of genuine interest in them. Support for this position comes from another of the Western Electric experiments to study how working conditions affect output. The researchers placed six young women in a relay assembly room, in which, over a two-year period, working conditions were purposely and drastically altered. At times, for example, the lighting was good, at others, terrible. No matter what experimental variables were introduced, the output of the girls continued to mount consistently. The research team concluded that this was because the girls believed that management was interested in them.[36]

In very similar fashion, children in guided group centers very soon become aware when adults are concerned about them. Behind the surly, hostile facade of the newcomer often lurks a badly frightened young person, half hopeful of establishing contact with adults who can be respected and trusted despite all that his previous experience with grownups may have taught him to the contrary.

The daily work activity and the interaction of the meetings soon begin to reduce the newcomer's feelings of isolation, and a certain degree of affection can slowly begin to manifest itself within the group. As this takes place, informal activities, part of the internal system, become more conspicuous, and the fights, insults, and mischief decrease, to be replaced by a willingness to assist one another in work assignments and in dealing with one another's problems. Initial resistance to interaction by the boys is succeeded by hours of informal talks together.

Homans' study of social disorganization within a New England town describes how, with the nearby rise of metropolitan centers and improved transportation, activities and interaction once common to the small town gradually disappear, and with that, common sentiments and action among the townspeople weaken, as old norms lose their former strength.[37] This disintegration of a group culture has parallels in the effectiveness of the group center in changing the sentiments and norms of its participants. As they are temporarily isolated from their former companions, activity and interaction with them are greatly decreased and indifference replaces interest. They begin to move away from their old associates, transferring their loyalty and affection to those who now share their lives. The stronger becomes the esprit de corps within the center, the looser the ties to their former home-town associates.

The Group Process and Self-Concept

In permitting delinquent boys to examine the validity of both antisocial and socially acceptable roles, the group leader touches one of the major pressure points: the self concept which "may be an underlying component in delinquent or nondelinquent conduct."[38]

This hypothesis was studied in 1956 when sixth grade teachers in high delinquency areas of a mid-western city were asked to name twelve-year old white boys in their classes "who would never, in their estimation, experience contact with the police or courts."[39] One hundred and twenty-five boys, so designated, were then interviewed, as were their mothers. The boys were also tested on several scales and measures, including the California Personality Inventory, with the conclusion that:

These 125 boys then at the threshold age for entry into delinquency, had developed and internalized law-abiding norms and concepts of self, which, as predicted, would protect them from future delinquencies . . . they defined themselves as good boys — boys who would not become entangled with the law.[40]

In a follow-up study four years later, one hundred and twenty-three of the original 125 were located and again interviewed, of whom only four had been involved, each in one single contact, with the police or courts. Three of these had been dealt with informally, the fourth boy had been placed on probation. Although an additional four boys had nominated themselves as potential delinquents, none of them had had any contact with the law. As for their self-concepts, after four years, as revealed by the interview and test scores, "the mean scores have remained stable and even improved."[41] The "good" boys still judged themselves favorably, suggesting that:

The results of this investigation may be interpreted to mean that once a favorable self-image has been internalized by pre-adolescents with respect to friends, parents, school and the law, there is every reason to believe that it is as difficult to alter as a delinquent self-image."[42]

Following this hypothesis further, a similar study was performed in 1958 with 101 white boys considered likely delinquents by teachers in the same slum sections of the same city.[43] Here the scores on interviews and tests were the opposite of those for the "good" boys of two years before. Four years later, in 1962, 70 of the original 101 "bad" boys were found and retested. The researchers found that "twenty-seven of the seventy vulnerable bad boys from the same slum neighborhoods had had serious and frequent contact with the court during the four-year interlude between the initial assessment at age twelve and assessment at sixteen years of age.[44] The scores for the "bad" boys again revealed their poor self-concepts:

We feel that components of the self-strength, such as favorable concept of self, act as an inner buffer or inner containment against deviancy, distraction, lure and pressures ... Conversely, the poor concept of self is indicative of a residual unfavorable socialization ... and indicative of weak inner direction (self or ego), which in turn does not deflect the boy from bad companions and street corner society, does not enable him to embrace middle class values, and gives him an awareness of being cut off from upward movement in the legitimate opportunity system.[45]

Using very different tests some years later, two sociologists found that 12-year old black boys who had been labeled potential delinquents by their teachers held themselves in low esteem, while those thought of as "good" viewed themselves equally favorably:

These data support the Reckless, et al, notion that two such nominated groups do have different qualities of self-concept.
These data ... may be considered support for a dissonance hypothesis of poor self-concept.[46]

In the group process, long-held negative concepts of self can apparently be altered, when boys discover that others have had similar problems, when shared stories of family misery and school failure make them realize that they are not unique, nor alone. Honest praise for jobs well done now comes from other boys and from the group leaders. Boys who have previously only thought of themselves as outcasts now realize that they are capable of giving support and encouragement to others whose situation may be more desperate even than their own. As the weeks pass, they become aware of the progress they are making in overcoming their own problems. The increasingly honest criticisms — or compliments — voted by the group begin now to force each individual to examine the reflection of his own personality as he sees it in the eyes of others — his "looking-glass self."[47]

If, as was said in the opening paragraphs of this chapter, the isolated individual is "sick," then through the guided group interaction process which ends that isolation and replaces it with positive feelings of identity with others similarly selected, the "sick" label no longer applies. Such a boy may well be on his way to becoming a person capable of reaching reasonable conclusions on his own, no longer responsive to his previous criminal subcultures or reference groups.[48] An apt parallel may be seen:

In the mental hospital, where the setting and the house rules press home to the patient that he is, after all, a mental case who has suffered some kind of social collapse on the outside, having failed in some overall way, and that here he is of little social weight, being hardly capable of acting like a full-fledged person at all ... Just as any normal member of his outside subculture would do, the patient often responds to this situation by attempting to assert a sad tale proving that he is not "sick," that the "little trouble" he did get into was somebody else's fault.[49]

In similar fashion, it is conceivable that the delinquent may attempt to justify deviance through "techniques of neutralization, denying responsibility for his situation, blaming his parents, environment, and bad companions. As long as he can thus convincingly rationalize to himself his antisocial conduct, he can successfully resist change and continue to view himself as more sinned against than sinning."[50]

Guided group interaction makes it difficult for its members to "neutralize" their misbehavior, by forcing them to come to terms with their peers rather than with an adult clinician. The group process within the noncustodial halfway house dissolves the usual dichotomy where the delinquent assumes the role of prisoner — with his peers and himself on one side, and the staff on the other. When he attempts to evade responsibility for his behavior, his own companions now ask, "What the hell are you — a baby?" If he attempts to attribute the source of his problems to others, he is silenced by "You're full of . . . " He is not permitted to regard himself as "sick," "lazy," perhaps "stupid" frequently, and even "criminal," yes — but not "sick." He is told over and over again by boys of his own age that only *he* can deal with his problems, if he ever really wants to make it on the outside.

In large institutions, the mental patient or the young offender is often stripped of his defenses and rationalizations — in clinic or at work — and then returned to his ward or cottage to deal with his shattered self as best he can. In the mental hospital, for example, an attendant may brutally discredit the patient's fabrications "in line with the practical psychiatry of bringing the patient down to reality,"[51] resulting only in bitter resentment on the part of the patient. The group process does, admittedly, tear away defenses, and does stress reality. But this stark confrontation within the group does not leave the group member distraught, or destroyed, for he knows that in the process others in the group are also dealing with their own problems. The guided group, in short, represents a therapeutic approach to the boy which, eschewing traditional psychotherapy:

. . .must include putting him into a situation where he can engage in self-satisfying action with some fair degree of success and where he can receive some degree of recognition by others for this success.[52]

The opinion held of them by other boys is of even greater significance to delinquents, for the understandable reason that persons with "a low level of self-esteem are much more sensitive to group opinion"[53] than is the average person. One who has long lived such a life at a low level of self-esteem can rise as a human being only as he comes to accept the realization that his contributions to the group are significant to them as well as to himself.

The Four Group States and Homans' Theory

Once the group culture has been established, the unfolding of the subsequent stages in its development is no longer so clearly discernible as when the participants assembled during their first months.[54]

When a new group comes together for the first time, four distinct stages may be observed.[55] In the first, when the members gather for their initial group meetings, they manifest both hostility and anxiety partially expressed in their search for a scapegoat for their difficulties. During the second stage, although there is some effort at differentiating the various problems which beset them, they begin to function in several cliques, rather than as one unit. By the time the third phase has arrived, the members tend now to begin to test the sincerity of the adult leader through the expression of considerable open hostility, an indication that the group is beginning to coalesce. Their sense of "we-ness" strengthens as they realize that adults are beginning to entrust to them the responsibility for making their own decisions. In the final stage, with a strong group culture established, individuals begin to be genuinely helpful to one another, and hostility to be replaced by concern for one another, and even by affection for a circle of intimates.

The four stages reflect the terms of Homans' theory of group process: when first assembled, with only the external system in evidence, the boys' sentiments and norms can be threatening to the very existence of the group. As the internal system begins to emerge from the external, it is observed that:

It gives rise to three interrelated generalizations: that group change is easier to bring about than is change of individuals separately, that its effects are more permanent, and that it is likely to be accepted if the individual participates in the decision.[56]

All three of these generalizations are directly relevant to the guided group interaction process.

Summary

The power of groups to influence human behavior can be described in terms of dynamics, based on leadership qualities through which adolescent group norms are brought into harmony with adult norms, resulting in basic alteration of the self-concepts, the roles, values and behavior of delinquents. Homans' theory of small group dynamics helps in an understanding of this process.

Despite the changes in delinquent norms brought about — and perceptibly — in the nonauthoritarian atmosphere of the guided group center, the long-term benefits of the process cannot be adequately assessed until greater continuity of treatment than at present exists, is available. When young delinquents return to criminogenic home and neighborhood environments, whatever positive change the halfway house has created is already affected:

What this implies for would-be changers of groups is that they simply cannot induce change and then lean back and rely on any "laws of permanence of group change," for under external pressures the whole group may shift back again just as completely and "permanently" as it did for the original group reformer.[57]

5   Guided Group Interaction

From its beginnings in the 1940's, what is known today as guided group interaction[1] has spread to halfway houses, correctional and reform institutions, parole and probation services, forestry camps and public schools. This specialized method of group therapy was originated during World War II. Lloyd McCorkle, a sociologist in the armed forces, worked at the Fort Knox Rehabilitation Center, under the direction of Dr. Alexander Wolf, in search of an effective way of dealing with military offenders on other than an individual basis. When the war ended, Lovell Bixby, McCorkle's supervisor, became Director of Corrections for New Jersey, and undertook to apply to delinquent adolescents the techniques which had been developed at Fort Knox.

The first small group-care home — for boys on probation — was opened at Highfields, housed in the former Lindbergh estate near Hopewell.[2] Here a completely open program was developed, with control deriving from the group process, instead of through reliance on traditional walls, fences, bars, deprivation of privileges and corporal punishment. The Highfields approach has since been greatly expanded and is found today in at least ten states: as far west as California as well as in Sweden and Australia. Many of today's leaders of guided group interaction programs received their initial training at Highfields.

The Group as an Entity

Instead of attempting to treat the individual within a group, guided group interaction aims to win the entire group over to certain attitudes and standards which, once accepted by them as a coherent entity, provide the motivation for the individuals within it to change.[3] If it can be accepted as valid that the norms and the conduct of social deviates are chiefly influenced and determined by their peer group, then when such a group is persuaded to change, the individuals within it may be expected, in turn, to alter their outlook and behavior.

As in the area of individual counseling, there is no technical difference or special mystique to distinguish such a group session from one in which noncriminals participate. It is expected that group standards will tend to reinforce therapeutic goals, with the aim of encouraging each individual to seek his own specific solutions rather than to accept conformity simply as it grows out of the discussion in a group setting.

Adolescents are especially responsive to group pressures. They are at an age when their drive toward independence turns them away from their parents and more closely toward their peers for support. Peer group pressure, then, is the main reliance of the guided group practitioner who strives to substitute socially approved behavior and values.[4] As the member of the group sees others with backgrounds like his own, in the process of modifying their values and conduct, he too tends to become receptive to change and to question his delinquent concepts. In the process he reinforces the standards of the group as they, reciprocally and in their turn, influence newcomers to the group.[5]

Where a program of guided group interaction functions well, the halfway house is marked by an esprit de corps and a perceptible atmosphere of mutual concern.[6] Most participants who have been in the program for some time have accepted the view that they "have problems," and are starting to perceive that alternatives to delinquent behavior are available — and attainable. With prompt and often scathing candor, they begin to confront one another's past and present misbehavior, revealing in the process an extraordinary ability to uncover the weak spots in one another's stories and their attempts to distort the truth in order to defend themselves.

The Group Sessions

The group meeting is the basis of the guided group interaction program, the number of individuals comprising it being usually limited to ten. In one exception found to this rule, a program in California holds daily meetings at which the entire population of forty-eight boys is in attendance, in a manner remarkably similar to the smaller meetings held elsewhere. The ease with which much highly intimate material is discussed here may well be due to the fact that all of the residents are accustomed to group procedures, for they also meet in small groups of six members, a minimum of three times weekly.[7]

The original New Jersey pattern called for the group to be closed to new members when it reached eight to ten boys,[8] in order that each group might develop a history and culture of its own.[9] In a halfway house of twenty boys, the two ten-member groups may strive to outdo one another in recognizing and solving problems. This is thought to aid both in the acceptance of conventional standards and in the rate at which delinquent modes are discarded. Most groups meet an average of five times a week (with never more than a two-day lapse) in order to develop and maintain the continuity and high level of individual involvement which is one of the most valued objectives of the process.[10] Meetings may last from one to one and a half hours. Opinion differs as to the best time of day for holding them;[11] some houses favoring night sessions and other, the daytime hours.[12]

Importance of Adult Leader

The distinctive culture and esprit de corps which marks each group are the lengthened shadow of the personality and the influence of the adult leader. Living close to his boys, the good group leader must possess — and demonstrate — genuine regard for them, plus a sufficient degree of maturity and objectivity to be able to permit them to express their feelings on all subjects — both as to staff and to one another alike — with complete freedom. By his sincerity, his leadership and his concern, he comes to be seen for what he is: an adult who can be trusted and who is worthy of being emulated. Once this has been achieved, a major battle in establishing a distinctive and healthy group culture has been won. For when this happens, it is now the group rather than the staff which plays the major role in coercing and helping the newcomer to alter his long-established concept of himself and his estimate of others, and of the larger society outside. Growing self-confidence is, as a result, projected outward and expressed as pride in the group or house program. Thereafter behavior problems which are the bane of all institutions — stealing, lying, fighting and homosexual activity — begin to decrease.

Types of Leadership

A clue to the success of the guided group leader may be found in a study of four clubs of eleven-year old boys whose reactions were observed to three different types of leadership: democratic, authoritarian, and laissez-faire.[13] When conducting themselves in democratic fashion, the leaders encouraged group discussion and decision. Instead of behaving in a manner which might indicate that their status was above that of the group members, the democratic leaders talked about nonclub activities, joked with the boys, and communicated with them in "man-to-man" fashion. There was nothing weak or passive in this approach, which, while minimizing status differences between leader and boys, offered suggestions to allow the latter to complete their tasks as efficiently as possible, as well as permitting them to decide which of several choices appeared best to them. Praise and criticism were forthcoming, but in objective and clear fashion. In short, the democratic leader behaved much as does the guided group leader described in this chapter.

In terms of work accomplished, the "democratic" groups did well, but, even more importantly in terms of changed attitudes and improved interpersonal relationships. Individual differences were not only permitted to come to the surface, but the boys also neither mocked nor humiliated fellow group members for manifesting unique or even bizarre behavior. When the adult leader intentionally absented himself from the room, the boys continued to work at their tasks.

The "laissez-faire" leader made few suggestions, and permitted his young club members to do virtually what they wished, in some respects behaving like the psychoanalytically oriented group leader who sits quietly and waits for the participants to break the silence. Although some of these groups did eventually produce positive results, others fell to pieces, the boys either sitting in sullen silence, or exploiting one another as scapegoats for their own hostility and anxiety. The complete absence of suggestions from such a leader sometimes resulted in the passage of months of confusion before the boys sensed what was expected of them.

The adult "authoritarian" leader behaved in a manner similar to that of the correctional administrator who remains apart from his charges and assumes responsibility only for the assignment of tasks and the making of decisions. Although groups functioning under such leaders accomplish considerably better results than did the laissez-faire groups, they did so to the accompaniment of two quite different, but undesirable, effects upon their participating members. Some boys resisted the adult leaders, banding together to rebel against orders and assignments. They also made several boys who were outside of such cliques the objects of scorn and abuse. Other boys were apathetic, performing what was demanded of them, but with no enthusiasm. In several respects, the groups under authoritarian leaders resembled, on a smaller scale, the traditional training school boys who, while they maintain their criminal norms, treat some of their peers as "scapegoats," rebel aggressively against authority, or passively and sullenly bide their time until released.

The sensitiveness and warmth of the capable adult guided group leader who attempts to influence values and behavior, so combines his special gifts and personal qualities as to induce boys to examine the consequences of their behavior. Among the elements of social control, there is a relationship between perception and interpersonal relations which has special application for the kind of young people who participate in groups within the community center:

The extent to which any particular perspective is used rests upon the sentiments that develop toward such individuals. Those who feel that they had been treated with affection and consideration usually regard their personal obligations as binding under all circumstances and find it difficult not to comply.[14]

Perhaps the most important element in the success of a leader is his ability to walk the very thin line between friendship and authority, combined with a willingness to permit group members to share in the decision-making responsibility. Although the design of the program of interaction may center upon him, the leader can never dominate – and only seldom direct: "If two people interact, with one frequently originating interaction for the other, the one who gets told what to do will hold respect or hostility for the other."[15] Hence the job of the leader is to initiate interaction, thereafter leaving the conversational exchange largely to the other participants. Since these have relatively equal status one with another, they can far more readily tolerate criticism and direction from one another than from the adult. The competent leader is usually a good listener, whose understanding and sensitiveness directs the maneuvers by which his followers reach their joint decision: "The leader will have to give fewer orders himself if other members of the group have seen for themselves what the orders ought to be."[16]

Success depends on the ability to suggest quietly several alternatives and then to permit the group to reach its own conclusion. As they weigh the possibility of discarding accustomed and long-held criminal attitudes in favor of socially acceptable norms, the group members undergo and manifest extreme anxiety. It is highly unlikely that any real change can take place without such tension.

If the group is kept small in size and the daily schedule of work and discussion induces close interaction, the leader can ultimately build sentiments of affection and concern within the group, as well as an atmosphere which will lead to the creation of change. Once the group culture has accepted the leader's norms, he loses his image as an adult authority figure and becomes accepted and respected in his own personal right.

Nonauthoritarianism — The Key Factor

Four essentials characterize the guided group approach: nonauthoritarian atmosphere, intensity of interaction, homogeneity of the group, and special emphasis on group structure. Of these, the nonauthoritarian atmosphere of the group is the single most decisive characteristic, one which carries over into and influences every part of the total program. When responsibility and decision-making power are given to the residents themselves in the absence of formal rules and complete absence of fences and locked doors, then it is not any longer up to the adult staff but to the boys themselves to make the rules, enforce the rules and indoctrinate the newcomer as to what is expected of him.[17] With this comes the realization that it is each boy's choice to decide whether or not he will be part of the program, for he senses that he is being trusted to a degree which the traditional training school, with its reliance on rule and restraint, can never dare to offer.

An outstanding residential center operating under guided group interaction principles permits the boys themselves to decide whether or not the outside door shall be closed or left open at night. Staff insists on compliance with only one or two formal rules: the residents devise all the rest of their own rather large number of regulations and themselves determine the penalties for violation of them, by means of assigned hours of extra work. A staff member may retain the veto over a decision made by the boys, but in most instances the members of the group determine both the penalty and its duration. Not a few programs permit the boys to have considerable say as to whether or not one of their members may remain in the program; whether he should receive a furlough; and when he is ready for a return to the community. In some places, the group itself prepares a report on each member at the end of the first thirty days in the program. This report, which goes to the staff, may either approve a visit off-campus or find the boy unready for the privilege. The group can reduce both the number of passes a boy may receive, and their length; they remove such privileges as smoking and even the carrying of cigarettes. Where the group culture is strong, the boys are involved in all decision-making and a staff member who countermands or alters a group decision is expected to explain — and defend — his reasons. The residents feel that they run the program — and in the sense that it could run in no other way — they do.

The dread kangaroo court known to operate — overtly or covertly — in many reform and penal institutions, where it frequently imposes its will or whim on a sizable segment of the population, can be avoided as long as the adult group leader properly plays his role, which is to cause the participants to examine what they are doing, and their reasons for doing so.[18]

Those who seek to avoid responsibility may find it forced on them. When a boy informs a staff member that one of his fellows plans to run away, he may well be told: "What do you want me to do? He's your buddy; he's part of your group. You can talk to him; sit on him if you have to; but it's up to all of you to help one another."[19] The guided groups were told that if they avoided, or were incapable of, making their own decisions, the director would have to start acting like a warden, mete out punishments, cancel the group meetings, and, as a result, be able to enjoy two hours more each day with his family.[20]

Placing responsibility for decision-making on the boys is but one of the many ways in which guided group leaders behave quite differently from traditional correctional officials. At group meetings they may say very little, permitting the boys to conduct the discussion. As much as ten or fifteen minutes may go by before they intervene, by asking a question, or briefly commenting, and then in a quiet and uncritical fashion which is received with attention on the part of the boys. The group leader neither lectures, criticizes nor rebukes, and if being new, he should attempt to assume an authoritative role, he may shortly be told to desist and permit the members to run their own meeting.[21]

The halfway house director makes himself readily available. He takes most of his meals with the boys, and leaves his office door open to make it easier for those who may want to, to come in and talk. Little emphasis is placed on status. If a driver is needed to drive a boy for an appointment, to the bus station, or to a movie, the director may well be that person.[22] He may go from room to room, bidding the boys "good-night" before he goes off duty, and in the morning coming in to waken them. Boys are addressed by their first names, and are quick to win praise for jobs well done. They mingle freely with the wives and families of resident staff members. House directors play cards with their residents, participate in athletic games, join them on picnics or overnight camp-outs.

This friendly, personal approach is found to unsettle some boys whom it forces to reappraise, and even revise, their views of their elders. Accustomed to inflexibility, they are baffled by its absence. Misconduct may be occasionally overlooked, and the runaway accepted back without recrimination, or with a minimum of disciplinary action being taken.[23]

An atmosphere conducive to change may be created when boys are made uncomfortable by not always knowing what to expect.[24] In the conventional training school, the experienced inmate knows that by "playing it cool," he can survive for many months without ever having his antisocial view of the world questioned or disturbed in any basic fashion. The close personal contact between boys and staff in the halfway house makes it impossible for such isolation to occur.

This nonauthoritarian approach is made known in many other ways. Mail is not censored; there is complete freedom for boys to wear whatever they like; snacks are available between meals; there is no inspection of personal lockers; boys may decorate their rooms as they wish; length and style of hair is a matter of individual preference.

During group sessions, boys speak with complete freedom of their reactions to staff and program; and may object to estimates made in the reports of their progress. Such objections are seriously considered, and reports may, as a result, be rewritten.[25] On trips to town, boys are permitted to enter stores, banks, barbershops, or places of amusement without staff supervision. At mealtimes, they speak freely, confident that what they discuss will go unreported. Parents and friends may visit, and boys are permitted to leave the grounds in their company. The house telephone is available for their use.

The traditional correctional official may view all this as a call to chaos, especially during the group sessions when no effort is made to regulate language which is frequently replete with profanity and obscenities.[26] Such talk is part of the culture of these boys, and is accepted as a natural and harmless form of release for the hostility characteristic of so many of them. The discovery that staff members will truly let them say whatever they want within the group meetings helps these young people to bridge the gulf that so often separates adolescents from adults, a gulf which is distinguished among other things, by marked difference in language.

This almost totally uninhibited and certainly nonauthoritarian atmosphere is the chief characteristic of the total environment created by and within the halfway house which is based on the principles and procedures of guided group interaction. In such a therapeutic setting, the barriers against exploration and acceptance of conventional values begin to weaken, and the way is made clear for the adoption of new modes of thought and behavior by many of the boys who participate in it.

Intensity of Interaction

The originators of the guided group approach maintain that constant interaction of its members is the prime essential in the creation of a strong group culture.[27] The daily meetings, while basic to the entire process, are viewed as only one aspect of the necessary and continual interaction of members at play, work and meal-time. Anything that happens during the day may become grist for the group's discussions. The boy who has shirked his work assignment is told so by his peers in no uncertain terms. The placing of four boys in a room is deliberate — aimed at forcing them to start to become aware of others.[28] Since the true delinquent is an almost totally self-centered individual, the group attacks at that very point, making it almost impossible for a newcomer to hide for long his true and total self from the other boys and from the staff. Guided group interaction may have value in settings where boys engage in individual programs of work or school, and where group emphasis is limited almost entirely to the evening discussions. But the evidence is fairly clear that the group culture is strongest where interaction takes place twenty-four hours a day and in as thoroughgoing a fashion as the capacity of staff and the needs of residents can make it.

Group Homogeneity

A fairly high degree of homogeneity in age, socio-economic background, previous criminal experience, intellectual competence and racial composition of the group participants seems desirable if the group culture is to arise and flourish. First offenders are seldom placed with boys with long histories of institutionalization.[29] Mental defectives or boys with acute emotional problems are not thought to be suitable candidates for guided group interaction.[30] Nor are those with histories of sexual aggression, arson, or narcotic addiction likely to adjust readily in a group also composed of the general run of property offenders or perpetrators of minor assaults. Efforts are generally made to keep the racial ratio in some kind of balance.

Despite this general rule regarding group homogeneity, there are notable exceptions which seem to work out well. A West Coast project operates five halfway units for a very mixed population. These are composed of persons ranging in age from their teens to the forties, blacks and whites, men and women, parolees, probationers, drug takers, school problems, and finally persons who walk in off the streets and request shelter. Group discussants include professionally trained guidance workers who ask to be included. With a total of some sixty persons in care in five separate houses, at some distance from one another, only one staff member, an extremely competent and dedicated person, serves them all. Management is otherwise assumed entirely by the group members themselves.

Group Structuring

Careful structuring is another key factor in the successful creation of the group culture. For example, new boys are assigned to a group which may be composed of those longest in the program, so that their first group exposure may be to an experienced nucleus. When enough such newcomers have entered the program, a new group is then spun off, which, with the passage of time, becomes the old group. This progressive arrangement serves several purposes: it indoctrinates newcomers in the culture and helps to intensify their sense of purpose; those who have been in the group for some time now find themselves assuming the role of guide and teacher, which inevitably leads them to think in terms of preparing themselves for return to the community.[31]

This division of boys into "old" and "new" groups plus the internalizing of acceptable social goals conduces to a certain rivalry which adds some pressure of time to the therapeutic process. A certain onus falls upon the boy who continues to "goof off" during the group sessions, because he is, in effect, delaying the release of the other members of the group. In the words of one participant: "When you come here from the court, you start off by 'conning.' You just pretend you're changing. But, as new boys come in, you know you're expected to be a leader. So what has been just pretend becomes for real. After all, if you're an old boy, you don't want to be left behind with all the new guys."[32]

Structuring also helps determine the style and procedure of the group meeting. As soon as a group is formed, several boys may formally request that they be given an opportunity to be the subject of the group's attention, what is known as "to get the meeting." A vote may then be taken, with the group deciding to give the entire ninety minute period to one boy, or perhaps to divide it between two of them.[33]

The boy now comes before the group as the exclusive focus of its attention and he starts out by telling his life history. This is a crucial moment, for the newcomer is now expected to tell the truth about himself, his family, his actions, feelings and aspirations.[34] He has been told in advance that he had better be completely honest about all this, for his group peers who listen to him have an uncanny ability to detect contradictions and lies, aided by what they have learned about him through previous weeks of informal contact.

Once the life story has been told, the evasions sifted and the truth more accurately assayed, the group members then proceed to present a diagnosis of the boy's problems as he has revealed them. The group may decide that these consist of lying, stealing, drinking, "wanting what you want when you want it," running away from problems, or "not thinking and not caring." Such a list may include as many as eleven separate items, and during the remainder of his stay, the boy is expected to work on these.[35] As the weeks pass, the group may add further items to his original list. The "problems" of its members are the grist of the group's discussion, and their solution its common concern.

Toward the close of each group meeting, a brief summation is made by either a staff member or one of the boys, bringing out what progress has taken place in regard to the boy whose problems have been on that day's agenda. The summation may pose some new questions to which answers are needed. Knowing that there are areas which still need to be explored, a boy can look forward to continuing assistance from his group.[36] The summation also relates to the general behavior of the group members during the meeting, whether their questions were genuinely helpful or antagonistic. The members leave the meeting with the key issues fresh in their minds.

Building the Culture

Procedures for initiating the guided group program vary. The traditional view holds that the group leader should give as little direction as possible.[37] Other practitioners insist that the therapist should set forth what the basic aims of the program are, and tell the group what is expected of it.[38] All agree that the initial stages in the creation of the group culture are fraught with difficulties. The reaction of the typical delinquent upon exposure to a guided group is one compounded of disbelief, confusion and understandable suspicion. Almost universally, such a boy later reveals that his first reaction was: "this is crazy," coupled with amusement with what he considers to be an ultrapermissive and therefore wholly unworkable program. Others, confused by the lack of formal regulations, may express the desire to be sent to a reformatory where they will at least know what is expected of them.[39] Most boys resent the implication that they have "problems," or the expectation that they should concern themselves with the problems of others.[40]

One director describes a harrowing experience which continued for six months. Boys in the group "rigged" the meetings, pretended to be telling the truth when, in fact, they were relating a series of falsehoods and credible improvisations. They brought in dope and liquor, often smuggled by their relatives on visits, and sniffed glue. They freely and loudly voiced their view that the group meetings were a waste of time, and if one boy did start to tell the truth regarding his past, others would fix him with a characteristic stare to stop him. Many boys failed during the first six months and had to be returned to court.

In this instance, the director had at the outset given the boys almost no cues as to what was expected of them. One boy, looked upon as a leader, when threatened with a six-month sentence for further misconduct, became frightened and finally began to tell the truth. Others in the group followed his example. The group culture here formed after so many initial difficulties, coalesced only gradually, but eventually became very strong in its effect on those who entered it.

The opposite method calls for the furnishing of guidelines to the group members at the outset. This view rejects the idea that long periods of sullen silence are inevitable. Instead it holds that the director must assume an active, almost evangelistic role.[41] During the first weeks, such leaders live in constant touch with their boys and find themselves doing most of the talking. When adults have proved themselves worthy of being trusted and capable of showing affection, an atmosphere is created where mutual concern can now begin to be displayed.[42]

Nonauthoritarian in its basic approach, the guided group center could scarcely achieve the desired group culture with hard core delinquents without reliance on some sanctions in the background, such as transfer to training school or reformatory.[43] If they become completely unmanageable, physically assaultive of staff and other residents, or run away, such boys must know that they will be brought before the court again. This dire possibility, combined with a real curiosity about the truth of this "crazy program" often suffices to discourage absconding.

The average delinquent may be in a group center for at least a month before he begins to start to show any change in attitude or behavior. The "moment of truth" often occurs when the first monthly report on him is read aloud by a staff member.[44] Suddenly made aware that his efforts to "con his way through" have been apparent right along to both adults and boys, he becomes frightened that he may be removed from the center. Once the group culture begins to take hold, this threat to his continued stay starts to fade as it is replaced by a positive feeling of belonging, and a growing sense of purpose and achievement.

Four Stages of Development

The culture of the group generally passes through several stages of development.[45] As many as four have been observed and described.[46] In the first stage, when the boys are strangers to one another and to the staff, no group structuring exists. At this point, boys are attempting to learn about one another and about the program, and are, understandably, highly defensive. At this point they may attempt to find a scapegoat upon whom they can focus their abuse and hostility.[47]

At the second stage, as boys begin to reveal their basic personalities and the truth of their previous behavior, they frequently exhibit extreme tension. Cliques begin to be created within the population, for although each boy now starts to recognize his own distinctive problems, he is not yet ready to function as a member of the group. The individual members are beginning to experiment with techniques of participating in and even running the group meetings, and while espousing redemption, nevertheless continue their ties to a delinquent value system.[48]

By the time the third phase has arrived, cliques and subgroups are beginning to fade and crumble. This period is marked by hostility, especially toward the adult leader, as former defensive patterns are seen as threatened. With the program about three months along, the larger group with a common sense of purpose can be seen beginning to form. As the boys begin to find alternatives to their previous delinquent and aggressive behavior, they are brought up to a point where they have to decide whether they truly want to change, or choose to maintain their former viewpoints. Those who have started to adopt a new value system now find themselves bound by a strong sense of group solidarity and identification. Those who are unable, or unwilling, to accept the new nondelinquent roles may react by running away. Others, openly antagonistic or consistently uncommunicative, may return to court for further disposition.[49] Where a strong group culture is maintained, boys and staff are in agreement that the number of group members who can consistently bluff their way through is very small.

The final stage finds the participants relying very little on the adult leader, but placing considerable confidence in their own ability and that of their companions to face problems and to make satisfactory adjustments to society.[50]

Delinquents who find themselves adopting new value systems now help to work on the defenses of boys more recently received into the program. Some of these "old" boys, in the words of one director, become "social workers on a twenty-four hour basis."[51] At this stage they are deemed ready to return to the outside world, and can well serve to indoctrinate groups of other delinquents in these same goals.

The situation for the staff, once the group culture has reached this stage, shifts from tension and discomfort to an easy and even harmonious role, as they now rarely have to assume an authoritarian stance, inasmuch as the group itself is now making the demands for socially acceptable behavior upon its own members.[52] Group discussion at this point moves quickly and with great intensity as the adolescent participants, more keenly perceptive than they are usually given credit for, seem to reach new heights of ability to communicate.[53]

The sense of mutual concern which prevails at virtually all centers where guided group interaction is practiced, is perhaps the single outstanding indicant that the delinquent value systems are in process of being dissolved and replaced. "Identification with one's fellow man, and empathy, generally are regarded as the natural basis for human morality."[54] It is not surprising that when a recently arrived boy continues to act with belligerence and suspicion, that his peers, who have only recently been in his condition, will labor cooperatively and persistently within the group to overcome his resistance and negativism, themselves gaining in self-confidence as they strive to show him socially acceptable routes to manhood. Like the adults in the Synanon sessions, boys who give help as well as receive it, develop affection and regard for one another as they simultaneously gain self-respect and self-confidence.[55] A boy may be criticized for being consistently unfriendly to another member of the group, and he will be pressed to see the other's good points. Drinking or being a passenger in a "borrowed car" while on furlough is strongly condemned because of its possible consequences for a fellow group member.

Most training schools countenance, because they cannot control, the existence of pressure groups comprised of the strongest, most aggressive boys who torture, sexually exploit and otherwise subjugate other youngsters. The result is a descending pecking order from which hardly any child, in the end, is exempt. In the centers where a strong group culture prevails, where boys range generally from sixteen to eighteen years, and with a considerable disparity in size, equal rights are nevertheless the rule. A boy moves with his group, in which the rights of the smallest and weakest have parity with those of the strongest. During a group meeting in which a boy has been granted the privilege of "telling his story," other members will protect his right to proceed without distraction or interruption. Even when the atmosphere of a meeting becomes so heated that some questions or comments are completely drowned out in the general clamor, no one seems to lose his temper, though some may seem angry at the epithets which are hurled. Once the ninety minute meeting closes, the heated exchanges end abruptly, without outward show of personal hostility, and boys who have been berating one another a few moments before, are now seen to leave the room together in friendly fashion. This perceptibly improved sense of self-control is perhaps the greatest contribution which guided group interaction makes to these young lives. When anger and frustration are allowed to be released verbally, the result seems to be almost a freedom from the need to resort to physical violence.

A well-developed group culture is characterized by boys entering the meeting room on time, without having to be coerced by staff members, as if eager to begin. In such places, it is not unusual for the boys to hold their own meetings in addition to those formally scheduled. Startling examples may be cited of the reversal of former customs as observed in the new attitude toward the misbehavior of their fellows. The typical delinquent view is that any such discussion is "ratting" and an unpardonable betrayal of solidarity.[56] Boys who have successfully passed through the four stages of group interaction know that their revelations of past or present delinquency will be kept in the confidence of the group, and that if fellow members are to be helped, it is essential for all to tell the truth. No longer under the threat of punishment or loss of privileges for what they may have done, they can presently freely discuss their own misdeeds as well as those of their friends.[57]

Still another reversal of delinquent attitudes is found in the boys' supervision of one another, or "checking," as some term it. While at work, a boy may be reminded that failure to do his share will not only bring a rebuke from the detail supervisor, but will indicate his lack of progress within the program. While on furlough, group members may visit one another's homes to make sure that no one is "hanging with the wrong crowd," an expression of their mutual determination to help resist the influence of "bad friends" [their term] in their neighborhoods.

The worker with delinquents well knows that they do not differ greatly from other young people in their view that almost all adults are to be regarded only with suspicion and hostility. In any altercation between adult and adolescent, the latter is seldom interested in hearing the details: in his distrust of all adults he has already rendered judgment against the older person. By contrast, members of guided group discussions often express a willingness to see the adult point of view. They may share an employer's attitude when they believe one of their group has been at fault, and even go to considerable efforts to understand and to rationalize parental behavior.

Adult visitors, who are occasionally permitted to witness group meetings, report that the boys, engrossed in their own discussions, pay them no heed. The secretiveness and feeling of "distance" which characterize most adult-adolescent relationships seems here to have evaporated. An analogy is that of the passenger in a glass-bottomed boat, where a transparent view is had into the depths of what is ordinarily completely opaque. This openness and candor are also found in the day-to-day friendly interaction with adults, in contrast with the neutral, even contemptuous fashion with which most training school inmates regard the casual visitor.

Inmate agreement with staff on a number of matters further indicates a move away from delinquent attitudes. In a center where television, ping pong, and other distractions are intentionally absent, the young resident may remark: "Those things would take too much time away from our problems."[58] Boys will accept pay as low as fifty cents or a dollar a day for their work, without complaint. At one nonresidential center, several of them voiced the idea that, with only a dollar or two in their pockets, they were not tempted to buy liquor, or otherwise get into trouble.[59]

Once the group culture has been established, problems with staff tend to diminish, and even rather rigid adults, who may be long accustomed to the traditional imposition of authority from above, begin to shed their defensive attitudes: "As the kids get nicer, the staff gets nicer, too."[60] From an administrative point of view an even happier result is that close controls and supervision are no longer needed. One center has created an honor system for regulating hours of extra work. During lunch, a staff member simply asks, "Who's got hours? How many of you have five hours, three hours, two hours, or one hour to work off?" Hands shoot up in response to the periods named. No formal record is kept of these hours, because the group culture reinforces the honor system. As a result, the number of employees can be reduced well below the level of the conventional correctional facility.[61]

An encouraging indication of the effectiveness of guided group programs is the frequent number of return visits made by those who have completed treatment. In contrast to the reluctance of most former delinquents to discuss their training school or reformatory past, a sense of loyalty and some pride is expressed by many of these graduates. Some residential and nonresidential group centers use the services of their graduates to help strengthen their group culture.[62] When a person who has completed treatment voluntarily returns to tell the residents how much the group meetings have helped him in the improvement of his own lot, he is likely to be listened to with attention.

The Depth of Guided Group Interaction

Guided group interaction does not aim to involve its participants in the reexperiencing of the trauma of early family relationships, but rather to focus on the difficulties which they presently confront in their relations with others.[63] Support for this point of view comes from a recent joint research effort from three major universities, covering a six-year span. The findings conclude that, instead of effort being directed at attempts to solve the emotional problems of delinquents, concentration on helping such children adjust to existing situations is likely to bring better results.[64]

While deep exploration is not the object of guided group interaction, in this process the most intimate and disturbing emotional trauma are frequently revealed and openly discussed. In confronting certain facts about themselves, children are helped to gain firm and abiding insights. Resulting changes in attitudes and behavior, far from being superficial, become internalized in the process. Although a meeting may begin casually with discussion of a minor event of the day, and although no effort may be made to probe deeply, the group often finds itself working with events long buried in individual pasts. Problems ordinarily considered too shocking for simple counseling sessions are brought to the surface, even including serious delinquent acts which may be unknown to the police, and not excluding incestuous experiences.

Suitability for Guided Group Interaction

The claim would hardly be made by even its most enthusiastic supporters that the guided group process is a panacea for all delinquent children.[65] Some may see it as best suited for those with only minor delinquent histories. But this does not appear to be the case, for many boys convicted of such offenses as malicious stabbing and assault, arson, grand larceny and burglary, vandalism, possession of narcotics, and repeated auto theft have responded well to this approach. Guided group interaction may actually be most effective with the aggressive gang boy from urban slums.[66]

Responding to the subculture in which they find themselves,[67] very often living by their wits, hiding behind a facade of toughness, highly dissatisfied and anxious, such children may well comprise three-quarters of all the delinquents currently in state custody.[68] Many black delinquents, usually the residents of our ghettos, are reported to respond well to the opportunity to adopt new roles, when placed in new surroundings.

Although aggressive delinquents may be the best candidates for the guided group process, teenagers with a deeply developed commitment to a criminal way of life may not be so readily amenable. These are likely to be devious, hardened youths badly damaged in early life, mistrustful of the world. Often bright and even sophisticated, they are usually without remorse. They frequently appear to do well in halfway house programs, performing whatever tasks are assigned, and participating freely in group sessions, but their contributions are likely to be more plausible than penetrating.[69] The number of such young people is relatively small in comparison with the total number of children involved in delinquent behavior. Their designation as "sociopaths" may more accurately reflect the current inadequacy of the clinician than the potential for treatment which such offenders represent.

Children from middle-class homes may not fare too well in the guided group program. The difficulties which they have had with the law seem to stem largely from emotional conflicts within their families, and when they find themselves quartered with gang boys from the city slums may feel themselves to be weak and inadequate, having little in common. Their delinquent history having consisted largely of drunkenness, attempts to outrun the police in the family car, vandalism, they may express distress at their forced association with "thieves." When expected to interact with boys from a lower socioeconomic level, they may seek to escape involvement either by being overly passive and withdrawn, or running away, generally within a few days after arrival. Such boys are uncomfortable because of their feelings of minority status among lower-income delinquents, and it may well be argued that if a center were to be created for them, guided group interaction might be more effective.[70]

Guided group interaction is not recommended for children under twelve, who do not move easily beyond the emotional confines of the family and therefore find the raw confrontation of the group session too unsettling. Young children are simply too immature to be able to face up to their problems and select alternative roles.[71] They tend to be excitable, to want to play, and find themselves generally incapable of taking seriously the stuff with which the group session is concerned. Levels of emotional and mental development differ, naturally, and there are many sixteen year old boys who are equally immature and therefore unable to take the hard thrust and probing of the group meeting.[72]

The original Highfields design ruled out offenders with long histories of institutionalization, on the grounds that they had become so imbued with the delinquent subculture that they could not experience the anxiety deemed essential for change.[73] Accustomed to "doing time," such youths, as a result, tend to give only surface conformity. Children who have lived in a succession of foster homes often exhibit a depth of apathy which can defeat any efforts to involve them in the group, except where a very strong group culture has been developed.

Boys who have been users of narcotics are not usually acceptable for the open, nonsecure facilities of the group center. In reality, a number of such boys, of average mental ability, have been successfully treated in these centers.[74] Two well-known programs for adult narcotic addicts — Synanon[75] and Daytop Village[76] — while they do not use the term "guided group interaction," nevertheless practice a method of treatment which much resembles it.

The large majority of convicted adolescent homosexuals have a history of involvement with older men, whom they "hustle" as a way of obtaining easy money. Seldom are lasting relationships formed with these men. Though it has been estimated that as high as 85% of delinquent boys in some group centers have either "hustled," or experienced homosexual relations during confinement in jails and institutions, such conduct does not seem to have lessened the heterosexual interests of most of them.[77] The extremely effeminate or seductive youth could be expected to disrupt the adolescent group culture, and cannot usually be accepted as a member of a group center.

Although some program directors claim that the excitability and emotional instability of girls make them more difficult to work with, at least two residential centers exist for girl probationers.[78] A policy of including older boys and girls together in the same group has long been followed at Synanon and at the Manhattan Project, both in Los Angeles.

Factors Destructive of Guided Groups

A strong group culture usually neither develops nor flourishes if the individuals composing it are overly diverse in background, intelligence and level of maturity. Compulsory attendance at group meetings can also work against formation of a group culture. Participation in meetings is not to be thought of in terms of punishment. It is a sign of weakness in the group culture when misbehavior results in mandatory five-night-a-week attendance, while good conduct can reduce the number of sessions to two or three. Where meetings are held infrequently, or at intervals of several days, the esprit de corps essential for change simply does not get a chance to develop. Only after adolescents have moved on from the intensity of the guided group to a more relaxed aftercare experience does it appear practical to reduce the number of meetings.

Major problems relate to intake and departure. If too many newcomers are received at any one time, the group culture, which may have been painstakingly developing over many weeks, may be completely disrupted in very short order.[79] Centers, therefore, attempt to limit intake to only one or two new participants at a time. In order that the ten or twelve member group may be maintained at full complement, newcomers are received at approximately the same time that other members leave. The semester schedule of the public schools makes it difficult at times to accommodate the center program to boys on the basis of their need, rather than on the basis of whether the school term is beginning or ending.[80] The adult leader is the key figure in the success or failure of a guided group program. If staff are too authoritarian, unable to share responsibility with their charges, unsure of themselves, or hostile, the process of interaction can never really get started. Where correctional administrators, politicians, the press, parents, and the general public express anxiety toward the apparent permissiveness of such programs, the program is likewise bound to suffer. Interestingly enough, such opposition may sometimes serve to build the group's esprit de corps; if they can survive such attacks, group members find themselves bound more firmly together by their common defensive efforts.[81]

The inability of a group leader to tolerate expressions of hostility toward himself or the program can also spell failure. This is vividly described by one teenage boy, relating how difficult it was to speak candidly before a particular group leader: "All you have to do is watch his eyes. You can see him getting madder and madder. It's just a question of time before he gets back at you."[82] Equally ineffective is the group leader who is cynical or verbally abusive toward the members of his group. While teenagers will accept such treatment from their peers, they strongly object to any adult who labels them insultingly in front of their fellows.

If a strong group culture is to emerge from what is originally a scattering of some twenty self-centered, distrustful boys, their ultimate acquisition of a major degree of self-responsibility is essential. Attitudes change when boys can believe they not only can make decisions about their lives, but that they also can do things for themselves.[83] When they are told they have decision-making power, and then find this is not the case, positive group feeling is impossible, resentment follows, and delinquent values remain undisturbed.

As long as the key personnel relate to adolescents in a mature, nonauthoritarian way, the group can even make positive use of dogmatic, overcritical lower-level staff.[84] At one center where the boys worked under an employee whose approach was one of anger and personal abuse, the boys were convinced, after they had discussed him that: "If we can make it with that cuss, we can make it with any boss we'd have on the outside."

Most halfway houses employing guided group interaction have met with favorable response from the press. Despite such support, the program can be jeopardized by a change in the political structure, which may result in a withdrawal of financial support. Legislators, likewise, pressured by parents, disgruntled neighbors of the center, or by their own anxiety about noncustodial and "nonsecurity" programs, may also withhold funds,[85] or insist upon the imposition of such measures as rules, reports, and formalized procedures.[86]

Guided Groups in Institutions

The initial opinion that the treatment center employing guided group interaction should not house more than twenty or twenty-four teenagers has been closely followed not only in all of the New Jersey installations, but in the forestry camps of Kentucky and in the New York START centers, as well as in programs which are privately funded. Inauguration of guided group interaction in existing training schools with large numbers of individuals is an almost impossible task.[87] Yet, despite the manifest difficulties, there are valid reasons why such groups should be able to function well even in large facilities, if certain safeguards are taken. A primary requirement is that staff as well as inmates be exposed to group procedures. Although considerable anxiety may exist at initial meetings, group sessions composed of staff at various levels can begin to function well in a matter of weeks when properly presented. Barriers can be broken down between employees, and the staff brought to a better understanding of what goes on in the teenage groups. Active participation is the best way to learn group techniques.[88] Staff involvement in groups requires, for its success, the wholehearted endorsement and participation of the institution director and all of his top-level assistants.

Various approaches have been used to break down inmate resistance to group procedures. One is to play to them tapes of group sessions recorded at other locations, so that they may hear the completely frank, and uninhibited comments of other adolescents. Still another method is to use persons who have passed through the group process, as group leaders.[89]

A successful instance of how a group of delinquents were won over took place when their adult leader placed the troublemakers of the school, the three- and four-time losers who controlled the institution subculture, in one cottage. He then moved in with them, and by convincing them that whatever was said at the meetings would not be used against them, he succeeded, after some six months, in establishing an esprit de corps which was evidenced by their prestige in the eyes of the other inmates, and the latter's expressed wish to be involved in the same group program.[90]

A large institution which operates on guided group interaction principles as its treatment approach can make provision in its original construction plans, as was done by an eastern state when in 1968 a new 900-man institution was built. The blueprints clearly show the plan for these men to function in small, rather than large, groups, as they work, sleep, eat, converse and spend their leisure as a small number of inmates sharing a specific area. It is planned that individuals with largely similar problems will be housed together. Not all inmates will be eligible for the guided group interaction program; the most severely disturbed will be treated in other ways by the psychological and psychiatric staff.[91]

In introducing guided group interaction into any large facility, the traditional, formal controls should be retained until a group culture begins to take shape. Old-line staff, however punitive in outlook, are essential for control during this interim period. The stick may not be removed until the lure of the carrot is found at least equally effective. All this takes time; there are bound to be setbacks as well as evident advances; in the end the institution can become, largely under self-management, more secure than when it was punitively controlled. In the process some of the traditionally minded, custodial staff will find themselves converted to the newer approach. Those who do not will find other posts for themselves in the more comfortable atmosphere of the custodially oriented institution.

Guided Groups in Probation and Parole

Some of the same objection to the guided group approach in large institutions may also be leveled at its use for persons on probation: that the group meeting strips away an individual's defenses leaving him ill-prepared to associate thereafter with others who are not similarly involved, or who may be actually unsympathetic to his anxiety. Partial efforts at guided group interaction for persons in the community may generate tensions which are then difficult to control adequately, resulting in harm not only to the individual involved but also to the program.[92] The basic question to be decided is whether change should be attempted under conditions which provide neither the support nor the controls found in the residential center.[93]

Perhaps the most effective approach is to expose the offender to guided group interaction within the supportive environment of the halfway house, and then when he is considered ready for aftercare, to carry over the group discussion as part of the parole process. The group member will presumably at this stage have already made the basic shift to socially acceptable attitudes. The traumatic stage is behind him, and what is needed most at this point is some measure of support to counter those family or neighborhood influences which played their part in the origins of his antisocial behavior. In short, if the guided group process has helped the offender for a four- to six-month period, it is only prudent to maintain contact with him while he is on parole where a modified group approach and a sufficiently small caseload can continue to permit real interaction between leader and boy.[94]

Developing Group Leaders

Advocates of guided group interaction place relatively little emphasis on formal academic training as a prerequisite for group leadership. While many leaders hold master's degrees, many of them interned at Highfield, or other established centers, and this experience, rather than formal training, is regarded as the key to their skills.[95] Most successful group leaders are not psychoanalytically oriented, considering themselves competent, rather, in the reality, or confrontation, approach to personal problems. Internship for two to six months is regarded as the most effective avenue for the training of a competent group leader.

One of the most exciting, as well as encouraging newer developments is the employment of former offenders as leaders of group sessions in a number of halfway houses. Each day finds growing support for the idea that young offenders can be expected to respond more positively to persons who have undergone experiences parallel to their own than to middle-class professionals with whose backgrounds and values they may find little in common.[96]

Present needs for correctional personnel simply do not allow sufficient time for candidates to complete years of training, even if this were considered desirable. Persons interested in becoming group session leaders, whether exoffenders or professionally trained social workers, should be persons of good intelligence, considerable empathy, patience, and courage. "These positions are more demanding of skill and dedication than almost any other work to be found in corrections. It is work that is confining and exhausting for both the worker and his family."[97]

A Typical Guided Group Interaction Meeting

A guided group interaction meeting usually runs for ninety minutes. Typically, ten or twelve boys file into the room promptly at the scheduled hour, dragging in their own chairs. The director may introduce a new boy to the others, explaining that he was there to help them with their problems, as the experienced members were to help him with his.

Immediately after such an introduction, Harvey, one of the group members who has been at the center for some months now, becomes the focus of attention describing, in a somewhat belligerent tone, a clash he has had that morning with his work supervisor. The latter had taken offense at a comment he had meant to be humorous, and had yelled at him. Harvey, in turn, had grabbed the employee's arm. The employee had then shouted, "Get your –– hands off of me." Although the narrator was giving a version of the incident favorable to his point of view, the other boys were hesitant to credit it, one after another criticizing him for having deliberately aggravated the employee: "What's wrong with you, Harvey? The man was simply doing his job." Harvey replies that he felt he had been humiliated, or "put down" by the employee, to which the others retort: "You put yourself down." Harvey, now aroused, states that he would not have grabbed the employee's arm if he had not "hollered and cussed at me," at which, he said, he himself had become excited and scared.

At this point, the leader intervenes, for the first time in fifteen minutes, quietly asking the group why they thought Harvey had acted as he did. The boys are quick to reply that, although he had been at the center for five months, Harvey could still be expected to make "smart" remarks and wisecracks. Almost half the group now hurl questions at Harvey, many of them simultaneously, all accusing him of being a troublemaker, a faker, and a "bad mouth." [These are euphemisms for more profane language.] Harvey at this point admits that the employee with whom he had argued probably agreed with the group's opinion of himself.

One boy then asks, "What will it take to get you interested in people?" When all he gets back is a muttered reply, another boy comments, "It would be easy to talk Harvey into committing a crime if he was 'on the outside.' " Here again (ten minutes having elapsed since his last question), the leader quietly asks, "Why?" The boy replies: "It doesn't matter much to him. Harvey seems like a weak person." The comments that follow are not all so negative, the boys admitting that, "Harvey does not enjoy hurting people like he used to."

The significance of this remark can better be judged by the fact that Harvey had had a long history of violent assault, his most recent act, the one resulting in his arrest and conviction. He had forced a grown man, at the point of a gun, to crawl, bare-chested, on a gravel road. After several hundred feet of such humiliation and torture, when the victim, his chest torn and bleeding, attempted to lift himself up from the road, he had been met with threats that his head would be blown off.

Harvey now voices his concern that he might get sent to the state training school. "Why do you enjoy wising off?" The leader asks this question, to which Harvey admits that he didn't think of the feelings of others. Then one of the group comments, "If Harvey doesn't like someone, he just messes over him. He doesn't care."

"Does Harvey intend to hurt people here, at this time?" the leader asks, to which one boy replies, "No, he didn't mean to. His smart remarks were more off the cuff."

The counselor cuts in: "Harvey is not really sorry about the employee. He is simply sorry because he knows the man will be riding him from here on. He's sorry for himself, not for what he did."

The conversation had now gone on for an hour, and Harvey was permitted to step down from the "hot seat." In his place came Stanley, a black boy who had hit another boy with a mop because: "He told me I was lying. I didn't want him lying on me."

"How did this affect you?" the group asked. "Why did it make you mad when the boy said you were lying?"

Stanley began to get angry. "I thought it was like a team here. I got attached to you guys, and then, when I tell you what I've done, you give me hell even though I said I was sorry."

The boys, thoroughly aroused, all reject his statements. "How come no one in the group can talk to you, Stan? What are you going to do about it, Stan?"

Incensed, Stanley remarks that he is "a cool gent," who does not have to justify himself to anybody. The others better not "mess" with him.

Harvey, now a discussant rather than the target of the group's concern, comments, "You're not near as cool as you think you are, Stan."

Another asks, "What does this 'cool' mean, Stan? Suppose you tell us just what this 'being cool' means."

Stanley becomes thoroughly belligerent at this point: "Anything I feel like doing, I'll do it. Besides, Harvey'd better watch himself, 'cause I don't like him messing with me."

The intensity of the attacks now increases: "What is this threatening stuff, Stan? Let's face it, Stan, you do threaten people."

Above the loud and angry attacks Stanley is heard defending himself: "That still stands. Ain't no one going to mess over me."

Another member of the group, stung but undaunted by his threats, asks, "What are you, Stan, a giant superman?"

Stanley fights back, "You just — with me and you'll find out. I won't let little boys like you — over me. I can handle myself pretty well. I ain't been — up like I have been. I been trying.

Suddenly he seems to change his tactics, and although still furious, pretends complete agreement though in a low monotone, "I'll go by what the group says. If you say I don't know what I'm doing, I guess I don't."

The others are not so easily placated. One comments, "Now you're playing games, Stan. You're acting like a baby. Your threats aren't bothering anybody."

Quite subdued, now, Stanley: "I don't mean it as a threat. I've been saying that kind of stuff all my life." As if he suddenly realizes that he himself has let drop his guard, Stanley shouts back angrily, "But nobody better tangle with Stan!"

Suddenly the air is thick with obscenities. A third boy, Frank, as angry as Stanley, now remarks, "You don't scare me none. Go ahead and make your move."

A fight appearing imminent, the leader who has been silent during all the foregoing, quietly asks, "What's the group doing now? Aren't you trying to force a challenge?"

The tension eases and one of the group says quietly, "We just want him to stop that kind of —."

Stanley rejoins, "I ain't going to like these boys, if they keep messing with me."

For the remaining quarter hour the leader now took over, giving a summary of what had taken place. He referred to Harvey's clash with the employee and his belief that progress had been made, because this was the first time that Harvey had admitted being afraid. He was confident of Harvey's ability to control himself even when other people shout at him. He pointed out that Harvey had acted belligerently because of his fear of being "put down" before the group. The leader then emphasized the boys' concern for one another by relating how, when Harvey had recently got himself into an embarrassing situation, it had been Stanley who had stepped forward and permitted Harvey to "save face."

He then referred to Stanley's attack with a mop on another boy, pointing out that Stanley had told the other boy he was sorry. "Stan says he's trying to change, and he complains that the group won't recognize this. The group, on the other hand, says it does care for Stan, but it's not afraid of him either. The group feels that Stan is trying to 'put them down' by making them afraid of Stan. But," he continued, "Stan is showing us some of his true feelings in contrast to Frank who has been playing it real 'cool' in keeping his feelings hidden."

Here Frank admitted that, "I've had these feelings for a long, long time," that he often felt angry, and that he tried to conceal it by "playing it cool."

The leader then criticized the group for not having stopped Frank at the point when he had challenged Stanley to "make his move."

"The group should have asked what was going on because Frank left the issue of helping Stan and simply got mad."

Frank, his head low, in an undertone: "I might as well let my anger out here, or I'll never get out of this place."

The leader assured him, "Don't worry about letting it out."

The meeting ended with Stanley, still appearing angry, remarking, "I don't know what to say."

With the other boys looking concerned, the director closed the meeting: "You boys recognize you've got problems, and you're doing something about them."

The Ordeal of Change

While little is known of the mechanics of the process by which insight into the basic problems of an individual comes about, there are, in the literature, not a few personal chronicles which permit us, now and again, to get behind the defenses put up by the anxiety-ridden — the boys who express their conflicts by acting out or running away from confrontation with the necessity to change.

In such boys, attitudes of independence and the ability to relate to others are seen as attempts to conceal basic problems or to mask the real discomfort and even pain which marks so many of these young people. The following is a transcript of the story of one such boy. Only names, dates and places have been disguised. The rest stands as it was recorded.[98]

My name is Joe and I came up here in June — the tenth. My charges are immorality, smoking marijuana and I been in and out of the Youth House all my life. I don't get along too well with my family — maybe because we don't understand each other. My mother and myself. My father died when I was young. She never treated me the way I wanted to be treated. I've always put the blame on her for the way I live — that's so far — but that's not true. I always wanted to be number one — on top. I always wanted to be good at everything I do — that I want to do.

I come up here to the Center and I disliked whites because of what I've seen done through the years. When I was "on the bricks" I used to go to the Mosque and listen to the minister preach. He just say things I wanted to hear — and I thought that was for me — I wanted to be a Muslim. But, after I kept goin' for a while I thought it was nothin' but a hustle. They was hustlin' people's money left and right — people didn't have no money — but they got it and they sapped them and conned and rapped on them and I didn't like this. After that I joined — I messed with the Black Nationalists. I used to work at a Afro-American shop. I used to talk all the time and they used to tell me about what they're goin' to do for us. I used to dig them because they didn't just tell you to go out on the street and do things, they went out there before you and they did more than any other black organization that I know about and I dug this and they had a peaceful existence, like everything was together — brothers.

And then the riot came and I went out in the street and looted. I thought this was good. We was tearin' down the fucked up system. Actually we was just tearin' down our own neighborhoods — our stuff — and when the riot was over we had to take charity, welfare — food and whatnot. Durin' the riot I got busted on my head by a negro detective when I was sneakin' out of a store and I hated him. Because to me he was Uncle Tom — you know, a traitor. Just some kind of a brainwashed negro. Later that day he took me to the precinct — he tried to talk to me and I nixed him off. Because he disgusted me. My head was bleedin', blood was drippin' all down the side of my face, dryin' up — my head was splittin' and he kept on talkin'. He had tears in his eyes — and I saw this — and I thought it's not his fault. He really don't know what's happening. A man would do many things for money — and I kind of dug him because he wasn't a phoney — he wasn't — like critical. He was tellin' me things which at the time didn't mean anything, but now it does.

When I come up here I got so I had this dislike for whites and I wouldn't talk to anybody. I wouldn't talk to any staff members because they were white. And I cliqued with four guys up here when I first came up. I rapped on them about how black people should stick together. I really meant it. After we got busted down for this clique and we talked about it I learned that a prejudice is not somethin' that can be ignored. It is somethin' you have to deal with, to understand, and after we talked about this my meetin' gave their viewpoint. I began to realize that regardless of what color you are, people are people. And there is very little hatred against race, it's more or less we are all selfish and we all want what we want and get what we want regardless of how the other feels. And this is a failure. This can't last.

And a month or so after I been here I started to open up. I felt more comfortable. And I remembered what happened on the 25th of December when I got a ride home by a white family and my own mother wasn't there. I remember I felt that this is fucked up — you know — my own mother's not here. And after — I fall back on the very people I thought I despised — and I shook and trembled in the car — I didn't know what to say so I kept quiet but they was so friendly that I felt like I was fucked up — not them — it must be me and I tried to talk and the words came out all jumbled and my hands started shakin' and I couldn't stop it. I'll never forget that. I feel that it was my emotions. One of deep rooted hatred and another of just the opposite. I dug it and I was trying to force myself to realize — you know — these people aren't the way I thought.

My meeting has helped me a lot and I feel toward them as a brother. I really do. But even now I feel that they haven't done as much for me as I would like to believe they could. They haven't really talked to me about me, except in the meeting. Partly this is because of I don't give them a chance — really not much of a chance.

I had my mother all wrong. She really did think about your future and that — how you're going to be — and I dropped out of school and caught myself hustlin' and fuck school — it didn't get you nowhere — you can't go very far — they won't let you go but so far. So I took to stealin' and hustlin' muggin' breakin' and entries and what not — to keep in shape — you know — I was kind of proud because — you know — I outsmarted the man — that's the way I felt — I was under pressure more or less. A challenge was always near and I always accepted this challenge and I felt that — you know — this was me. This was the way I was meant to be. And that was another one of my foolish, egotistic desires. I was on the wrong track but now I see that didn't do any good for me or my people. I'm just another hood — a young punk — want a car — smokin' marijuana — school was square to me fucked up — you know — that's for chumps — pussies — not for me. I am hard, cold — but I am not — that was just a role — I am finding out — still I am really — because I don't know whether I am that or this — what I am now. Am I really me? Is this me? Or was that me? I know one thing I would rather play this role than play the other. And I know nothing can stop me from doing what I want to do. I want to — and now that I found where I really want to be I am going to travel around the world, go many places — that takes money and I am going to get it — I am going to be a millionaire with a mansion one day. I do feel alone — all alone — you know — like there's just me — out there in the fuckin' world — and I still have to look where I am goin'. Watch out for anybody who would attempt to mess me around. But I been doin' this all my life — you know . . .

I don't worry about anything. I found out that nobody can help me — much as I can help myself — and I'm really not sure if anybody else thinks that I'm helped. But I *know* that I am. I look at myself now and I see changes — changes in the way I think — the way I behave — and it's for real — it's there — let's stop here, even though I still am selfish I am goin' to try and do as much as I can to change things in the world. I hope to be some day in a position where I can do this. I know the only way I can get there is by hard work, very little pleasure, and determination. Most of all I will depend on my pride to keep me going. My pride — that's very important to me — very important.

Mr. X — I always thought he was more of a machine than a man. He seems so unreal. He just knew too much and I tried to figure him out. What kind of a man is this — you know — but you can't! I respect him very much because he's not afraid to say what he wants to say — nor do what he wants to do. He must have an awful lot of understanding of himself and I hope one day to have just as much and if possible more. He really is a nice guy — really is a nice guy — beautiful person — and I am sure that everyone in my meeting will stay out there "on the bricks" and do more than they could possibly really do in the past because they *got* it now. And I wish them all the best of luck. I'll try to keep in contact with them by mail — as many of them as possible.

As for narcotics — I don't need it and I never did need narcotics. It never did make me feel any stronger than I was but at the same time it gave me a feeling of peace. I always felt peaceful when I was high as if I could do things no one else could do. I could see it in the way no one else could see it, and it really did something good to me because I became interested in art. I could actually dig art. And I used to create my own things — such as — I used to like to write — I was planning to write a book — and jazz — I love jazz — and these are beautiful to me and marijuana — I still don't think it's right for one man to determine whether another man can enjoy the kind of pleasure that he wants because what I'm saying is liquor is just as bad and in some cases much worse. But now that I've fucked myself around and spoiled my plans I am going to give up. Fuck it — I could do without. I also noticed what it had done to me because my mind was screwed up — actually fucked up. When I was high any little thing would annoy me. If someone played the wrong record I would get pissed off and start cursing and shit. I never could understand that. I could be hurt while under this drug — I could be hurt because I was wide open. I couldn't take no shit — as far as more could possibly happen because I knew I had everything up tight and under control and I had no reason to look out and something much worse could happen than this. I once tried to commit suicide. I had run away from home again. I was just tired of livin'. The pressure was on my back heavy and I just wanted to give the whole show up — take the easy way out — lay back. I figured there would be no problems — it would be quick — and I'll be high before I do it and everything would be all right. But a man like myself can not do this — destroy yourself — I can't do it. Really I don't think anyone can do it unless he is in a, or she is in a, state of delirium. I have learned a whole lot up here — more than I can even tell — more than I can tell — about people, the way I am — myself — my family. When I was down in my — what causes trouble and the things I do. Why it is a problem? What makes it a problem? I know these things and I guess it's been said a million times before me. Well, I'll just say that. I won't stop what I'm doin'. If anything I'll improve and I am not talking about stealin' smokin' drinkin' and stuff. I'll do something for myself and something I can contribute to society. Society needs a change and I want to help it.

Summary

Since its inception at Highfields in 1950, guided group interaction has won increasing recognition and favor as a treatment technique for delinquent youths and is now found in many states, in both residential and nonresidential centers. Although the consensus is that it functions best in facilities for from 20 to 30, some believe it can be successfully adapted to persons in larger institutions, as well as to those on probation and parole.

In its inception stages, guided group interaction can be distressing to both adult leader and group member. Four recognizable and distinct stages follow one another when a new guided group center is created. Not until these stages have evolved will a cohesive social group characterized by common goals be established. It is impossible for delinquent behavior and attitudes to change as long as the impact of the group can be evaded. But as it develops a culture and norms, it starts to function as an entity, it becomes oriented toward change, and individual members feel themselves pressured to conform. A commitment to alter one's way of life does not take place without anxiety, tension, and potential explosiveness enroute, or unless the individual is motivated to change and is also helped to internalize the new, proffered standards.

Crucial to this success is the personality of the group leader. In addition to concern and interest, he must be agreeable to granting considerable decision-making responsibility to his group members. By allowing complete frankness in speech, he helps to bridge the gulf that too often tragically separates today's generations. Through intelligent and empathic handling, he aims to conduct open, noncustodial programs uncluttered by the impersonalness, severity and security of the conventional institution. The approach is not so permissive as it may appear; subtle pressures are constantly exerted to lead group members to examine critically their previous life styles.

Initially, part of this pressure depends on the threat of imprisonment, for until an esprit de corps develops among the group, some external controls are needed to induce conformity. This can be eased as the culture begins to form and the group develops its own internal controls, when a relaxed and informal atmosphere gradually emerges. A sense of mutual concern and respect ensues, tempers seem to abate, and adults are now approached in a friendly, even eager, way by their young charges.

The meetings are frequent, usually an hour and a half in length, five times a week. Constant interaction takes place, not only during the discussion periods, but also at work, meals, and play. It is through this constant interaction that group norms and common purpose develop, especially when the participants derive from similar socioeconomic backgrounds and have a common delinquent history. While there is no stress on urgency, a feeling emerges that time is important, and through the use of "old" and "new" groups, boys are made aware that they should move through the program within a maximum of six months.

The establishment of a positive group culture requires certain preconditions. Boys will not become involved if they are allowed to participate on a "take-it or leave-it" basis. If there is no pressure of time, they will not experience the anxiety essential for change. If they lack respect for, or confidence in, the adult group leadership, a delinquent subculture will take over and flourish. Intake must be carefully controlled, for the too-rapid admission of a large number of new boys can disrupt an already established positive group culture. Experience indicates that the following will, in all likelihood, make poor subjects for group participation: those who have difficulty communicating with others because of cultural or personality disparities, who have been institutionalized for many years, who differ considerably in their social and emotional maturity, and finally, those with severe emotional problems.

Guided group interaction seems more likely to be effective with members of lower socioeconomic groups and less so with offenders from middle-class backgrounds. Some questions remain as to the efficacy of guided group interaction with the young drug addicts, the active homosexuals and those with an apparently long and deep commitment to a criminal way of life.

In the inauguration of a new group, and for its culture to unfold properly thereafter, much time and distress can be saved if the young participants are provided with some guidance and encouragement. Despite initial resistance, once the group members know what is expected of them, they can then proceed to assume greater responsibility, after which the leader can begin to withdraw from his prominent role at the earliest — and most graceful — opportunity. It is the group rather than the leader which is the chief instrument in producing change. He is merely the catalyst — and the more expert he is in the art, the more effective is he likely to be. Too constant intervention on his part will only make the group members overly dependent upon him: "a distraction and an excuse for evading their problems and ducking responsibility."[99]

Tape recordings of established groups, when played before young persons assembled for the first time in a newly started group, give the newcomer an awareness that it is possible to reveal the most sensitive areas of his life before his peers. Another technique is to employ former delinquents, who have already moved through the halfway house experience, to "seed" the inexperienced group.

While there are very real difficulties in introducing this treatment method in large, well-established institutions, one approach which has worked is for the adult leader deliberately to search out the recognized leaders of the inmate subculture. If these "dukes" can be successfully drawn into group interaction, the task of reaching others is eased and, in fact, once their own outlook has changed, such former delinquents can conduct new groups. Architects for newly proposed institutions should be urged to so design facilities as to permit division into small groups to enhance the opportunity for member interaction.

The use of guided group interaction for probationers and parolees is feasible where such persons have already been exposed to the intensive treatment phase within a center. They may then be expected to move successfully to a less rigorous program of group interaction while under probation or parole supervision. Skilled group leaders can be developed without years of training, through intern programs in the necessary techniques.

Guided group interaction confronts its participants with the "here-and-now" realities of their lives. When youngsters are given an outlet for the expression of their hostility and frustration, aggressive behavior can be greatly reduced and replaced by a culture or esprit de corps which can then redirect values and resultant behavior. Through constant interaction, a spirit of honesty, mutual trust and even affection is attainable. "The group cohesion is the major factor in enforcing the goal of change."[100] The role of the staff member is vital in guiding and evaluating the process, and easing the travail whereby young people can be helped to bring about fundamental changes in their attitudes and lives.

Varieties of Treatment in
the Community

6 Group Foster Homes

Rationale

Delinquent children can be placed in group care foster homes instead of singly in the conventional foster home when they are unable to tolerate a close one-to-one relationship with foster parents.[1] The average adolescent's eagerness to escape from adult control is expressed in hostility toward anyone in authority but, when placed with others of his own age within a group setting, he may find it less difficult to accept the control of substitute parents than in a setting which does not provide opportunity for association with his peers.

By living in a group, he avoids the more intimate living situation of the ordinary foster home, while the presence of others of his own age gives him support at a time when he is both anxious and awkward about close contact with adults, and in need of help in changing his antisocial attitudes.

Location

Recent years have seen increasing interest by a number of jurisdictions in developing group care foster home programs for delinquents. Oregon has established group homes throughout the state;[2] California is experimenting with five distinct types to meet the needs of different classes of young offenders;[3] Colorado has opened group homes which operate under its county welfare departments.[4] The most notable expansion is found however in the midwest chiefly in Wisconsin, Minnesota, Ohio, Iowa and Michigan.

Specific designations describe the two types. While "boarding homes" refer to the traditional foster home caring for from one to four delinquent children; the "group home" usually accommodates four or more children.[5] The growth of these two facilities as with the halfway house itself, has been so rapid that it is impossible to list them all. In 1967, for example, Wisconsin had available at least 260 boarding homes, many housing more than one child.[6] Ohio in that same year had between 35 and 50 boarding homes in operation. Iowa over one hundred.[7]

Wisconsin was the original pioneer in this form of correctional treatment in 1955, and twelve years later reported 31 group homes caring for a total of 133 boys and girls. Of the 290 foster homes licensed by the Division of Corrections, approximately one-tenth are group homes.[8] Minnesota followed Wisconsin's development in 1964, when its Citizens Council on Delinquency and Crime, a private statewide organization which supports progressive penal legislation, strongly endorsed the group home concept. A council survey had discovered that too many children in the state training schools were being detained beyond their optimum release dates because their own homes were considered unfit to receive them again, while foster home facilities were inadequate to provide care to all who needed this type of care. In just two years, 250 boys and girls had waited from three to almost five months beyond their release dates for this reason. Of all the absconders from the State Training School, almost one-fourth were boys whose placement in a foster home had been delayed.[9]

Largely as a result of the efforts of the Citizen's Council, based on the results of their survey, the Minnesota State Legislature appropriated $108,000 in 1965 to set up seven group homes, and in the following year delinquent children began to be placed in the community. One half were children released from state schools; the others were first offenders. Two years later the legislature appropriated additional funds which made possible the doubling of the number of group care foster homes.[10] These efforts on the state level had been preceded in Ramsey County by those of its juvenile court judge who had been instrumental in establishing group homes for delinquent girls in the St. Paul — Minneapolis area.

Payment

States which operate successful group foster home programs for delinquents make considerably higher payments for the services of the foster parents then those usually paid for the care of dependent children largely because of the greater difficulty of dealing with children who manifest behavior problems. Three forms of payment may be noted: a monthly boarding fee; a boarding fee supplimented by a monthly "bed subsidy": a specified per diem for each day that the delinquent child is in care. In California the Youth Authority has a somewhat unique arrangement whereby a monthly subsidy of as high as $310 may be paid to a group foster couple plus a fee of $94 a month for each child in care.[11] The boarding fee may run as high as $140 per month per child; where he is old enough to work a part of this cost is expected to be borne by the boy out of his earnings.[12]

Wisconsin, Minnesota, Iowa, and Michigan provide a flat monthly subsidy to a foster couple for each bed which they make available in their home, whether the bed is occupied or not. This sum ranges from $30 a month in Minnesota to $50 in Michigan,[13] depending on the skill and experience of the foster parents and their years of service to delinquent children. The top monthly subsidy per bed can be paid at the end of seven years of service, on the recommendation of the state parole authorities. The guaranteed subsidy per bed, paid as soon as the foster home license has been granted, provides a desirable financial cushion for the foster parents, for even if the house is only half-full, their monthly income is not too adversely affected. In this way the authorities are assured of a fairly constant foster home service availability.

In addition to the bed allotment, Wisconsin, Minnesota, Iowa and Michigan pay a monthly boarding fee once a child is in residence, ranging from $75 to

$115. Sums even beyond the maximum may be paid, upon authorization by the state foster home administration.[14]

An annually renewable contract is entered into with the prospective foster parents, in order to minimize the possibility of misunderstanding as to their role vis-a-vis the state agency. A yearly medical examination is expected of the parents, at which time the fitness of the home is reevaluated.[15] At least one state requires fire inspection at regular intervals. Either party to the contract may terminate it after a thirty-day notification. In return for its subsidies, Iowa expects its group-care parents to receive whatever children the agency believes might benefit from placement with them, in contrast to the ordinary foster or boarding home where the parents are first consulted.[16] In Wisconsin and Minnesota any foster parents, in group as well as in boarding homes, may refuse to take any child whose previous history may make them doubtful of their ability to keep him in care.

Additional payments are made for clothing, medical and dental care, and pocket money. In order that foster parents may have an opportunity for time away from their charges, Wisconsin also pays relief parents when the regular parents are on vacation or become ill. Ohio is representative of those jurisdictions which pay a per diem, here ranging from $4.00 to $5.50.[17]

Because of the difficulty of finding enough qualified homes and foster parents to care for the numbers of delinquents whom they would like to place, correctional authorities acknowledge that the rates for such services must be expected to run from $20 to $55 a month higher than those paid for the care of dependent boys and girls. Parents who are willing to care for a sizable number of children may have to buy or rent a large residence; a large number of children in care makes it all the more essential that the foster parents be enabled to take time off from what is at best a difficult and emotionally exhausting responsibility.

Experience has proved the value of correctional agencies, such as parole departments, assuming of the assignment to find foster homes for delinquent children. In the great majority of instances, delinquent and dependent children do not appear to get on well together under the same roof. Nor can welfare department personnel, who are charged with finding homes for dependent children, be relied upon to search out the special foster home situation which is likely to be receptive to the idea of caring for delinquent children. This is not to say that such foster parents are easy to find under the best possible circumstances. However, at least one instance may be cited where the judge of a county juvenile court turned, in desperation, to press and radio to persuade citizens to offer their homes for children who would otherwise have to be committed to institutional care.[18]

Foster Parents

The best substitute parents for delinquent children in group homes seem to be those people who have had experience in caring for foster children of other types and thereafter seem to adapt most easily to delinquents. Such persons feel less threatened by such acting-out behavior as temper tantrums, or by physical and verbal aggression than do those whose experience as parents has been limited to dealing only with their own children. The following composite well describes the average foster couple:

Group home parents generally will be middle aged (40 to 55) with experience in raising children of their own. Some may have cared for foster children. Most group home mothers will not have gone beyond high school. Some fathers may have some college. Most of the fathers will probably be skilled laborers and will continue their regular occupation as in normal living. The mothers should not work outside the group home.[19]

When Minnesota prepared to embark on a group foster home program, it sought for foster parents among "mature, stable, people with high standards and good values for themselves and others, but with the ability and flexibility to understand and accept problem behavior."[20] While some foster parents are young couples with small children of their own,[21] others equally effective are older persons, whose own children have grown up and moved out of the home. In one Wisconsin home, eight delinquent girls reside with a farm couple who have a sixteen-year-old son. The foster mother, a most sensible woman, was all in favor of the experiment: "He's not girl crazy. Although he's in the same school with the girls, he doesn't see too much of them there because other students would tease him. At home, we get along fine, although the girls sometimes complain that he tries to advise them about whom they should date."

Some foster parents, rather than seeing the delinquent teenager as a detrimental influence on their own children, often describe the association as mutually beneficial both to their own and to their foster children.[22] Others describe the mixture as not always a happy one, failure being partially attributed in not a few instances, to "sibling rivalry" between foster and natural children, especially young children:

Wisconsin does have some comparatively young couples but we do not favor this age group for foster home parents. They are the exception, not the rule; and they are given very close guidance and support by the supervising parole agent.[23]

Group home foster parents have one need in common: attention, advice, encouragement from experienced supervisors, and reinforcement. Delinquent children are not infrequently both angry and fearful in their dealings with adults, alternating just as easily — and ambivalently — between aggression and dependence. Some authorities therefore recommend that foster parents about to receive such children should take an initial indoctrination course of some kind, others advocate a term of in-service training which will give them contact with delinquents at the state training school as well as limited formal instruction, with materials specifically aimed at persons with sixth and eighth grade reading abilities.[24] Wisconsin, however, has no program of formal training for its group home parents in the belief that this might hinder the natural, open fashion in which their foster parents accept delinquent children into the home.[25]

Placement Policies

When different foster homes are available for various offenders, the assignment of each child to the home best suited to him becomes a test of skill and patience on the part of those who are responsible for the placement.

Despite what has been said above, about the desirability of not commingling the two groups of children, Iowa uses group homes to serve both its delinquent and its nondelinquent children. So does Colorado, when its supervisory staff believes that foster parents with dependent children can live comfortably with children released from the training school.[26] Children who bear the label of "dependent" are bound to have other problems as well, many of them similar to the problems presented by the child who happens to have been adjudicated a "delinquent."

Most delinquents in Wisconsin group homes are parolees from state training schools. Some 10% of them, however, are young people under the jurisdiction of the local courts who have not yet been committed to the Division of Corrections. Placed in the same group foster homes, and supervised by parole officers, these relatively inexperienced delinquents who come directly from the court seem to get on well with parolees released from the training school.[27] Michigan also places these two groups of offenders in the same homes.[28] Minnesota, however, separates the two groups, housing the "first-timers" together, while sending those with more extensive records of delinquency to other group homes.

Number of Children Per Home

The optimum capacity of the average group home appears to be five, with an upper limit usually of eight, for reasons of fire and safety, as well as in order to avoid any appearance of a small institution. Furthermore, a home of very large capacity would be prohibitively expensive for the private home owner; transportation would also present a problem. Minnesota, while generally limiting the maximum number of children in its group homes to six, makes one exception by reason of the particular skill of an unusual pair of foster parents who are entrusted with eight boys, all of them with serious criminal histories.[29]

The "group home" designation does not apply in Ohio to homes with less than six children, but larger group homes may hold as many as twelve, with at least one that has cared for fifteen parolees from the training school.[30]

Girls and Boys

Of interest is that two-thirds of the Wisconsin group foster homes care for delinquent girls,[31] as do five of the seven group homes in St. Paul, Minnesota.[32] Although some correctional administrators maintain that girl offenders are more difficult to handle than boys, others apparently have greater success in convincing prospective foster parents to accept them into their homes. Most boys have records of offences against persons and property. The girls are more frequently in custody for sexual misconduct or for running away: to the average citizen, the stereotype of waywardness arouses less fear. This is probably the underlying reason that, in at least two midwestern states, the ratio of group foster care for girls is much higher than it is for boys.[33]

Development of the Group Home

Much of the success of the group foster home program depends upon the initiative of individual parole agents, especially if these are well trained and well paid. Where the agent favors this form of placement, good foster homes are more likely to be found, and a higher ratio of children to be placed in them. The group home has the advantage of caring for several children in the same caseload in the one home. At the same time, if the authorities place children from all over the state in the same home, the agent will find himself serving children who were not originally from his sector of the state.

Support from administrative headquarters is equally vital for the development of a strong foster home program. States where these programs seem to do well favor the appointment of a specialist — the Foster Home Administrator — both to supervise foster home programs, and to encourage the group home idea. One state encourages the calling together of foster home parents in periodic meetings for an exchange of views and a discussion of common problems. Much is being done to stimulate the interest of parole agents, to promote the program through public relations efforts, to develop training programs, and actively to search through advertising and other ways, for additional foster homes.

Because of the anxiety which children experience at the prospect of removal to a foster home, attempts are made for the transition from the state institution to a group home to be made as smooth as possible for them. Orientation classes may be held for these children while they are still at the training school.[34] A brief pamphlet, with photographs and a description of the prospective foster parents, their children and their community, is given to the child. He may also be invited to make a trial visit to his prospective home, and when the placement plan is final, the parole agent will personally drive him there.[35]

Treatment and Program

The group foster home aims to provide for its children a degree of stability of family life which most of them have never previously known. With trustworthy and accepting adults serving as a model for him, the delinquent teenager can be helped through identification to find some stability and purpose in his own life. The same parole agent usually serves all children in one group home, and although he may meet with them from time to time either singly or in a group, this relationship is a minor part of the treatment program. Foster care is seen primarily as a substitute to parental, providing, at a minimum, a temporary custodial or "holding" service, such that:

This attitudinal position is directly related in practice. . .foster parents are not recruited, nor are foster care placements implemented, for the purpose of facilitating attitudinal and behavioral change on the part of the youth placed.[36]

The Wisconsin program typically leaves decisions as to a child's school and social activities largely to the discretion of the foster parent and the parole agent, the two agreeing to the rules regarding hours, frequency and times for visits from the child's own parents, and such other family matters as social contacts and responsibility for household chores.[37]

Visits to a number of these group homes rate them high in physical appearance and the caliber of their foster parents. Warmth and affection are often immediately apparent, with many foster parents seeming to enjoy their situation as much as do their charges. In some homes, wards are quite evidently made to feel as if they were family members. In others, where the same high degree of intimacy may not be attained, relations between adults and child are nevertheless good. Recreational opportunities seen in most foster homes were ample, though living conditions were occasionally found to be crowded. There may not always seem to be enough lavatories; basement rooms may now and then be used; but even such places appear neat and cheerful with a perceptible feeling of "home."

Advantages and Disadvantages

Programs of group care foster homes for delinquent children present many advantages. In contrast to the violent community opposition that is sometimes encountered when a conventional halfway house is opened anywhere but in the most deteriorated sections of a large city, little resentment is voiced by the neighbors to a group foster home, because the foster parents are already local residents, and especially in those instances where approval of the local judge, police, and schools has first been obtained.[38] In Minnesota, each group home has an intake committee comprised of prominent local citizens, who serve also as a local public relations group.[39]

In terms of cost, group foster homes offer demonstrable advantages over institutional care. Because foster parents either own or rent their homes, the state is spared any capital outlay as well as the problem of hiring staff. Even where bed subsidies and monthly payments are comparatively generous, the costs per child in foster care are less than half that of institutional care — even at $1800 per annum. Moreover, once funds have been appropriated, the group foster care program can be established, especially if any prior recruiting of interested foster parents has already been done.

The drawbacks that inhere to the group foster care home may take a bit longer to set forth than the advantages of this program, but are perhaps not so cogent. Where the foster parents are the key figures in its success, persons willing to accept as many as eight delinquent children into their homes often find their lives rather confined as a result. Their death or illness may necessitate immediate removal of the children.[40] Children are placed in these homes at the sufferance of the foster parent and when sudden disagreements arise between them and their wards, the latter must be removed if the parents insist upon it. This can be most unsettling to children, many of whose lives have seen a steady succession of one adult after another. The "life expectancy" of a group foster home is about five years, because of the demanding, not to say exhausting, nature of this close involvement with young delinquents.[41] It is of interest here to show a parallel with leaders of intensive guided group interaction programs, who report much the same experience.

Many foster homes are in rural areas, yet the majority of their charges are from the city, which makes visits difficult and may further weaken whatever ties with parents or other relatives that do exist.[42] The local school authorities may not only resent the inclusion of delinquents in their classes, but may object as well to the added cost of children from other parts of the state. This can be easily handled by paying for the school costs of such children, a measure which can go far to offset local animosity to "outsiders" sharing in local facilities.[43]

Care in the recruitment of foster homes indicates as a prime prerequisite, that an investigation be made of them beforehand. Once established, group foster homes need regular supervision, for what is a good home one year may not be the next, as foster parents become drained or apathetic. Much depends upon the continued interest of the parole or probation agent in assuring that children are placed with adults who will have genuine — and sustained — concern for them.

Some Foster Parents

In one midwestern city, a restaurant owner and his wife became foster parents for delinquent boys, after an experience in which they had picked up a young lad who had collapsed in the street outside. The boy was very drunk and after he had recovered sufficiently, they telephoned his mother who told them to "dump him back in the gutter where you found him." Instead, they gave him a room in the apartment over their restaurant. As more such homeless boys discovered that here they could find shelter, the apartment soon became too small. The couple then purchased an old mansion in a semi-industrial area of the city, which now accommodates sixteen boys. The father continues to operate the restaurant, returning to his busy household at night.

This private home has taken exceedingly difficult older youths from private agencies, some referrals from the county court, probationers from the county detention facility, and parolees from the state correctional school. State and county authorities agree that it has been amazingly successful with older boys, many of whom have had serious criminal histories.[44] In many ways, this home violates several basic principles of social work: there is no professional staff, some of the boys may share double beds, some of the furniture is worn and in need of replacement. Upon entering the home, these conditions give the visitor pause, but the atmosphere within thereafter conveys a vivid impression of happiness in a large and friendly family group.

The boys are given considerable freedom, attending school half a day, and employed in the afternoon at jobs obtained for them through the school. A boy who maintains a satisfactory academic level is permitted to remain out until 11:00 on week nights; Friday and Saturday nights until 2:00 a.m. Three of the boys in residence when this visit was made had their own cars, which they had bought with their earnings. If a boy is arrested for speeding, the foster father takes his license away until both agree that the boy is prepared to act more responsibly.

In addition to the unmistakable personal warmth of the foster parents, much of the success of this halfway house is attributable to their willingness to grant to their boys considerable decision-making power. Each week the couple meets with a council of four boys elected by all the residents, who together discuss any problems or plans which the boys may wish to bring up.

The entire group occasionally comes together for a house meeting, as when one boy has a serious complaint about a fellow member. The household then gathers around the dining-room table. The boy requesting the meeting makes his charge, which is supported or rebutted by the others. The accused then has his opportunity to reply. Questions are fired around the table so rapidly that invariably one or more are caught in their own lies. Majority votes determine all final decisions. Occasionally the group may remain in session until past midnight. On one such occasion the group was insistent that the guilty boy be removed from the house at once. A squad car was called and the police took him downtown to detention. This did not mean that the group had given up on him, however. Two days later, after the initial antagonism of the other boys had subsided, the group consented to approach the court, requesting that the boy be given another trial in the household.

Court and correctional personnel testify that only a few of the boys who move on from this group care home are later involved with the authorities. That many boys with long criminal histories can succeed here without recourse to any professional assistance, seems attributable to this unusual couple, to their affection for the boys, the confidence placed in their ability to act responsibly, to a regarding of these young people as they would their own children, had they had any.

The foster parents share their summer camp with the boys and invite them as guests to the husband's men's club. The group foster mother, though not a physically hardy woman, has an unusually gentle and patient manner. When on one occasion she returned from several weeks at the hospital, the boys arranged a celebration to welcome her home.

Summary

Group care foster homes for delinquent children have increased in numbers rapidly, since Wisconsin began this program in 1955. Activity in other states has also taken place largely in the past decade, chiefly in the midwest. Most group homes provide care for young people upon release from a training school, who lack suitable homes of their own, although some homes have also been established for children placed on probation by the courts.

Group homes report a rate of failure for children placed in them which is lower than for those returned directly to their own parents. The chief reason for the success of these programs is the high caliber of the foster parents themselves, and it is important that their efforts be coordinated by an administrator with responsibility for the expansion and improvement of the program, preferably under state correctional agency auspices.

Strong group home programs flourish where foster parents receive adequate remuneration, in addition to funds for clothing, medical and dental care and spending money for the children placed with them. Since the work is confining and the responsibility considerable, it is essential that foster parents be adequately reimbursed for the very large personal investment which they make of their homes, their time — and themselves.

In general, foster parents are recruited from the ranks of middle-aged couples who have raised children of their own. Yet young foster parents who are raising their own children can often be found, and who display understanding and a tolerance of difficult adolescent behavior plus the energy to cope with it. Although some programs advocate formal training for foster parents dealing with delinquents, others prefer to recruit from among persons with some experience of foster children.

Placement in a group foster home can hardly be called formal "treatment," yet many children with serious criminal histories seem to benefit from living with adults who can proffer security, guidance, and affection. Permitting close association with others of their own age, the group situation is often easier for the adolescent to live with than placement in a foster home by himself would be. In order to relieve some of the anxiety and fear experienced by parolees before transfer from training school to group foster homes, trial visits, orientation sessions, and information about the prospective home are offered.

Death or illness of parents, or personality conflict, can disrupt an excellent placement, however carefully the foster parents have been selected and supervised. When city children are placed a distance from their home areas, relations with, and visits from, their own families may be limited. Group foster homes have other compensatory advantages to offer. With no capital expenses, and at costs one-half or less than those of most custodial institutions, they can relieve overcrowding in training schools and provide care for probationers whom the courts may wish to place in the community and in open settings. Such children are permitted to live in ways that represent what their own homes should have been.

7

Prerelease Guidance Centers

One of the earliest references to the concern of the federal government in the general area of community care of the released offender is found in a report on institutional treatment prepared under the direction of the Attorney General of the United States in connection with a National Conference on Juvenile Delinquency which he had convened in 1946.

A post-training school hostel would solve many of the difficulties arising from emotional disturbances when release is delayed, and ease the transition from the institution to the community. For various reasons it seems advisable that the hostel should be controlled by the training school itself and should be regarded as a part of the institution set-up . . .

Such a program, providing home atmosphere in a community setting reduces the possibility of stigma to a minimum and permits the youngster to pursue his schooling or work with a minimum of distortion and interruption. Because of its comparatively low per-capita cost, the hostel can afford to provide many of the special services which the conventional type of training school must forego. The hostel is a development that will merit study and observation in the coming decades.[1]

This farsighted prediction of a development which has since come to pass sets out many of the arguments which are found valid as justification for today's community residences for offenders. And yet some years had to pass before the first attempts were to be made to put into practice these early aims.

Research had meanwhile pointed up two important findings. The first was that of those released offenders who failed in the community, the great majority did so within the first few months following release. A corollary finding was that motivation for change, if it existed at all, was perhaps strongest in the offender at just that moment of release. If his attitudes had been constructively influenced during his term at the institution, then some bridge back into full community life was required at this step, in order to give additional supportive aid.[2]

Awareness began to mount that perhaps a good deal of the onus that was attached to the institution for its failure to rehabilitate a larger proportion of the offenders who passed through it should be placed rather on the failure of the correctional system as a whole to provide some link between the institution and the community at this crucial point of first return.

Various devices began to appear in response to this awareness. An important innovation, for example, was the so-called prerelease camp, which originated in the Midwest. These camps were operated by the institution, and formed a part of it, even though located at some distance away from it. Preparation for return to the community was by means of group reorientation programs and the relaxation of strict custodial and other regulations. However, because such prerelease camps were isolated from the community and usually in rural areas, they could not provide the interaction with the community which is the essence of the residential idea. They nevertheless have made a valuable pioneering contribution.[3]

At about the same time, the Federal Bureau of Prisons undertook a survey to discover what were some of the hurdles confronting released offenders, what were some of the ways in which federal prisons and reformatories were failing to prepare for entrance into the community those persons who were released on parole or discharged because their full sentence had been served.[4]

Two relatively minor — but by no means insignificant — areas, fairly easy to control, were turned up. The first was the matter of the clothes in which the ex-prisoner would face the world; the second was the amount of money he would have to start life again as an economically independent person. One may recall the pre-World War II movie "Captain of Kopernick," where the first thing a convict released from penal servitude did was to shed his prison donated suit in exchange for the uniform of a captain of the German army, purchased at a second-hand shop. The point is clear: the last thing a man just released from prison wants to look like is a man just released from prison. The Federal Bureau of Prisons, when it initiated during the war a program of releasing selected individuals from its institutions to service in the Army as a condition of parole, made much of the importance of outfitting them in a variety of garb, no two alike, so that they would be indistinguishable from other draftees when they appeared at the induction centers.[5]

The matter of money is likewise of importance. Every correctional institution is limited by law or regulations as to the amount it may give to the man whom it turns out of its gates. Even today such persons are frequently given no more than $5 in cash to take with them. Others may have earned and saved larger sums while in the institution, which may be given to them at the time they are released. As witness, one released prisoner is reported to have spent $75 of the $150 which represented his total savings on a taxi ride from the prison gate to his home. While this incident is admittedly exceptional, it does illustrate the great need which persons who for years have not handled money in their daily life within institutional confines have for help and guidance in the spending and handling of funds.

Having money to spend wisely and to save presumes that the released offender will have some earning capacity — of a legally acceptable nature — and a job. This is an assumption not always borne out in practice. While a precondition for parole or full-release may specify that a man must have a job to go to, such a job has been often, and even notoriously, of an ephemeral nature, just sufficient in many cases to meet the letter of the regulation, but frequently not bona fide. In addition, the man who gets a job on the outside, whether through his own efforts or those of a parole officer, rarely if ever sees his prospective employer and is certainly not permitted to visit his place of intended employment until he reports — hopefully — for work.

The same requirement also applies to the home to which the releasee will go. This must likewise be a specific address: frequently it may be the home of his wife, relative, or a friend. Such resources may not be readily available, with the result that many homeless men in institutions must depend on someone on the outside to help them to locate a precise place where they may say that they will go before they can be released.

Clothes, money, job and home all provided in the best of all possible circumstances, what now of other considerations which will confront the released offender in the freedom he has dreamed would be his when he was again outside? Surely it is at this point that his prior isolation from the community, the limitations of his social contacts largely to persons in the same condition as himself and to guards and other staff members, takes its toll. The prospect of mixing with persons of the opposite sex, the simple risks of crossing heavily trafficked streets, to cite but two, present challenges which many find, if not insuperable, at best fraught with strain, anxiety, and in many cases, plain inability to cope.

For the experience of passing an extensive period of time within an institution inevitably fades out many patterns of conduct brought from the outside and replaces them with newly acquired modes of behavior. This is graphically illustrated by the experience of a parolee who was interviewed after he had been released into the community after twenty years of imprisonment. When he was finally released, he told how, each time that he came to a closed door — in a house, an office or a public building — he would halt stock still and wait for someone to open it for him. For a score of years he had been conditioned never to turn a knob or raise a latch without first having to stop and await the intervention of another person — a guard or other prison official, with the necessary key or buzzer. In the outside world there is no simpler act than that of pushing open a door. In confinement, there is no act less subject to the individual inmate's control.

The establishing of more complex patterns of behavior brings with it a related concern — how persons who have had their lives planned for them for some considerable period, will deal constructively with the leisure which will fill at least two-thirds of their time, assuming a normal work week. This host of problems (which many persons who have not been in correctional situations may never fully master) adds up to a total burden which not all newly released offenders can be expected to carry without help. The wonder is that more of them do not fail on their first, sudden confrontation with the outside world.

At the time of demobilization, also at the end of World War II, in recognition of the difficulties which would be met in that transition period by men preparing for release or discharge, some institutions, notably those under federal authority, initiated what was called "prerelease" preparation. This took on different forms, but consisted chiefly of discussion meetings, usually led by representatives of the outside community.

A typical series of such meetings might consist, for example, of the following. The first would be conducted by a parole officer who would explain and interpret the meaning of parole. As in the remaining meetings in the series, opportunity was provided for discussion. Thereafter, representatives of public employment services would outline both the opportunities available and the steps to be taken in order to find a job. Employers might discuss how to apply for a job, the filling of forms, the employment interview as well as what was expected in way of performance, and how to handle the matter of their prison record in discussions with fellow employees. The local union representative would then discuss such matters as membership and permits, fees and initiation; how to contact the local union, the complexities of social security.

While such prerelease programs were centered in a special wing of the institution, and literally under its shadow, the prisoner who participated in it was given certain opportunities at the same time to establish contact with the outside world. Tours were conducted, for example, to places of interest in a nearby large city, and to the plants of prospective employers. In addition, each participant was granted a day's leave from the institution to visit with his family, if he so desired. Before his departure he was given a free choice of the work and dress clothing he would take with him when he left. Some prerelease programs permitted their participants to wear civilian clothes during this period.

While admittedly inadequate, for their time and certainly in the light of what has since developed (as will be shown below) these prerelease programs within institutions were both innovative and auspicious. For, as a result of these early attempts, the Attorney General of the United States in 1961 recommended to Congress that funds be appropriated for the establishment by the Bureau of Prisons of an experimental community program.

Although this first federal impetus was in behalf of younger offenders, the creation of these residential units which came to be known as prerelease guidance centers, reflected a far-reaching re-orientation in the thinking of federal correctional administrators. Partly as a result of their apparent success, the Prisoner Rehabilitation Act of 1965 provided for the establishment by the Bureau of Prisons of community-based residences for older offenders as well. Two years later, three of these were inaugurated to serve men between ages twenty and forty, and entitled "community treatment centers." At this writing, the Federal Bureau anticipates that an increasingly large percentage of younger men will in the future either be dealt with by state correctional agencies or placed under probation.[6] In time the concept of the prerelease guidance center may then be replaced by a more comprehensive and all-purpose facility, the community treatment center.

Rapid Expansion

Within a matter of months after the Attorney General's initial recommendation to Congress, the first three prerelease guidance centers were opened in New York and Chicago in 1961. At one time, it appeared that as many as thirty-five such centers might be projected throughout the United States, a likelihood that has diminished with the publication of the Report of the President's Commission on Law Enforcement and the Administration of Justice, which recommended that: "The Federal Government should divest itself systematically of much of its present direct service to offenders. It should operate fewer institutions and community correctional programs."[7] Preference was indicated for greater reliance on state facilities with Federal assistance, which would offer a wider range of services for offenders. Today, the Federal Bureau of Prisons operates seven of these centers.

The Basic Models

The prerelease guidance center concept exhibits a wide diversity in program, location, and — to some degree — in treatment philosophy, as well as in staff ratios and types of men served. Three basic pilot models were originally approved. The first was to be operated directly by the Bureau of Prisons. A minor variation was experimented with in another center, where a co-operative effort between federal and state correctional systems is reflected in most of the staff being paid by the Bureau of Prisons, while one member is on the State payroll.[8]

The second model depended on other Federal agencies to establish and operate the center, under contract. A university, for example, might establish and operate a center which would serve both federal and state prisoners at the same time. With the university paid a fee for such service, this arrangement seemed desirable where the number of federal releases did not justify the creation of a separate facility.

Locations

In contrast to some of the unpleasant experiences reported by privately established halfway houses, the prerelease guidance centers have experienced little public hostility, largely because they have been located in areas zoned for apartments or commercial purposes rather than in private residential neighborhoods.[9]

YMCA's have also been favorite locations for several of the first prerelease guidance centers, whether occupying one floor or only a block of rooms on a floor. Most of the federal centers are in separate buildings: a former children's home, a former small college building, staff quarters for prison officers attached to a penitentiary in a neighborhood which has traditionally housed a number of such staff.

One center, rather exceptionally, occupies rooms previously leased by the Public Health Service on a floor of a government office building in the downtown area of a large southern city.

Centers which are not units within YMCA's or office buildings usually operate their own cooking and dining facilities, although opinion varies as to the desirability of this arrangement. Some believe that eating together produces a spirit of greater sociability and opportunities for friendly, informal counseling and other staff-resident interaction. On the other hand, it is argued that the saving which results when a center can divest itself both of the staff and of the equipment necessary for preparing and serving meals will usually determine the final outcome. Residents generally occupy single rooms, though some two-man rooms and dormitories are also found.

The Residents

Federal prerelease center residents are given the opportunity to complete their institutional time under conditions of minimum security while still legally and administratively in the custody of the Bureau of Prisons. Three to four months prior to their parole date they are transferred from the institution to a center. They know that such placement is a step precedent to parole, that good behavior in the center may result in their parole dates being advanced, that misconduct may cause that original date to be postponed.[10]

The sentences of some men exclude them from parole consideration, usually those who are serving short terms, who must be released without further supervision at the end of a fixed period. Other offenders are generally scheduled for a 30 to 180 day program in the Federal centers, 72 days being the average in fiscal year 1969. At present, offenders are released by parole, mandatory release, expiration of sentence and return to a Federal court at completion of diagnostic study. There are a few other, seldom used, methods of program termination, but these are not pertinent here.

Not long after the original program was initiated, the centers were used for another variety of offenders, those whom a Federal judge might have been reluctant to commit to an institution for whom a period of study and observation seemed to be indicated. Such persons were not placed on probation, but were rather committed by the judge to the custody of the Attorney General, with the recommendation that they be placed in a center for a specified period of time. If the offender should be able to adjust adequately, imprisonment was thus avoided, and plans for subsequent supervision by a federal probation officer could then be developed.

Failure to adjust in the prerelease center, or on parole, does not automatically deny a man the opportunity for a second placement. Not every first sally into the community can be expected to be totally successful, and it is not unlikely that such centers will eventually become available for selected probationers, possibly those with unsatisfactory home conditions, as well as for minor parole violators, rather than committing them to prison or reformatory.[11]

While men in prison and in prerelease centers are legally in the custody of the Attorney General, probationers and parolees are not and, until this technicality is remedied by legislation, they cannot properly be placed in a federal halfway center. Federal probationers or parolees can now be placed in a center only after a formal charge as a violator. Some federal centers also admit state prisoners. The intermingling of federal and state prisoners, under a shared cost plan seems to work out well, with the result that the Federal Bureau of Prisons continues to place men in state or privately operated halfway centers.

Intake Changes

The original policy of the Bureau of Prisons restricted the persons who could be accepted at these centers to those under 25 who were committed under the Federal Youth Corrections Act or to those below 18 under the Federal Juvenile Delinquency Act.[12] Although some boys as young as sixteen have been accepted, the mean age of the young men accepted into the early centers was twenty-two.[13]

Satisfied with the results obtained with young offenders the Bureau of Prisons since September, 1965, has been authorized to place adults in existing prerelease centers. Centers in Atlanta and Houston will specifically provide for men twenty-six and older, while the Oakland, California center will receive young adults who are between twenty-two and thirty.[14]

A challenging and hitherto unpublicized development is taking place in a large midwestern city where the YMCA based center occasionally receives women releasees, in rooms set aside for them several floors above that of the men. In another in-town YMCA which houses a federal center, the director contracts with a nearby hotel to accommodate women prereleasees.

Age and sex requirements have been broadened since the first centers were opened, and so have the offense categories. Although men with severe physical, mental, or emotional handicaps are still unlikely candidates, chiefly because of the difficulty of finding employment for them, and men with histories of violent crimes are still excluded, those with records of homosexuality, narcotics or alcoholism may now be accepted on a selective basis.

Residents' Characteristics

Most young prisoners in the original populations of the prerelease centers had committed such property offenses as auto theft, check forgery and postal theft.[15] Although the literature tends to describe auto thieves generally as of a higher caliber than other offenders, a recent federal study reaches quite different conclusions: that these offenders present serious behavioral problems to correctional administrators, are therefore less likely to be recommended for parole, and more likely to fail on parole when it is granted.[16] A hopeful note is sounded by a subsequent study which indicates that car-thief recidivists seem to benefit most from the prerelease programs.[17]

The general characteristics of state offenders are somewhat different from those of the federal prisoners, including the fact that their offenses tend to be more serious, more likely to include more blacks, more likely to have lower IQ's, and to be lower in educational attainment.[18]

Originally, the plans of the Federal Bureau of Prisons specified that the prerelease centers would receive offenders who were residents within a fifty-mile radius of the center location, to the end that this experience would ease their transition from prison to community. Assisted in obtaining jobs, which, hopefully, they would obtain on leaving, they could also be facilitated in making regular contact with their families. Exceptions to this policy do occur, however, for several reasons. Some federal prisoners come from states where there are no centers, or where state prisoners are also served; some residents come from rural areas.[19]

Staff

Staff at prerelease centers generally include: a director, a caseworker-researcher who serves as assistant director, an employment specialist, two or more correctional counselors, a secretary, several part-time intern assistants such as university students, and perhaps a cook.

Student assistants help by answering the telephone at night, making bedchecks, awakening the men and providing supervisory coverage on weekends and holidays.[20] Some students also conduct both individual and group counseling sessions. At least three centers report that counseling by women is working out successfully with immediate reaction from the men indicated by their being more neatly dressed, better behaved, and softer spoken.[21] One woman counselor plays pool with the men, and expresses a preference for informal conversation rather than formal counseling with them.[22] Qualifications for staff members are broad and varied and, as a result, clergymen, lawyers, sociologists, social workers and teachers are found serving as directors.[23] Top-level personnel are required to have completed college, but more than one new director has been promoted from a lower-level job without this qualification: some caseworkers have MSW degrees, others do not. At least one center makes available a consulting psychiatrist and social worker, as well as the services of a psychotherapist from a nearby medical school who also conducts weekly in-service staff training sessions.[24]

Typical Ninety Day Schedule

When a federal prisoner is assigned to a center, he may travel from the institution in the company of another inmate if the two happen to be released at the same time. Otherwise no one accompanies him as he travels on his own by public transportation:[25]

Very often nowadays the offender who is placed in the Guidance Center has been previously on Work Release and leaves the institution in "store bought" clothing in the latest style.

The amount of money he has in his pockets may vary from five dollars to sixty, seventy dollars or more, depending on how far he must travel to the Center. His other possible funds are forwarded to the Center by check and made available to him on his arrival.[26]

When he reports in, the newcomer is informed of the rules: he may not associate with fellow residents outside the center: he is not permitted to drive a car: he must adhere to the scheduled curfew and participate in the counseling sessions.[27]

He is also expected to seek work, enroll in a training program of some sort, or enter school full-time. While he is unemployed, the center provides him with three dollars in meal tickets per day, plus six dollars a week for pocket money. Throughout his stay he is not expected to pay room rent or medical expenses. Once he finds employment, however, he must pay for his meals out of the forty-five dollars which is all he is permitted to spend per week, without obtaining special permission. Anything above this amount goes into an enforced saving account. He is not to drink any liquor; women, drugs and gambling are not permitted within the building. He is expected to keep his room and person in good order.

During his first two days at the center, the newcomer is interviewed by the caseworkers, the employment specialist, and by the counselor assigned to him for the duration of his stay. The caseload maximum is usually eight. Except when accompanied by a staff member to seek employment or for medical reasons or other such purposes, he is not yet permitted to leave the center, but is encouraged to invite his family to visit him. He is otherwise free to make use of television, library, cafeteria, or other services available within the building.

At the end of his first week he is allowed to spend Saturday or Sunday with his family, on condition that he return by nine that same evening. During his second week he may now visit at home on both Saturday and Sunday, but may not stay out overnight. After the third week he no longer has to spend all his off hours within the center. He must sign in when he comes from work, but may now sign out until nine o'clock on those nights when no group discussion is scheduled. During the fourth week, the evening curfew is advanced to eleven, but men are still required to sign in upon return from work, and then out for the evening, recording the intended time of return and destination. This latter requirement is never discontinued. The resident may now enjoy an uninterrupted weekend at home on an overnight pass if his record has been satisfactory. After two months, the weekend family visit may now extend from Friday through Sunday evening.

This schedule of expanding privileges finally permits a small number of those men who do well, who demonstrate emotional maturity and who have jobs at some distance from the center to live without close supervision. These "out-counts" may live at home, or occupy their own apartments, as long as they telephone the center at designated times (such as when they start for work) and provided that they also return to the center for group sessions and other discussions. They now live in all major aspects as free citizens. In a few instances men have been placed on "out-count" after only three or four weeks in a center, but most residents have to wait until the last month of their stay for this special status.

Men placed in these prerelease guidance centers are distinctly advantaged in that they realize they are in pre-parole status, and that assignment here represents an early escape from the tight rein of the institution, and therefore a real "break." This factor is only one of several which gives these centers a stronger hold on their residents, particularly those who might otherwise persist in recalcitrant behavior. Only one-fifth of the men placed in prerelease guidance centers arc returned either for running away, for failure to adjust to center regulations, or for a new violation of the law.[28] Although a "run" can be viewed as an "escape" for which an additional penalty may be inflicted, such men are usually returned to the institution without that charge being formally leveled.

Staff of the center also have a voice in recommending the date for a man's parole. If his performance is unusually good, this may be requested at a time earlier than originally scheduled. The reverse, of course, is also possible.[29]

Major sanctions for poor behavior include both return to incarceration and postponement of the original parole date. Other lesser sanctions include reprimands, restriction to the building, or to the room, denial of the privilege of leaving the center after work, or canceling of the weekend visit to the family. As a next to last resort, a man may be temporarily transferred to a local jail for several days' detention.[30]

Despite availability of these stronger controls over residents than is found in other halfway houses, some staff members are, on the whole, reluctant to be punitive. This, in turn, presents problems, for if a counselor hesitates to enforce the curfew or fails to discipline a man for drunkenness, his fellow residents will know about it, and call his attention to such seeming favoritism. For this reason the search for more positive sanctions goes on.[31] For example, a "points" system has been suggested whereby the resident is rewarded for his good work and savings habits, for consistently abiding by the rules, and for cleanliness. Although no man could have his points taken away, his failure to earn merely the prescribed minimum each week would result in his demotion to a lower stage. Three stages or phases, have been proposed, with extensive freedom and privileges made available in the last. To make a man less dependent on regulations, and encourage greater self-reliance in the free community, an excellent work record and a proved ability to manage his financial and social affairs would earn the greatest number of points during this final phase. The end-result is well summed up in the following:

The Pre-release Guidance Centers permit daily awareness of an offender's behavior when he first reenters the free community, and thus an opportunity for immediate staff reaction both to assist, and if necessary, to control. As long as some confinement institutions are necessary for protection of society from those persons who would otherwise commit serious crimes in the free community, graduated release arrangements will augment the protection that society gets from such confinement.[32]

Pros and Cons on YMCA Locations

Centrally located in an urban area, the prerelease guidance center makes no claim to present the homelike atmosphere of a privately operated halfway house. The placement of several centers in YMCA's has brought mixed reactions. YMCA's are generally in downtown areas near bars where homosexual contacts are easily made.[33] While such contacts may be initiated by YMCA guests, it is also evident that many of the young residents of the prerelease centers are not inexperienced in this regard. For this reason, among others, difficulties occasionally arise between them and the regular guests, as well as with some Y employees.[34] In some instances the latter may be overly sympathetic; in others, they may blame anything that goes wrong on the halfway house residents, if only because these comprise an easily identifiable group.

In several instances, the high number of escapes from the program may be attributable to the open criticism by YMCA staff of the dress and conduct of the young releasees, resulting in considerable tension and resistance on their part to such criticism.

One large YMCA provides a rich and varied program of social, recreational and athletic activities but reports that many center residents make little effort to use these, and those who do tend to be the minority with middle-class backgrounds. Girls are invited to attend the dances, but the eagerness of some residents to become further acquainted with them gives some Y personnel second thoughts about the desirability of such contacts.[35]

This very diversity of activities and resources may even cause some residents to become overly dependent: when restaurants, educational training, entertainment and the rest are all available under the one roof, many may find little reason to venture outside.[36] Finally, the close presence of other guests who are in no way related to the prerelease center inhibits young men from engaging in the physical activity which they may need, but which is possible only in a separate facility.[37]

On the other hand, separate buildings which house only released prisoners may tend to become too narrow and isolated and, as a result, more likely to turn into small institutions to say nothing of the greater expense involved.[38] Costly to build or to renovate, once they are in operation, such separate centers require staff on a twenty-four hour a day basis, in contrast to a center located in a downtown YMCA, which has experimented with no staff coverage whatsoever at night.[39]

With the exception of making their beds and taking care of their clothes and other personal items, residents in a YMCA center may receive the same maid and janitorial service as do other guests. The view has been expressed that in the usual halfway centers, concern over cleanliness of rooms, preparation of meals and other chores, creates tensions and impedes interaction between residents and staff. One of these comments pointedly: "When a man comes home from work he's tired. The average citizen doesn't have to clean latrines or polish stair rails after a day's work. Why should our men?"[40] From this point of view, it is interesting to note that more than one prerelease program advocates the renting of rooms in well-run, low cost hotels in working-class neighborhoods, which offer a happy compromise between a YMCA and a separate facility.[41]

Goals and Means

The federal prerelease guidance centers base their program on a recognition of the necessity for facilitating the transition of ex-prisoners into life in the community to the end that recidivism will be reduced.[42] They therefore help center residents find employment, establish relationships with other persons and agencies in a mature and constructive fashion, recognize and deal with other personal problems, develop a sense of money management, and accept parole supervision as a necessary precondition to their ultimate return to society. All this is provided in a comparatively open setting which encompasses access to relatives, friends and a variety of community services. A major tool in carrying out these goals is counseling — individually and in groups.[43] For the most part the approach is aimed not at the alteration of personality patterns and the gaining of insight, but rather at the resolution of day-to-day problems.[44]

Full-time employment is the core of any such program.[45] To this end, the employment specialist helps find jobs for his men, in the course of which he finds himself performing a public education function with unions and with the business community. He is honest about the past history of his client, including his previous work record, even if this is not exemplary.[46] In receiving factual and honest information on a prospective employee, the employer can assure himself that he knows more about the applicant from a federal center than he would about an unknown, casual jobseeker who comes in off the street.

The employment counselor helps his client learn how to fill out an application form, what to wear, and how to conduct himself during an employment interview: even to such details as what to do with his coat and hat, whether to stand or sit, whether or not to smoke, and how to acknowledge an introduction. In order to help him not to become overly dependent, the young man is encouraged to do as much as possible for and by himself. When finally primed and ready to set out for the job interview, he goes alone. He also makes his own arrangements for Social Security coverage. Most residents find themselves employed fulltime within ten days after their arrival at the center.[47]

Weekly group discussions are held in some centers, at which attendance is usually mandatory, and to which employers, labor leaders, and state employment counselors are invited.[48] The use of group counseling varies from center to center. One center program schedules three meetings a week to discuss such basic aspects of living as how to buy a car, to open a bank account or to order a meal in a restaurant. These meetings also feature, as speakers, marriage counselors, spokesmen for Alcoholics Anonymous and from mental health agencies. Informative movies are also shown.

Subsequent sessions, less structured than the earlier ones, give the men an opportunity to bring up their own problems and to express themselves freely about such matters of immediate concern as staff, other residents, and the center as a whole. Several centers make a practice of inviting graduates of the program to return to give talks on their experiences or to lead group discussions.

Money management is a topic of both importance and vital interest. In addition to an enforced savings program, the resident may be expected to show his paycheck to his counselor who records it. The resident then cashes the check, deposits all earnings above $45 and returns his bank book as proof. Occasional major purchases are permitted, but ordinarily the weekly allotment is expected to cover meals, clothing, recreation, transportation and incidental expenses. When the resident leaves the center his savings are entirely his. Many a resident manages to take with him an amount in the hundreds of dollars — which represents for many of them more money than they have ever had before.

A recreation director can encourage and help arrange for avocational and leisure-time interests, games and sports events.[49] Theater parties are reported by one center to have been so successful that the groups have to be limited to five or six men so that after the performance they can have supper together and discuss the play. Those with jobs paid their own way: the unemployed paid one-half the cost of the ticket.

Final transfer to parole supervision is made gradually by building a relationship between the releasee and his probation officer, who visits the newcomer within forty-eight hours of his arrival. (In the federal correctional system, the Probation Service supervises both probationers and parolees.) As the weeks pass, the probation officer is expected to assume increasing responsibility for guidance and supervision and no decision regarding program or parole date is made without his active involvement.

Both individual and group counseling are found in the federal centers, some under the leadership of trained and qualified counselors. Group sessions may meet once a week, or more often, and the discussion may range from fifteen minutes to over an hour, with attendance expected of all residents. Several centers report, however, that they have completely discontinued any attempt at group therapy on the grounds that these tend to deteriorate into gripe sessions. Here the preference is for individual contacts between resident and counselor whenever any personal problem is under consideration.[50] One such center which had discontinued all formal individual and group counseling services simply made staff members available for informal conversations from 7:00 a.m. until 9:00 p.m., later enlisting the services of clergymen to visit and talk with residents. Plans were also projected to use some residents as subprofessional staff, to interview new arrivals, tabulate research data, conduct group sessions, and help develop employment opportunities.

Individual center directors are encouraged to experiment, with their staff, in a variety of designs: the holding of group sessions either within or outside of the center, the releasing of counselors from all administrative functions in order to devote full time to group session work, the retaining in the group of some participants who have moved from the center to parole supervision.[51] Although the original policy forbade parolees from returning to the centers for counseling sessions or visits once they had left, individual directors are permitted to use their own discretion as to whether or not to allow this. Some directors even encourage group members to take part in discussion of how best to discipline an uncooperative member. Willingness on the part of the Bureau of Prisons to permit these and other bold and original approaches may be said to be a major element in the effectiveness and vitality of their program.

Summary

Since 1961, the Federal Bureau of Prisons has rapidly developed a program for men leaving federal correctional institutions prior to the granting of parole, as well as for a very few who are still under court jurisdiction. Originally, for younger offenders, these prerelease guidance centers or community treatment centers have been established under several different sponsorships and in many different locations. Some offenders have been placed in houses serving state parolees and, on occasion, including female offenders. The rapid growth of these facilities in the community has led to the recommendation that the states now be encouraged to assume a larger role in this field, and to provide facilities which may be used for federal prisoners as well.

Residents, who are not yet officially on parole, in prerelease and community treatment centers are permitted to live under close supervision in the community for three to four months earlier than they would otherwise have been. During this period they are assisted in finding employment and in dealing with day-to-day problems. They are helped to budget their earnings, to visit their families and gradually to learn to accommodate to the outside world. As it is an easy matter to return them to prison if they violate the rules, tight controls are not needed.

Some of the earliest centers were situated in YMCA's but today's trend seems more favorably inclined toward separate buildings. Because these are located in business or apartment neighborhoods, public opposition has been generally slight. As each man resides at a center for from three to four months, 110 men, on the average, can move through treatment within a single year.[52]

Center staff of eight or ten people, some employed on a part-time basis, are drawn from a variety of backgrounds. While the director is expected to be a college graduate, many counselors have moved up through the ranks of the federal prison system. Considerable discretion is given in the designing of treatment. Some centers have tried casework: major emphasis elsewhere is not placed on reshaping the personality or helping a resident with his deep personal problems. Admittedly not a therapeutic community, the center is primarily a place where a man can eat and sleep, learn to budget his money, find a job and renew contacts with his family and with the outside community. If he refrains from violating the law and otherwise stays out of trouble, the aim of the program has been achieved.

Federal prerelease and community treatment programs represent a courageous and innovative effort on the part of federal correctional authorities. With reconviction rates certainly no worse than those for prisoners released directly to the community from the institutions, they represent an enlightened attempt to assist offenders to build or restore their community ties. While these men are given considerable opportunity to show responsibility for their actions, the public also benefits by reason of the closer supervision which is provided for these men than for those on parole. From the viewpoint of the federal prison administration, these centers also serve a valuable staff-training function. When a custodial officer is transferred to a prerelease center, he is given an opportunity to gain first-hand knowledge of the problems faced by prisoners as they attempt to reestablish themselves in the community.

8 Halfway Houses

While religious and other private agencies originated the early halfway houses, largely for adult offenders, it is significant that government has in more recent years played the major role in providing such facilities for the younger offender. Because most state training schools (83% in 1967) operate at or beyond their capacity[1] and because of the growing conviction that these traditional programs have little success in correcting delinquent careers, judges and child-welfare workers have found themselves increasingly at a loss to provide other placement resources. Heavy probation and parole caseloads preclude any attempt to supervise adequately. It is for these reasons that some state legislatures, never overgenerous in appropriating funds for delinquents, have begun to vote funds to innovative services for juveniles.

Michigan provides an example of state involvement in the halfway house movement resulting from a crisis situation. Here in 1964 a Detroit juvenile court judge was advised by correctional authorities that their overcrowded institution was unable to accept any further commitments, unless suitable places were found to which children ready for release could be sent. As a result of aroused public interest, an appropriation of better than a quarter of a million dollars was quickly forthcoming for the creation of ten halfway houses for young offenders.[2]

Historical reasons and traditional methods may help to explain why private agencies evince less interest in youthful offenders than in the adult. Small group-care facilities, under private auspices in a number of states, have undertaken, over a period of many years, to care for a wide variety of conditions of children in the hope of sparing them from a training school experience, but they hardly look upon such activities as constituting a halfway house program.

The behavior of many of the children served by these agencies may fall into a category which could be as readily labeled delinquency as dependency but the former appellation is resisted for fear of the agency's losing local financial support. Such terms as "troubled boys" or "children in need of supervision" conveniently — if euphemistically — describe their wards.

Halfway centers for delinquent children have been slow in developing because private agencies are, in most instances, hesitant — if not reluctant — to deal with teenage antisocial children.[3] Many of these have been in institutions since an early age, have experienced almost total rejection and are therefore characteristically openly hostile to adult authority. Such temporary residences, unless carefully controlled, may turn into small group-living facilities where children can reside for years. Unless provision is made to prepare its young residents for eventual release to a foster home, the halfway house may find its turnover greatly reduced, thereby defeating its basic purpose.

Sharp delineations between delinquent and dependent children are more easily made by law than in practice. The neglected child, who was originally dubbed a dependent at the age of eight or ten, may more likely than not have committed a delinquent act by the time he has reached adolescence. Whether he is now to be given a delinquent label depends on the authorities who are responsible for him. More than one juvenile judge will prefer to adjudicate the children he places in a local halfway house as dependent and neglected though their illegal acts may be well known to the court. Children in need of care whether placed in a dependent or in a delinquent category, are more similar than diverse.[4]

Location and Characteristics

Halfway houses for adolescents are found more frequently in urban than in rural areas. In order to avoid the cost of buying land, houses may be established on the grounds of existing institutions, where they are looked upon as independent and separate entities. Their children either work or attend public school in the community, and in other ways follow a pattern of living which is unlike that of other children in the institution.

A halfway house can generally be established without much opposition on public property or in a rural area. It is for this same reason that halfway houses are most often located in lower-income neighborhoods in the city. More vocal and better organized opposition usually results when an attempt is made to set up a halfway house in a suburban or middle-class area. Commercial locations or those undergoing transition or redevelopment, marked by little neighborhood cohesiveness and a resultant anonymity, are favored sites for the establishment of a halfway house. Community opposition can also be circumvented when the center is set up within an already existing institution, such as a YM or YWCA.

A halfway house in a heavily populated area is best advised to establish itself in a zone marked by heterogeneity, with a minimum of bars and night spots nearby. Such transitional neighborhoods, which are not yet slums, offer several advantages not least of which is that they are unlikely to mount any hostile objection. There is the further fact that most young residents come from just such homes and neighborhoods in the inner city, and can therefore be more realistically helped to confront whatever detrimental influences may exist there. When residents leave the halfway house for independent placement or return to their families, the center is also easily accessible to those who may feel a desire to return for advice, or a need for interim support. Finally, and most practically, residents must be able to reach schools, employment, and a variety of other places by means of public transportation which is generally more readily available close to the core of the city. The most valid argument for establishing a halfway house in an urban area, rather than in a remote location is that at the same time the most basic: it serves to bring home to the community at large its share of responsibility for the creation of conditions conducive to delinquency, and its consequent responsibility to deal with the results of those conditions. A halfway house located miles outside the metropolitan area helps to conceal this double responsibility from the citizenry.[5]

In their interior arrangements, residences usually resemble homes rather than institutions or schools. Because their chief focus is on the development and improvement of social skills, these residences do not, as a general rule, provide within their premises for workshops, classroom, health or avocational programs. Residence staffs emphasize that to furnish such facilities would be to detract from the main emphasis — reliance on outside resources. Community centers provide sleeping and living quarters, kitchen and dining areas and some minimum facilities for home recreation.

Ample financial support has been known in a few isolated instances to result in too much money being diverted to equipment and furnishings which, while not deluxe by middle-class standards, may actually prove to be detrimental to a rehabilitative program for children from lower-income homes. An extremely exceptional instance is one privately supported halfway house which features wall-to-wall carpeting, modern teak furniture, expensive table lamps, ornate bathrooms, air conditioning and even a stereo system wired to every room.

In contrast, some residential centers can be found, even those with adequate financial support, which present an almost barren appearance, with beds so neatly placed and spaced, and the entire residence so immaculate that it is sure to recall to the minds of its residents the traditional training school polished floors and unused sterile visiting rooms.

Opinion differs as to the desirability of single rooms, both from the economic and treatment viewpoints. Some large mission-type houses may provide dormitories for their men, but those centers which attempt to administer any treatment program usually provide private rooms. Where interaction is an element of the guided group process, two, three or four boys may be placed in the same room in order to facilitate constant communication among them. Other residential centers prefer to provide a single room for each resident, holding the view that if meaningful change is to take place, constant interaction is not desirable, that opportunity must be allowed young people for introspection, reflection, and self-appraisal. Assignment of a single room is also used in some places as a reward for improvement in conduct.

Community Relations

The halfway house routine permits its residents a type of freedom which runs counter to the old established probation and parole regulation that persons under supervision after serving a sentence for a criminal offense may not associate with one another. But the principle that the community should assume some part of the responsibility for its nonconforming members is a more cogent countervailing argument, especially since close to 100% of all persons in confinement at any one time are ultimately returned to freedom in the community.

Neighborhoods in transition may offer the best locations for halfway houses in urban areas, but this is no indication that their inhabitants are necessarily more tolerant than their middle-class cousins. Nevertheless, since any large metropolis has areas that meet this description, persons searching for a halfway house location will be gratified to discover that the larger the city, the less difficulty they are likely to experience in finding a location where a minimum of opposition will be raised. When a halfway house is to be established, it appears to be the better part of wisdom to make some attempt in advance to inform the neighbors. The opposite approach was attempted in a large eastern city. Here an old home in an integrated neighborhood was acquired quietly and with no publicity in the hope that success would be gradually demonstrated by the acceptable behavior of the residents for whom the house was planned.

Despite the residential nature of the area and its mixed population, neighborhood opposition developed when over one-half the families on the street signed a petition demanding that the house not be licensed on the grounds that it would stimulate crime and their property values consequently would go down. Legal action on the part of these families resulted in a court injunction against the use of the house for parolees, which ultimately came before the state supreme court for review. In a decision of far-reaching significance that court set aside the injunction declaring:

This present fear of what may happen in the future, although genuinely felt, rests completely on supposition. . .We can only hold that, under the present circumstances, there has been an insufficient factual showing that the defendant will make any unreasonable use of the property or that the prospective residents of the halfway house will engage in unlawful activities in the surrounding neighborhood.[6]

Police records on the West Coast similarly fail to substantiate the fear that an increase in crime in the neighborhood follows the establishment of a residential center for delinquent boys, or that property would decline.[7]

As aroused as the public may be by the idea of narcotics, if, for example, halfway houses for addicts are supported by the courts (as in some instances they have been)[8] then surely facilities for young delinquents should fare well in their attempts to establish themselves, particularly when they have made attempts — in advance — to inform their neighbors of their interest.

One final incident may be cited to show that determined efforts on the part of the backers of a halfway house can dissolve neighborhood opposition. Efforts in the suburb of a New England city to establish a residential center for women parolees from the state reformatory aroused the residents on the street to hire attorneys, make the issue part of a local political campaign and demand that the mayor and the city council deny the halfway house a license. Its sponsors turned to newspapers, radio and television to present their case and finally invited people on the street to a bus ride to visit the reformatory and meet their prospective neighbors. Although only a handful of neighbors accepted, those who did helped to persuade the opposition that their fears were ungrounded. The women residents moved in and were found to act like anyone else on the street. In this instance, the support of the board of directors, a representative group of community citizens, was largely instrumental in guiding the strategy which led to this successful outcome. For once a group of local residents have participated in such a project, they come to feel a stake in it and a personal responsibility for its successful continuance. They can become involved in the planning, in deciding intake policies, and ultimately in knowing personally some of the young residents. Thereafter they can hardly stand aside when others begin to attack "their" project.

Houses serving children who are within the compulsory school attendance age try to maintain good relations with school administrators whose preoccupation with preparation of their students for college entrance or indifference or outright hostility to delinquent children might otherwise militate against any halfway house students who may be enrolled in their classes.

Community Participation

Ideally, halfway house programs provide their young people with opportunities to form and maintain contact with the community, the local barber, the doctor and the dentist. In addition, they are encouraged to participate in choral groups, dramatic societies, and athletic teams. They have access to community stores, libraries and churches, theaters, swimming pools, and bowling lanes. Staff obtain for them tickets to athletic events, dances, plays and concerts and encourage their parents to visit and to take them out on outings, weekends and vacations.

The smaller the staff of the halfway house, and the less structured the program, the easier it is to create an atmosphere of tolerance and acceptance by the neighborhood in much the same fashion as if it were a large family. At a halfway house operated for women parolees from a reformatory, for example, the visitor is struck with the atmosphere of casualness and informality. No posted chart specifies when each resident is expected to perform her household stint. As the girls return from work, they drop in to the kitchen for a visit with the house mother, and over a cup of coffee are casually invited by her to help in preparation of the evening meal, depending on how the girl may feel, her available time, and the interval of time elapsed since she was last asked to help.

Given the present ineffectiveness of most American prisons and reform schools in influencing the attitudes and the behavior of their inmates, the sudden and sharp contrast between the ordered existence of the institution and the freedom of the outside world poses problems for most released offenders. The longer their stay within a closed institution, the more difficult the transition. A long-time member of the armed forces experiences anxiety when he leaves the security and orderly routine of military existence. The trauma and tension felt by persons released from correctional confinement makes all the more understandable their need for a decent place to live, an opportunity to attend school, assistance in finding employment and some degree of acceptance — or at least tolerance — on the part of the community. Persons who are without concerned families or friends are even more dependent on such outside aid at this critical juncture in their lives. At the same time, when given an opportunity for concrete expression of its interest, the community may be educated to alter what is an all too prevailing attitude — that the criminal is the exclusive concern and responsibility of public officials — police, judges, probation and parole officers, custodial institutions — and to accept some portion of that concern as an end for its own.

The Manhattan Project — A Combination of Residential and Nonresidential Programs

A most unique halfway house program in Los Angeles which combines both residential and day-care features is worthy of some detailed description at this point. Of some sixty-five people involved, all but one quarter are occupants of the five residences. The others live elsewhere but participate daily in the group discussions and seminars which are the main feature of the program. Additionally, nine junior high school students come together in their own group meeting at one of the residences.[9]

The population is representative of the widest possible spectrum: adult parolees, state or federal probationers, and psychiatric referrals. Now and then a man or woman will literally walk in off the street and request admission. Professional parole officers, psychologists and social workers, impressed by what the project had done for their own clients have been known to ask to enter and themselves to participate in the program as nonresidents. One-half the population is under twenty-one years of age: of its total population, 80% have been in trouble with the law or have been referred because of narcotic drug use by the state narcotic unit.

Now and then a runaway from another state may be referred for admission to the program. The project operates a 24-hour emergency service in several city junior high and high schools, and teachers and counselors know that young persons with behavior and personality problems can be referred to the director of the project at any time. Efforts are thereafter made to involve such young people, on a voluntary basis, in group discussions and seminars together with the adult participants, a step which was taken at their own request. Some group people who do not reside at the project may be admitted as "live-in" guests for weekends.

The two-hour group discussions and seminars for the adults take place five nights a week. The younger residents meet for shorter sessions on a once-a-week schedule supplemented by a program of recreational and educational trips.[10]

Residents are expected to contribute fifteen dollars a week to the program, of which three dollars go into a house account to purchase such items as are available to, and shared by, all the members. The remaining twelve dollars pays rent, utilities, equipment and repairs. All residents are expected to buy and prepare their own food, cooperating with others if they are so inclined. Since the adult members of the project work, they have little difficulty paying the weekly fee. Most of the younger participants are wards of public agencies who underwrite their treatment costs which run, in some instances, as high as $240 per month.

The project has not always been a success. When it was first opened in 1960, efforts were made to assist the residents through one-to-one casework methods with a professionally trained staff. When this approach did not appear overly successful, a group psychoanalytic approach was instituted, but the turnover rate of residents did not indicate that this approach was any more effective. With only eighteen persons remaining, the director announced that the house would close. If any of the residents cared to continue the program, he suggested, they were invited to join him at lunch on the following day to discuss ways of giving the residents themselves the responsibility for reorganizing the program, and for its continuance.

Of the eighteen, only five appeared the next day. Concerned that the project was worthwhile, and agreeing to assume responsibility for major decisions from the outset, they agreed to draft their own constitution and to pick a new location. This same group of five, with the director, then formed the first executive committee of the project, which today is comprised of persons selected by the executive boards of each of the five residences.

Once the residents had assumed full responsibility, they came to the conclusion that they no longer considered professional staff to be necessary. Controls began to emerge from the group itself; newcomers who entered the program with little or no status moved upward as they demonstrated maturity and responsibility. Nor is age the prime determinant of these qualities: two seventeen-year old boys were recently elected to the board of one of the residences, one of whom was thereafter elevated to serve on the twelve-member governing body of the entire project.

Project participants move through several stages. Newcomers at the lowest level have little to say about the management of the residence and leave the halfway house premises only to go to work or to school. When they go out, they must tell the individual in charge where they are going. They are taken shopping by more experienced program participants who help them in their purchases of food and other items to make sure that they spend their money carefully.

Those who fail generally do so within the first two weeks after admission.[11]

If the newcomer can withstand the shock of this initial humbling (but not demeaning) experience, he may eventually graduate, usually after a month and an evaluation by the executive committee, to a more responsible role. At this stage, he is considered "capable." He can now become a group leader, or conduct a seminar. He may be given responsibility for one of the residences for the entire weekend which means that he is in charge of the house, even to collecting the weekly fee from residents. If he misbehaves at any point in his stay, he can be called before the executive committee who may restrict him to the residence for a period of time, or even remove him from the program for up to four weeks.

The top level participants are "the responsibles." These serve as department heads, sitting in on board and executive meetings, but without vote. They organize shopping expeditions for the newcomers, may be placed in charge of kitchen details and supervise the work of others lower down in the program.

A limit of two or three visitors may be permitted to sit in on the group meetings for one or two sessions, but no more, unless they are willing to become personally involved: by sharing their own problems, by abandoning their role as onlookers, and, in the words of the project, by being willing "to make a commitment."[12] Without a trained staff or a variety of resources available to assist the newcomer, the project is interested in the contribution which he is prepared to make to the group. The key question is not "How can we help you?" but rather "What do you have to offer us?"

Treatment here is based on the reality approach found in similar programs for narcotics offenders.[13] Borrowing from the guided group approach (described in an earlier chapter) individual participants confront one another — and themselves — with such behavior as lying, stealing, shirking work assignments or other unacceptable behavior toward fellow group members.

The seminars encourage a variety of activities, including role playing and psychodrama if group members decide that these will help portray the problem. A seminar member may be asked to confront a large mirror and, as he stares at his own image, is urged to tell himself and all those in the group what he sees as the positive and the negative aspects of his own personality. A particularly confused or angry participant may request that he be the central figure in a "mad session," where he can pour out his frustrations and hostilities, even to the extent of demolishing a makeshift table specifically constructed for that purpose, which is then rebuilt for similar use later on.[14]

Underlying what must appear at times to be a brutal confrontation, is an atmosphere of mutual concern and total acceptance. For the project participants know that no matter what they may have done, or how offensive their actions might seem to others outside the group, within the intimacy and understanding of the group they can speak and act openly and unashamedly.

The establishment of a group culture favorable to social goals is obviously more difficult in the nonresidential setting than in a residential center. The young person who attends a center by day, returning home at night, maintains daily contact with family and peer associates, and for this very reason is more likely to be torn by conflicting loyalties. For if the halfway house program is dynamic, and he begins to develop a "we-feeling" for staff and fellow participants, his nightly return in his home neighborhood is bound to induce conflict with his new-found identification.

Nevertheless a strong case can be made for the nonresidential center. Obviously, some children are temperamentally unsuited for a residential program, either because of immaturity or inability to accept and deal with the constant interaction with, and pressure from, the group. Many, as a result, run away from residential centers; in some places the rate may run as high as fifty percent:

It seems logical to assume that, even though a delinquent may be subjected to many controls and some pressures, the chance to return home each night rather than having to live 24 hours each day with those pressures, and the people who generate them, may have a salutary effect.[15]

Nonresidential centers are also more accessible, being located in areas of high population density. This makes it easier for parents to participate in the program. Such houses have other unique advantages. Among these are their lower costs, by reason of not having to furnish living, sleeping and eating facilities. Meals, for example, are provided by means of tickets to local restaurants, by a catering service, or by arranging for the institutions where the boys work to feed them. Fewer staff members are necessary as well: a director, his assistant, a work supervisor, and a secretary may be all that are required.

Like their residential counterparts, the nonresidential centers chiefly serve young male offenders, although California operates two for girls, as well as programs which involve both girls and boys in guided group interaction. It is reported that the commingling of boys and girls in the same building has created no major problems, nor has the age range among the girls, who compose a third of the members. More difficulty has arisen by reason of the age range of the boys. Despite an attempt to stagger the age groups out of a desire to reduce conflict, the presence of younger boys in the same building can result in some conflict with the older boys.[16]

California's Community Treatment Project, while essentially nonresidential in nature, incorporates some elements of residential treatment, in that approximately one-fourth of its young participants are placed in foster homes. Originally established in 1961 for delinquent boys and girls from Sacramento and Stockton, it was later extended to San Francisco and subsequently to the Watts area of Los Angeles.[17]

The theory underlying the treatment procedures in these programs is based on the finding that, as there are different types of delinquent youth, no one of these fits a common mold, and they will not all respond satisfactorily, therefore, to a single treatment formula. Children are differentiated on the basis of their maturity levels, further subclassified into seven successive stages, based upon how they perceive themselves and others around them. At the lowest stage of maturity, the individual's interpersonal interactions are almost those of an infant. At the top, or seventh stage, an individual would have to manifest such keen judgment, and be so extremely competent in his relations with others that he would be a rarity, if, indeed, he could be found at all.[18]

Some young people never move beyond the low-level stages, and while their comparative immaturity in both perception and behavior does not necessarily lead them into delinquency, their very limitations make them more likely candidates for this kind of behavior than persons at higher maturity levels. Most delinquents are found to fall generally into stages 2, 3, and 4.[19] Stage 2 is characteristic of the completely impulsive, self-centered person; stage 3 of an individual concerned with others only to the extent that he can manipulate them to serve his own aims; stage 4 of an individual with guilt feelings, whose discomfort over his failure to meet the standards of persons he respects may be expressed in neurotic or antisocial behavior. Within these three stages are nine delinquent subtypes, for each of which a different treatment approach is indicated.[20]

Children become eligible for the Community Treatment Project when they are committed to the Youth Authority's diagnostic centers for the first time.[21] They may have failed repeatedly on probation, but they now come newly to the authority's jurisdiction. In age they range from fourteen to eighteen, and unless they demonstrate serious emotional imbalance or have committed a crime so serious or bizarre that there might be repercussions from their home community, they are considered eligible for the experimental project. Within certain experimental areas in which the project is currently operating, about 75% of the boys and 90% of the girls admitted to the authority for the first time are accepted.[22] Since boys in state custody outnumber girls by roughly five to one; they are admitted to the community-based programs in about that proportion. Once accepted, they are assigned on a random basis either to a correctional institution or to the Community Programs.

Interviews and observation at the diagnostic center determine the subtype into which each delinquent falls: "Each type of ward is assigned to a Community Agent who has been selected for his ability to relate to and operationalize a treatment-control plan for one or more specific subtypes."[23] One agent, for example, may have shown himself to be particularly patient and generous with his time with certain children, as with the subtype known as "asocial, passive," who is further described as "in tremendous need of supportive structure."[24] Caseloads are small, twelve to fifteen being the usual number of children assigned to any one agent.

The unpretentious buildings which house the experimental programs are best described as nonresidential halfway houses. They contain offices for the agents, class and conference rooms, and a large indoor recreation space in addition to the outside play area. An individual child's use of this building depends on the program designed for him in accordance with his appropriate subtype. If individual counseling with the boy and his family is prescribed, for example, the boy might only rarely come to the center, the parole agent calling frequently at his home to meet with him and his parents. If a boy is believed more likely to benefit from interaction with his peers, he is then involved in group discussions several times a week at the center.

About eighty parolees, boys and girls and of various ages, are served by one nonresidential center.[25] Children in their early teens are expected to attend school; those who are beyond compulsory school age, and with no interest in continuing their education, are expected to work. If academic failure has been a factor in their pattern of delinquent conduct, then attendance at the center may be compulsory on one or two evenings a week, where classes are small, and individual tutoring can be done. When the condition of a child's home appears to be a directly causative factor in his delinquency, he is placed elsewhere. A single child is usually placed with foster parents, but some group homes are also in existence, one such, in Watts, being located directly across the street from the nonresidential center.

A visit to a Community Treatment Center on a late afternoon brings to mind a neighborhood settlement house. Outside, several boys may be shooting baskets, or talking. Inside, the pool tables are busy while the record-player, at top volume, blasts out the latest tunes. Not all the boys present are parolees: some may be their friends who have wandered over after school. Some are there because they find the center a place where they can enjoy themselves. Others wait for their meeting or a conference to take place. The atmosphere is informal, the exchanges which take place between boys and adults — the supervisor, his assistant, or a parole agent — seem friendly. As evening approaches, older youths may appear, up until closing time at 9:00 P.M. The building is open three or four nights a week for counseling and instruction and also for dances and parties. Such activities, as well as weekend outings, are jointly planned by the young people and the staff.[26]

Summary

The first halfway houses were started and supported by private religious or secular groups. Since World War II, their number has increased, especially as government interest has been expressed in the area of juvenile and adolescent delinquency, and largely as a result of growing disillusionment over the effectiveness of public training and reform school regimens.

Criteria for admission to a new halfway house tend to become less so with the passage of time. Some halfway houses originally created for parolees now also admit young people who are not delinquent, as well as first offenders. No sharp distinction can be drawn between those children who are dependent and those who are delinquent, especially because the older a dependent or neglected child becomes, the more likely will have been his involvement in antisocial conduct. Halfway houses set up for probationers usually refuse to accept parolees in the belief that their institution experience has made them less amenable to care. Staff in halfway houses for parolees concentrate on placing young people in schools, training programs or employment. Probation halfway houses more frequently place their emphasis on attempts to restructure attitudes and values and induce changes in behavior.

Halfway houses are found in both city and rural settings, Those in urban areas are often located in transitional neighborhoods where lack of community cohesion and anonymity make public protest less likely. Furthermore, many residents come from similar neighborhoods, will return to them, and therefore need help in coping with the conditions there prevailing.

Center programs vary so greatly as to make almost impossible a list of their common characteristics. If the house is small and the budget modest, the treatment program may be largely unstructured, the chief aim being to provide a tolerant and supportive setting where efforts can be made to enroll children in school or to find jobs for them. Their prior records, lack of education and absence of skills, together with their basically hostile and defeatist attitudes, makes the finding of jobs for them no easy matter. Vocational training programs and active public and private employment services can help to offset these drawbacks.

Residential programs which are treatment oriented tend to impose relatively rigid admission criteria, as they are geared to deal with young people who are likely to respond positively to the group treatment program which is their hallmark.

Nonresidential centers are able to offer more intensive supervision than does conventional probation, and are decidedly less costly to operate than residential programs. When centrally located, they are more accessible to both boy and parents. For the child who is unable to tolerate the more intense atmosphere of a residential center, they can help reduce the urge to give up and flee the program.

Some Specifics

Leadership and Staff

The most significant ingredient in the successful operation of a facility which cares for people is the caliber and motivation of the staff who man it. The shadow cast by these persons, more especially of the person at the top, determines the nature of the atmosphere which will prevail, the quality of the relationships developed between staff and residents, and what will be the standards of performance of both.

Many of the early halfway house programs in the United States were established by just such dedicated persons, who made up in the depth of their commitment what they may have lacked in professional training. As in the probation hostels of Europe, married couples would devote their lives to caring for and counseling with offenders, or a concerned clergyman might find the site for a house, enlist community support and raise the necessary funds. Dismas House in St. Louis, like St. Leonard's in Chicago, came about in the 1950's as the result of the enthusiasm and tireless efforts of a priest who personally involved himself in assuming responsibility for men released from prison.

Changing Times

But the growth of halfway houses in recent years has been so rapid that individual enthusiasm and personal dedication no longer suffice. The "founding father" who runs his center alone may be too engrossed in his enterprise to realize that it may stop when he does, with serious consequences for the lives of its residents, many of whom have already experienced considerable trauma in their relationships with others. The ideal halfway house is a community effort, well-led, preferably under "a director with a strong personality, but one who is not building the project as an extension of his own personality."[1]

There will, of course, always be a number of people who put dedication above remuneration, and this number is perhaps more substantial than ever, as young people look for satisfying careers in nonprofit occupations, whether as a reaction to the affluence which they see about them, or as a protest against the reification of human beings in what they regard as a materialistically ridden society.

But even such devoted candidates for the correctional field have to be reimbursed. Work in halfway centers is long and arduous, confining and exhausting. Status and success with their difficult charges are the rewards, but to this must be added decent rates of pay. Annual salaries of directors of halfway houses may run as high as $14,000; there is hardly any minimum, and lower echelons of staff are paid proportionately to the level of their training and responsibilities.

Difficulty in Finding Staff

Finding good halfway house personnel is far from easy, especially in the historically underpaid correctional field, with its traditionally low social status. With few exceptions, most halfway house staff members are underpaid, especially in the privately sponsored centers. This low-salary range discourages many professionally trained persons from entering the halfway house field, which by its nature brings the director and his staff into very close personal contact with frequently hostile and rebellious youth. To cap it all, the hours are long and the work is both immediately demanding and seemingly never-ending.

The Director

The director is without question the key person in the halfway house. He may frequently combine the roles of both healer and promoter; the establishment is bound to reflect the total outlook and attitude which he brings to it. His staff look to him for guidance by both precept and example. If he is a fearful man, the program will be marked by a number of formal regulations and the more institution-like will the house become. If, on the other hand, he is a tolerant and relaxed person in working with released offenders, if he can be flexible without being weak or overpermissive, his house can help to ease, and even ultimately displace for some of its residents, their longtime distrustful and manipulative attitudes.

Like an actor in the old-fashioned stock company, the director must be able to play whatever role the occasion demands: the administrator, chief therapist, confidant and father figure to both staff and resident, as well as the "face" of the house to parents, the court, public agencies and the community at large.

The ideal halfway house director has been sketched by one with notable experience in the field. He:

Should be of stable personality whose feelings about himself reveal a sense of confidence (not cockiness) in his ability to do things. Should find it easy to meet people and relate with them. Must come across as warm and understanding, as one who is able to listen as well as talk. Should not be one whose own hangups make it difficult for him to be firm or to take chances.

Must be able to make decisions and not be afraid of sometimes making the wrong ones. Must have the ability to rethink situations from other perspectives, and not find it difficult to adapt to different or changing circumstances.

Should not be dependent upon others for approval and should be able to operate relatively independently. On the other hand, must be able to accept supervision.

Should be professionally trained (psychology, sociology, social work and perhaps education would seem appropriate) in order that he can operationalize theory and conceptualize practice. Should be able to promote training programs and encourage and expand the educational attainments of both boys and staff.

Must be the type of person who inspires confidence in others and demonstrates qualities of leadership but should not be particularly concerned with status.

Should not be a person who needs to be liked and feels uncomfortable when it may become necessary for him not to be liked. He should have the ability to laugh at himself and let his hair down when need be. Should feel comfortable in roles where the tie is both on and off.

Should not be hung up on being so dedicated that his absorption in his work leads to his becoming myopic about other things in life.

Should feel comfortable and find necessary his working with the community and community agencies. Can relate on many levels and be confident and constructive in dealing with problems, hostility, and the sometimes not too legitimate demands which community leaders may place upon the agency. In other words, should be realistic about the difficulties and demands of community programming.

Need not have come up through the school of "hard knocks," although being groomed in the streets and polished in the university is a combination hard to beat. I do not mean the person who has been "busted" several times but rather the guy who certainly could have been on several occasions, and recognizes why and how come. The umbilicus to the street, however, needs to be severed.

Can realistically recognize and understand that the rewards may be fewer and frustrations more frequent and neither announces his decision to become involved because of it nor in spite of it. Plainly and simply he must enjoy working with kids and be the type of person with whom kids would want to be involved.[2]

A close relationship between the director and his staff is inevitable, considering their small number and the necessity for a meeting of the minds in matters of both philosophy and practice. Although the director is usually the chief therapist, the staff is also involved in decision-making. This is particularly true in guided group programs. Here, if the director openly encourages others to speak up in staff meetings, the more strongly may they oppose him when they disagree, and if dissatisfied with his decision, may either fail to carry it out, or communicate their disapproval to the residents.[3]

In the residential halfway house, the director's apartment may be located in the building, or close by, so that the presence of wife and children may at times be a source of irritation. An able director establishes and maintains strong bonds with his staff; a change in directors can mean an abrupt shift in policy and program, which may be resisted by the old staff.

Staff members are not without their own reasons for anxiety. Because of the small size of the center, they are closely and directly under the eye of the director so that: "Potentially the most threatening aspect to staff is the intimate knowledge that the director has of their job and role performance."[4]

When first exposed to the informal program of a halfway house, a staff member may be caused further anxiety:

The difficulty for staff involved in treatment settings where program rules and regulations are few and then not even clearly defined, invites opposition from staff, who could be expected to function with much more assuredness (albeit perhaps less effectively) in a less ambiguous working situation.

Staff may be expected to find it difficult to talk openly at staff meetings when in opposition to policy or decisions affecting youngsters with which they disagree. This is especially true in the beginning of any operation. It is important to recognize that directors' decisions or policies in most large settings are not open to discussion and analysis by all staff.[5]

Where the treatment plan calls for the frequent involvement of residents in group meetings, the completely candid discussion may cause staff members to realize that their own inadequacies are likely to become the subject. Where group members are given responsibility in making many decisions about the operation of the house, some staff people may feel their own authority reduced — or even evaded.

If guided group interaction is the treatment program, the influencing and altering of attitudes and behavior is in large measure — and deliberately — placed in the hands of the group members themselves. Thereafter if one of these participants is invited to become a member of the staff, an old-line employee may feel himself threatened by this dramatic reversal of roles.

Since constant contact with young offenders is exhausting both physically and emotionally, this necessitates adequate time off, and frequent shifts in working schedules. A long weekend, attendance at professional meetings or enrollment in relevant courses of study can help in part to revitalize a staff member whose energies and emotions have been drained by the demands made upon him by the intensity of this work.

It is these very demands which make it impossible to run an open program without conflict and tension. When the fostering of anxiety in the population is part of treatment, avoidance of problems cannot be the prime concern:

Things cannot, and indeed should not, run smoothly in such programs. The difficulties created for staff are as obvious and perhaps necessary as the difficulties created for program participants . . . the name of the game itself is problems and to avoid it means perhaps to run something other than what could truly be described as a treatment program.[6]

Professional Training

The prime requisite for top staff is that they should have a deep personal commitment to people. Young persons in difficulty can be helped if they sense that adults are genuinely interested in them and have concern for them. As in education and religion, only the sincerely committed adult can have a genuine and lasting effect upon the young.

Many people who neither understand nor relate to other human beings can earn degrees, but if without empathy or if burdened by their own neurotic needs, even highly trained graduate social workers may find themselves failing in this highly demanding field. Nor is psychiatric training an unfailing guarantee of success with the kind of problems with which the halfway house has to deal.

There is some growing evidence to support the view that juvenile offenders require different care — different in degree as well as kind — from other types of young people in need.[7] These latter may be well served by traditional social work techniques, but young offenders may need workers who posses other assets, including knowledge of such disciplines as education, psychology and sociology, as well as field experience in dealing with delinquents:

Social casework provides persons with a commitment to one specific orientation, and yet the day is long since past when all the problems of the delinquent youngster can be solved on a one-to-one basis, or with inner-psychic methods. A new bureaucracy composed of those without administrative skills in some cases, and without administrative training in most cases has grown up, composed chiefly of social workers. They seem to have little qualifications and little skills for weighty new assignments that include finance, personnel, management and public relations problems.[8]

The problem therefore arises as to where this special combination of skills can be acquired, especially in view of the fact that few universities provide any training in corrections. Most halfway house staff members acquire, rather than learn, their skills, which gives added relevance to the following statement by an authority in the field of correctional manpower:

Corrections is a multidisciplinary field. No one profession, discipline, or school of thought should have priority or dominance. All recognized disciplines and professions should be encouraged and aided to initiate and support educational and training developments in the correctional field.[9]

A halfway house policy of permissiveness may well strengthen rather than lessen the self-centered belligerent attitudes of delinquent boys, and unless staff are possessed of genuine and sensitive perceptions, their efforts to duplicate the freedom and camaraderie of England's famous Summerhill School, can easily result in chaos.[10] Failure to enforce reasonable regulations, or disregard of unacceptable behavior, can threaten the entire program and, if continued, arouse a level of public protest which can easily jeopardize the community centered treatment movement.

All of this bespeaks the need for mature, balanced and responsible adult leadership, whether these be lay persons with genuine concern for other human beings or trained professionals. The role of such leadership is supported by a recent study of 250 former convicts who were questioned as to what factor or factors influenced them to turn from their prior criminal involvement. More than one-half — 131 — stated they had changed during the course of their imprisonment, of whom approximately one-half, again, said that a specific staff member had been largely influential in their reformation: custodial officers or work supervisors who had taken a personal interest in them. Caseworkers were rarely mentioned. The ex-prisoner credited the persons who had helped him for the fairness and dignity with which he had been treated, not for their having been lax or permissive. Significant relationships between inmates and staff in reform and penal stations develop more often despite rather than because of the institution. Limiting staff to communication with prisoners almost exclusively on a formal basis, together with the deliberate effort to isolate men from one another, are among the many tragedies of the American reformatory and training school, inescapable perhaps in view of its huge size and the low pay level of its custodial personnel.

Directors and other personnel in halfway house work are recruited from various sources — holders of the master's degree in social work, psychology or sociology. Others come from education, bringing such skills as music appreciation, athletic coaching, counseling and guidance. Many of the earliest halfway house directors were clergymen: several came from probation or parole work. Some directors have come from maximum-security institutions, finding themselves drawn by the challenge of an open community-based facility. Others have abandoned careers in business. Nor is there any likelihood that this range of recruitment resources will diminish. For even if the behavioral sciences held all the answers to the problems of crime, the need is so great in the field of rehabilitation, and the supply of likely and competent candidates so limited, that all possible sources of recruitment must be continually tapped.

However attracted or otherwise recruited into the halfway house field, the number of staff employed in a halfway house depends on its size and the complexity of its program. A residential facility will customarily require, for example, more staff than a day-care center. If meals are served, a cook is needed, even if other staff prepare occasional meals and residents handle the chores. Where hours of work are limited to forty per week, more workers are needed than where staff live in and are expected to be on call at almost any hour. Houses for twenty to thirty residents often have from six to eight staff members, including relief employees.

The director who is unable to select his own staff must be prepared to indoctrinate those already on the scene with his own philosophy through staff meetings and informal conversation. Where several halfway houses are run under one agency, one of the directors may serve as coordinator of an in-service training program. The services of such outside consultants as psychologists can be helpful in staff training. In California, custodial officers who have passed civil service examinations and been carefully screened, are given on-the-job instruction by a halfway house director who reports that many of these later prove to be sensitive and competent group leaders.[11] Students in New Jersey centers acquire experience as group leaders through intern programs of several months' duration, under the tutelage of experienced group leaders.[12]

The following description of her job by a house mother in a halfway house for girls gives little clue that its author had been, for twenty years, an officer in a reformatory for women which had formerly operated under the rule of strict silence:

First of all, she has to like the girls. They can sense it if she doesn't. The fact that she's willing to live with them makes them have some respect for her. After all, it's the first time anyone has shown any interest in them. But, like any kids, they'll test her. And this is where it takes a particular type of person — one that's not easy to find. It's not enough to succeed: when there's conflict, she'll not last. Remember, she can't rely on locked doors and keys. All she has is her own personality. When she hands out discipline — such as ordering a girl to her room — the girl has to have enough respect for the housemother that she'll go there and stay there.[13]

If, it may be argued, ex-guards can be trained to make excellent halfway house staff members, why not ex-prisoners? For, if correctional administrators accept their own conviction regarding the worth of their efforts, they can hardly ask other employers to hire ex-offenders without being willing to take some few steps in this same direction themselves. Additionally, since former offenders come mainly from the same general socioeconomic background as offenders presently in care, they can be expected to communicate more easily. Unlike many professionals, they share the same argot, and having undergone similar experiences, are unlikely to be readily deceived by their young charges. What has been eloquently said about the public welfare field has relevance to the utilization of ex-offenders as correctional manpower:

A massive infusion of the poor into public service can result in a better response of the client to the proferred assistance. The poor person in service can relate more easily to a client in similar circumstances. He is a privileged communicant to information not shared with the more remote middle-class practitioner. He can provide valuable feedback on the attitudes and needs of the poor to which the professional does not have access. His style and value system do not antagonize the client. He provides visible evidence that there is opportunity for the poor to improve their state. The utilization of large numbers of the poor in public service is rehabilitative in its own right. The persons giving service are able to obtain the gratification − the sense of belonging, the sense of confidence, the sense of making a meaningful contribution − which are restorative of personal worth and dignity.[14]

That this is more than an idle hope may be seen in the use of former narcotic addicts as treatment personnel in at least two centers. Boys who were previously public wards are today working as counselors in youth centers or employed as tutors in the Mobilization for Youth program. In teaching others to read, the young teachers were found to improve rapidly their own reading skill, as well as their self-concepts.[15] Prisoners have worked as staff members in prison research projects,[16] while ex-inmates have been hired to lead group sessions involving adult parolees.[17] That a man is an ex-convict does not necessarily mean that he can handle other ex-offenders successfully without proper guidance and training, however:

The "ex-con" is someone whom I think we can do more for rather than the opposite. If we recognize this as such, I think then a policy of hiring "ex-cons" is not only valuable, but perhaps incumbent upon us.

There are few Leopolds around. Most eligible "ex-cons" who could otherwise qualify to work as staff would, if lumped together with all other eligibles, rank far from the top. This is only to be expected, and, I believe, a sad perhaps rather cold, but realistic fact.

In terms of the insight that the "ex-con" brings with him, again it is usually no more and often less than that of those who grew up in the streets and did not end up in corrections. It seems to me that to believe that incarceration any better qualified one to work with delinquents is somewhat unrealistic. This again is not to say that there are not certainly exceptions to the rule, but that is exactly the point. The ideal "ex-con" staff member is someone who probably never belonged in prison in the first place. It is not that he is better qualified because he is an "ex-con," but rather in spite of the fact.[18]

Volunteers from the community are another valuable resource for halfway houses and can, if properly motivated, screened and oriented, establish good relations with young people. University students, for example, make excellent "big brothers," especially if they have time to engage in sports and other activities with the house residents. Junior Chambers of Commerce and other civic group members can be invited to get involved in fund-raising and other activities in behalf of the halfway houses. Volunteers need direction, but with time and patience they can serve as tutors and help supervise such activities as picnics, games and camp excursions. Such involvement and the satisfaction they derive from it may lead these volunteers to support and work publicly in behalf of pertinent legislation relative to community-based programs.

Summary

Although many early pioneers of the halfway house movement were singularly dedicated individuals, this area of corrections has expanded so rapidly that government agencies have entered the field. Today, the move is toward higher salaries, reasonable workloads and adequate auxiliary staff.

Halfway houses are more difficult to administer than security institutions, for incidents must be dealt with as they occur, without any help from security measures and in situations frequently marked by verbal abuse and physical, even violent, aggression. Much of the administrator's time is devoted to working closely with his staff, and, in some programs, with parents as well.

Although the small size of the halfway house has many advantages, it also presents difficulties for the man who leads it. The atmosphere is informal, residents and staff have easy access to him, he is a prime target for attempts at manipulation from both. If he encourages his staff to function without formal rules and to make their own decisions, he may later find himself forced to countermand their judgment. If he encourages them to speak freely, he lays himself open to challenge and even to opposition.

Direction of such a program therefore requires an individual of an unusual combination of talents. The ideal profile is that of a strong personality who is nevertheless nonauthoritarian in manner, without being either weak or over-permissive. His many roles include that of administrator, therapist, public relations specialist, lobbyist — and fund raiser. Professional in attitude, and often in training, he easily manifests his liking for people, his empathy and common sense, plus an ability to communicate with both staff and residents. No one center director can possibly combine all these qualities, attitudes and roles in equal number or felicity, yet many practitioners of what is, in effect, an art do so to an astonishing degree.

Such persons come from all walks of life, and the searching for them usually specifies some academic qualifications, together with some knowledge of and experience with social deviants. At present, psychology, sociology, anthropology, education, psychiatry, law and social work all have a contribution to make to the halfway house field. Social work training, largely based on clinical practice with middle-class persons, has generally neglected exploration into effective methods of treating antisocial behavior. The need for personnel is so critical that universities might now well consider the expansion of curricula for correctional personnel, with particular stress on community-based facilities.

The manpower shortage in corrections may in some small part be alleviated by the use of ex-offenders as staff members in halfway houses. Other lower-level staff can be recruited through advertisements and from among housewives, substitute teachers, and other qualified persons. Many older persons in retirement are currently making a positive contribution in the halfway house field, as are volunteers and others with a wide variety of backgrounds. Every community abounds in untapped talent — people engaged in interesting endeavors who only await invitation by the resourceful staff of the halfway house — to be drawn into this work for the benefit of the community.

10 Rules and Sanctions

Halfway houses, being open community stations, obviously do not have to operate in the restrictive way that correctional institutions do, but they still require rules and regulations in order to function effectively. Generally speaking, these apply to such behavior as antisocial conduct in the residence or out in the community, work or school attendance, and the banning of liquor, firearms, drugs, or women from the premises (although this last is reported to be treated rather lightly in at least one halfway house for young men in Denmark).[1]

Except for the above, wide variations are found in halfway houses across the country. Most residents are expected to keep themselves, their rooms and their personal possessions in good order and to contribute some of their free time to the cleanliness and upkeep of the house. A few places, such as YMCA's, may have maid and janitorial services available. While some insist that residents be punctual at meals, others given their residents free access to the kitchen or provide them with meal tickets to outside eating places.

Typical curfew regulations may be 10:00 to 11:00 on weekday nights, but some centers overlook curfew entirely as long as the resident is up to go to work next morning. Some centers permit their adolescent boys to spend weekends away from the center with their families or in other homes, as long as they have informed the staff where they will be. Houses under government auspices usually demand a strict accounting of the whereabouts of their residents, who are required to sign in and out as they leave and return.

Consumption of liquor whether on or off the premises may be regarded rather seriously by some halfway houses for adolescents. Houses with a wider age range are chiefly concerned that the drinker not create a disturbance either in the neighborhood or within the house.

Some halfway house staff insist that all residents attend regularly scheduled individual and group sessions. In others, reliance may be had upon informal contacts to discuss such matters as employment and personal problems. Some of the federal guidance centers allow their men to choose whether or not they wish to take part in regular group meetings, and if they agree to attend, some pressure is applied if they thereafter decide to absent themselves.

Rates of payment for board and room by residents vary widely. Some houses fix either a flat daily fee, or a percentage based on wages. Others make no charge but require their residents to save a certain proportion against the day of their release. Until then they are required to live within a budget, arrived at by discussion and agreement with their counselors.

The widest possible variation is found in the length of stay. Some centers ask prospective residents to agree to stay for three months, but this condition may be frequently disregarded. Government sponsored houses usually exercise rather strict control over their residents. But many private places, especially those for adults released from prison, find that some arrivals have no intention of remaining with them for longer than a very brief stay. Hostile even to the most lenient rules, many of them have sought admission to the halfway house solely as a means of meeting parole requirements for release. Younger men who leave prison are usually the most resistive to halfway house placement, and despite previous orientation and programs designed to meet their needs, some of these have been known to depart a few minutes after they have entered the door.

Strenuous opposition is often encountered to the most reasonable of regulations, and strikes, walkouts, sitdowns and just plain refusal to cooperate have been the experience — at one time or another — of most centers. Therefore, however few or numerous, rigid or flexible, the rules may be, there is need of sanctions for those who disregard or overstep them. These sanctions are of two types — positive and negative.

Negative Sanctions — Incarceration

The most powerful negative sanction, of course, is the threat of incarceration. Those persons who have been assigned to a center by the court know that consistent misbehavior on their part may result in an order of commitment. Persons coming from prison who are not yet formally on parole are aware that they are certain to be returned if they abscond, that this will postpone their parole date and earn them extra years of confinement in addition.

Knowing this, federal prisoners are generally content to accept the regulations of the prerelease guidance centers, cognizant that if they were not there, they would still be in prison. In contrast, the state offender in a private facility may resent his placement, realizing that because he lacks family or friends to sponsor him, this stay is, in effect, an extension of his prison sentence, and at the least, less desirable than parole under ordinary conditions.

Halfway houses sponsored by private agencies and lacking official connection with correctional agencies do not have as easy a recourse to the threat of imprisonment, even if their regulations appear to be just as severe as those of the publicly supported facility. Their comparative tolerance is attuned to the caliber of their residents: men who have served time in prisons and reformatories who would understandably resist placement in houses which were too authoritarian or restrictive. The halfway house would then come to be seen as an extension of the institution they have just left rather than as an aid to adjustment in the future. As a result, when staff demands become too rigid, the population often declines.[2]

Temporary Detention

Temporary detention is a negative sanction second in severity to the threat of commitment. Young residents may be placed in jail, reception center or detention hall for several days or weeks, when cancellation of privileges and extra work do not bring compliance, physical punishment is forbidden, and institution commitment is not regarded as desirable. The nature and condition of the detention facility is pertinent to any decision to invoke this sanction. In an unusual group foster home for sixteen delinquents, the foster father simply telephones police if one of the boys becomes unruly or comes home drunk. Within a matter of minutes, a squad car comes to take the boy into temporary custody at police headquarters, where he is not mistreated and where conditions are up to professional standards. Such infrequent resorts to temporary detention can have a salutary effect on the management of the house.

Temporary detention is a valuable last resort for a facility which operates without any other physical constraints available to it for the occasional unmanageable young resident.

Ostracism

Where a relatively strong group culture has been brought into being, the mere threat of removing him from the program may be all that is needed to bring a recalcitrant youth under control. One halfway house which serves adolescent boys, many of whom have committed an offense, cannot legally resort to jail placement as a threat, as its boys are officially classified as dependents. Here the strong esprit de corps enforces a highly effective negative sanction which places the problem boy in the "cooling off unit," which in effect ostracizes him from the group by forcing him to leave the immediate premises of the house (a section of a metropolitan YMCA). Such a boy is assigned to a room on another floor of the building, and is not permitted to return to his group or communicate with the others until he has modified his behavior.[3]

Other forms of exclusion by the group as an effective way of gaining compliance may require the recalcitrant resident to sleep in a room away from his friends, or to eat alone, after the group has finished, or he may be "bunked" — that is, sent like a young child with a tantrum to his room by himself.[4] Houses serving adults also resort to removal from the group as an effective sanction. A board, consisting of the director and several residents, may order a resident to move out of the house for a week or two, or "ban" him, that is, deny him contact with any other resident of the house for a period as long as a month.[5]

Loss of Privileges

Restrictions and loss of privileges may be particularly effective in houses where peers rather than staff are permitted to make decisions affecting one another. The group may vote to limit the number of home visits, to reduce the amount of "free time" in the community, to prohibit the carrying of cigarettes or determine the exact number that may be smoked.

On the other hand, where staff are chiefly responsible for such decisions, they may attempt to avoid prescribing a specific punishment for a specific infraction. Impudence and belligerence to staff, for example, do not automatically result in loss of privileges. The original Highfields principle is that there should be no predetermined rules or penalties, that it is preferable that the boys be kept unsure — and guessing.[6]

Extra Work

In many of the halfway houses for probationers, extra work may be assigned as punishment — the peer group deciding exactly how much this should be.[7] For a rather severe dereliction of duty, or for consistent failure to tell the truth, one residential center may give a boy a certain number of hours in "the pit," a nearby hillside, where he spends his time with a shovel digging holes in the hillside or moving earth from one spot to another, and alone. More common as a penalty is the use of "hours," for a boy who fails to keep his room properly, goldbricks on work detail, is careless with matches or otherwise "messes up." One or more hours of extra work are then assigned, consisting usually of a cleaning or maintenance task.[8]

Staff can impose "hours," and in a center in Kentucky, the boys give them to one another. A boy who fails to clean up his room may be told by another, "You've got an hour for that." If the culprit refuses to accept the judgment, the matter is brought up at the group meeting and if they confirm the initial judgment, the group culture is sufficiently strong to assure the successful operation of the honor system. During lunch, a staff member asks the boys how many hours they may have to work off. Although each boy keeps his own time, a consistent evader would quickly be brought to book by his peers.

Complete delegation of authority to adolescents can create problems too, for in their enthusiasm to bring about conformity in others or to parade their own virtue, young people sometimes assign punishments which can be humiliating or physically injurious. Final authority must therefore always rest with staff, in order that the bizarre and occasionally sadistic rites typical of some high school and college secret societies may be avoided.

One federal center has developed a program which enables its residents, by a system of points, to move through three treatment phases, employing both positive and negative sanctions.[9] In the initial phase, the newcomer is graded largely on the basis of his conduct within the center. If he is to earn increased responsibility and privileges, he is expected to devote himself to his job and the management of his money and other personal affairs. Bonus points which help speed his move to complete independence can be earned through excellent work reports, as well as by punctuality at group meetings and conferences with staff.

Each phase of the program has a specific number of points associated with it. Progression to the next higher phase requires a resident to earn more points. If he fails to earn the required number in any one week, he is dropped to a lower phase with reduced privileges. Failure to earn the minimum number required for Phase I, the entering stage, results in removal from the house and return to the correctional institution. The scheme is, of course, reminiscent of the "mark system" inaugurated by Maconichie in the first reformatory he established in 1830.

Another guided group center employs a similar system which gives boys who are doing well and are nearing the stage of independent placement the privilege of moving from the cluster of rooms comprising the center facility to another floor of the same building which houses the center.[10] High above the city on the twenty-sixth floor, a boy here enjoys a room with carpeting and deluxe furnishing unknown to him in the halfway house — or unlikely in his own house. One-third of the total population resides in this comparative splendor as both reward and recognition, before they are finally released.

This same center also operates with a system of monetary rewards and penalties. This type of control is deemed advisable because the boys scatter each day to their individual jobs and school programs, and the group culture is, as a consequence, not strong enough by itself to enforce compliance. Also, since the boys have not been officially adjudicated as delinquents, no immediate threat of imprisonment can confront them. For attending school, a boy receives fifteen cents a day and an equal amount for attending the group meeting each night. If the group votes him an active, contributing member to the center, these sums may be doubled. An excellent school attendance record brings additional pay, as does the performance of chores, out of a fund, into which every resident pays a "service tax" of ten cents a week. The director may now and then jokingly remark that the excellent performance of the boys is costing the program too much money! Financial penalties are also leveled: a boy who fails to get up in the morning must pay a penny for every minute he oversleeps, and a like charge for every minute he comes in beyond the nightly curfew.

Not all systems of using money to control behavior have been successful, and some have had to be discontinued. Residents may object that those who are rewarded would have behaved positively without this incentive, while the less adequate were unfairly handicapped, for their best efforts could not bring them up to the level of those with greater maturity or more advantaged backgrounds. Finally, staff may object to being placed in a position where they have to evaluate one resident against another and in monetary terms.

Summary and Observations

All halfway houses have certain rules and regulations, some far less than others. Group living is impossible without certain expectations regarding behavior both inside and outside the house. Negative sanctions aimed at fostering desirable conduct include the threat of incarceration, temporary detention, ostracism or isolation from the group, loss of privilege and extra work. The threat of transfer to a correctional institution appears to be more effective with probationers than with parolees.

Individualization of the resident's condition and situation before imposing sanctions is indicative of the greater concern for the individual which marks the halfway house movement interested in personal responsibility rather than in formal controls. In the open atmosphere of the halfway house, therefore, sanctions can hardly be imposed, particularly on adults, without tolerance and flexibility. Where attempts have been made to impose many formal regulations, a high failure rate frequently results. Men paroled from security institutions may refuse to remain in a halfway house which is too reminiscent of prison, and opt for other placement.

Halfway houses, especially under private auspices, may settle for fairly elemental levels of expectation: that residents show some regard for the rights of others, and that they report for school, work, group meeting, and other house responsibilities. The higher the level of staff competence, the higher the level of performance which can be obtained by the establishment of meaningful relations between residents and staff. Such goals are more lastingly achieved through informal counseling than through fixed directives.

Adolescents seem to require a more extensive system of regulations, and in coping with their exuberance and their constant testing of adult authority, considerable skill is called for in the open setting. The guided group interaction approach relies on the group culture and its list of rules may therefore be fewer, because the group becomes the measure — and imponent — of social control. Sanctions can be accepted without resentment by young people, if they are responsible for their imposition on one another. Injunctions which would never be internalized if imposed by adults are more readily accepted by boys and girls under the group pressure which they themselves help to bring to bear on their unruly or uncooperative peers.

11 Costs

While the soaring impact of inflation makes it difficult to present precise figures for care in community centers, some idea of the range of what it costs to provide such a facility, to staff it adequately and maintain its residents, may be drawn from the following figures — which will probably be outdated by the time they appear in print. A halfway house may be an old apartment with a few rooms, or a brand new building constructed especially to its purpose. Capital expenses and per diem costs differ as widely as do these facilities.

An old home for ten boys may be purchased for $20,000: construction of a center for twice as many boys has been built by a state agency for twelve times that amount.[1] Construction costs may be expected to vary with labor conditions in different parts of the country, as well as with the program which the facility is built to contain. Where staff are expected to live in, for example, living quarters are needed for the director and his family, his assistant and family, as well as the married couple who work as housefather and cook. Renovation costs for old accommodations can be as expensive as newly built. For example, one suburban house large enough to accommodate 26 boys cost $2000 per boy to purchase, and an additional $3000 per boy to refurbish.[2] Manhattan real estate is apt to run much higher: $3000 per boy to purchase; $6000 per boy to remodel. These costs should be compared with the $15,000 to $20,000 capital cost required to provide living quarters for each boy or girl at a state correctional institution of conventional design.

Group care foster homes are the least expensive to acquire, since the house is usually already leased or owned by the foster parents. As a rule, capital costs of private agency-operated homes run below government sponsored facilities. Federal prerelease and community centers seem to be the most expensive of all. The absence of security hardware, moreover, facilitates their evéntual resale. Some forward-looking states in planning new structures design them so as to be convertible at a later date to other purposes — apartments, hospitals, nursing homes, schools and the like — when present need will some day have passed.

Rentals

Renting of an existing structure instead of purchasing it has certain advantages, as it can always be returned to its owner if the halfway house is, for whatever reason, discontinued. Monthly per capita costs for these accommodations run from $35 to $40. Such relatively high rentals are caused by the fact that a public agency must meet fire, safety and sanitation codes which are far stricter than those required of private dwellings.

Group foster homes for delinquents which generally pay a subsidy to foster parents well above that paid for dependent children, report an average annual cost per child of $1800, compared to annual per capita institutional care for such children which is rapidly climbing into the $5000 — $10,000 range.

Even where halfway house per diem costs run close to those for training schools and reformatories, it should be borne in mind that the treatment period is usually much shorter: few centers keep their residents beyond a year, most of them for periods ranging from two to six months.[3] The average cost of supporting a boy during his stay at Highfields in 1958 was a little over $500.[4]

Costs Vary with Programs

In those private facilities where the number of staff exceed residents, and where ample funds permit experimentation in treatment techniques, per diem costs may run as high as $30. Government-sponsored houses report per diem costs of from $8 to $13.

Some halfway houses pay monthly salaries to houseparents as low as $325 a month, which includes rent, food, and utilities (these emoluments coming to them tax-free). Far higher salary costs are found, of course, where no such living-in accommodations are provided and where civil service regulations limit the work week to forty hours.

Bookkeeping procedures made it difficult to fix precise or comparable costs. A publicly operated facility may be spared such central office administrative expenses as record-keeping and procurement, may have the wages of its boys employed in other public institutions paid by them in addition to medical service to both residents and staff.[5]

A halfway house associated with a county probation department may employ some persons who are on the payroll of that department. A director of court services, for example, may also be the "ex officio" director of the house, assisted by other members of his professional staff, even including psychological and psychiatric personnel. Some halfway houses operate with several part-time employees: the director serving as the only full-time staff person; his housekeeper, secretary, and relief supervisors may devote only a few hours of their day to the residence.[6] In halfway apartments with a couple in charge, the mother may be cook and housemother while the father who may hold down a regular job, receives some compensation for the time he spends with the boys evenings and weekends, in addition to receiving his quarters and food.

Where educational and remedial or tutorial services are furnished by the local public schools,[7] the house does not have to bear these costs. Public welfare recipients, students and volunteers can help to reduce costs, as well. Mothers on ADC (Aid to Dependent Children) can be enlisted to assume some of the responsibilities of cook, housekeeper and laundress. In one midwestern center such women have rendered excellent service. Their influence as the maternal figure — especially in tending to the cares of boys and the "giving" which is so closely identified with the serving of food — can be highly effective. Students can be hired for part-time positions at minimal cost through work study programs. They may begin as night supervisors, typists or switchboard operators and go on, as many do, to train themselves for work as counselors with residents.[8] Properly organized and supervised volunteers can provide much needed services. One halfway house, which cares for adult alcoholics located in a former police station, counts on the services of fifty volunteers.[9] Surplus food and other supplies also help to reduce expenses, obtainable through school-lunch programs or as the result of drives for donations, made by friends of the house.

Two currently operating transitional residences for released adult prisoners present a contrast in both cost — and the services provided. One, in Canada, has sixteen men in care at a per capita cost of $2600 per year. Across the border, the other reports an annual cost of close to $6000 per man, which includes provision of a legal aid clinic, an employment service, a narcotic program, and help on a nonresidential basis to both men and women offenders.

Halfway houses which serve adults primarily will charge their residents a weekly fee ranging up to $20; most of those serving adolescents do not make such a high charge. No uniformity can be found in the allocation of such payments by residents against the operating budget. Some houses impose no charge until the resident has been employed for at least two weeks and has had a chance to save a little money. Others charge from the first day of entrance, with the resident expected to repay the house any debts so contracted, out of his eventual savings. Some halfway houses for youthful offenders apply a sliding scale, usually based on a percentage of the weekly wages. Most houses for young probationers do not require them to pay anything; the practice is more common in houses serving parolees, where a maximum of ten dollars a week usually applies.[10]

Most residences keep a small revolving fund which they may draw upon for such eventualities as extending credit to a man who may have exhausted his funds and needs money for lunches, carfare and personal expenses while he seeks work. An advance may also be made for such necessities as work clothes, tools, union fees and dues or special licenses which are beyond the resources of a person just starting on a new job.

Where federal halfway houses occupy existing buildings, such as YMCA's or office buildings, no capital costs are involved, but operating budgets are reported to run between $90,000 and $120,000 a year.[11] An average population of from twenty to twenty-five men can cost between $11 and $13 per man per day, compared to the $7 per diem rate in a federal penal institution. Any such comparison of costs should take into account that center residents contribute to the general economy by holding jobs, paying taxes and accumulating savings. Many of their families, in contrast to those of other inmates, are thereby helped to avoid dependence on public welfare aid.

The nonresidential halfway center should be expected to operate at lower costs than the residential center if only because the expenses of equipment and furnishings, catering facilities and staff should be considerably less. Still, some excellent day centers run on rather large budgets, depending on their salary scale and the extensiveness of the treatment program.

Establishment and operation of an agency-sponsored halfway house for twenty or twenty-five delinquent adolescents can be done within the range of the following budget and payroll which is the result of the analysis of a large number of representative and well functioning facilities.

Where an old residence can be converted, the rent might well run from $600 to $800 a month. A new and quite adequate facility, prudently planned and constructed, can be built for approximately $200,000. This would include two apartments — one adjacent to the main building for the director and his family; the other, and smaller quarters for the houseparents, would be in the building with the boys.

A staff of six to eight persons could be included in an annual operating budget in the vicinity of $125,000 of which approximately one-half would go for salaries. A six person staff pattern would include: a director ($12,000 to $14,000); assistant ($10,000 to $12,000); a work supervisor ($7000 to $8000); house father ($7000); cook ($5000 to $6000) and secretary ($5000 to $6000). The budget could absorb the cost of a car, meals and the nominal wage paid to the boys for their work in a public project. A nonresidential center serving the same number of boys can operate effectively with four staff members for an annual budget of approximately $40,000.

Financial Problems

Many halfway house programs have been financed by a demonstration grant from private or public funds, but when it does not see to the replacement of such funds from other sources, it may have to close its doors. This has been the fate of three excellent nonresidential programs: Pinehills in Provo, Utah; Essexfields in Newark, New Jersey; and Parkland Center for younger boys in Louisville, Kentucky.

Originating and obtaining financial support for government-operated halfway houses is the responsibility of public officials. In some counties the local judge and his probation staff have often taken the lead. In order to obtain appropriations the director of the state correctional department or agency must first be persuaded of the value of such a project, for it is through him that the support of the governor and influential legislators is generally forthcoming. Citizen groups very often provide both stimulus to the creation of community center programs, as well as help in obtaining the passage of enabling legislation, and the raising of funds.

Initial activity in behalf of the locally supported halfway house is often the result of one keenly interested individual who, through enthusiasm and dedication, can kindle others. He must first prove the need for such a halfway facility by demonstrating that a sizable number of youngsters can benefit from such treatment, especially where the state training schools are forced to delay the release of certain children because their homes are unsatisfactory or unfit. The halfway house advocate should be well known and respected so that he may organize the board of directors who can attract financial support from the community.

In many instances the original promoter of a halfway house eventually finds himself its first director. Once assured of basic financing, he may rent an old home and furnish it with donations from its supporters. As the first residents are assigned by the court, interest heightens and a wider base of popular support and involvement for the residence is more readily forthcoming.

Continued financial backing may now be sought through direct mail solicitation and through personal appeals to civic and business groups. The fees paid by state correctional agencies for children placed outside their own homes usually do not cover the amounts necessary to keep a child in halfway house care. Here, local groups can be approached: women's clubs for example, have held cake or rummage sales, stores have permitted board members to man a booth during a promotion or — as in one instance — a local track offered to donate the winnings from the final race of the evening. Halfway house boards have sponsored movie openings, concerts and exhibitions.

The young residents are often the best spokesmen for the house, when business and community leaders are invited in for meals, or to an open house or Christmas party. Many other avenues are available to receive the message: radio and television publicity can be obtained without charge, under public service requirements of the Federal Communications Commission. Broadcasting program directors are always interested to invite persons who are able to present new and unusual community projects, and newspapers induced to carry feature stories and photographs. Citizens can be induced to make bequests to the halfway house, any such contributions being, of course, tax exempt.

For the small privately operated halfway house, affiliation with the annual community welfare appeal may end the ceaseless quest for funds. Such affiliation may, of course, bring other problems: outside budget controls, job specifications for staff members and restrictions on individual fund-raising efforts.[12]

Summary

Halfway houses can be constructed for considerably less than custodial institutions housing similar numbers. Capital expenditures for facilities to care for twenty or twenty-five persons can range all the way up to $250,000. Rental costs also show wide disparity. Annual operating budgets of some small private halfway houses are as low as $8000, while government-operated residences may well run twelve times that figure. Group care foster homes represent the least expensive venture, requiring virtually no capital outlay and even under generous boarding and bed subsidy fees, per diem costs average about the same as in agency-operated halfway houses for ten or more children. Several houses report daily per capita costs as high as $20 or $30, chiefly because of high staff-child ratios. Their shorter term of treatment means that they can process more young people per year, reducing the cost per child for his stay in them. Most government operated places report much larger budgets than do the privately supported.

Although grants from federal agencies and private foundations have launched a number of experimental projects, there is danger in relying permanently on such sources. State-operated programs are usually initiated by the director of correctional services, whose task it is then to obtain the approval — and financial support — of the executive and legislative branches. County-operated halfway houses have, of course, to assume the responsibility for obtaining necessary appropriations, and if they can enlist the support of citizens' groups, their task is made that much easier.

The small, privately operated halfway house wages a never-ending struggle for funds from many sources. Equally important for continued survival is support from the media — as well as from a board drawn from the community. Any consideration of affiliation with other social agencies in the area should take into account the possible consequent loss of some autonomy.

By Way of Conclusion

12 Research and Evaluation

Gross Research Efforts

Until recent years only the grossest methods have been applied to assess the results and the effectiveness of correctional programs. As but one example, the Illinois Youth Commission, like most state correctional agencies, weighs recidivism purely on the basis of the safe return of former inmates to the commission's own facilities. Its former older adolescent wards who are later committed to an adult correctional institution do not figure in its recidivism statistics, and therefore such boys are not considered "failures." The commission's forestry camps claim a lower failure rate than the commission's other facilities, but any comparative evaluation of the success rates of camps versus closed institutions is without validity because the selection process which takes place at time of intake sends only the less serious offenders to open institutions.[1]

Most state correctional agencies do not undertake controlled surveys, reporting rather in the most general terms on their rates of success without consideration for random assignment, matched groups, or comparison with the effectiveness of other agencies. The New York Division for Youth, characterized by progressive programming, announced in 1964 that for every twelve children leaving its camps, START centers and "urban homes," only one was later committed to a custodial institution, and only one out of every eight was arrested and convicted.[2] While such results on the aftercareers of 441 delinquent children are impressive, they are too general to make possible any comparison with other correctional programs. Selective in its intake policy, the Division accepts children who are still on probation, if they agree to accept such placement. The Division, in turn, can reject those whom it deems unsuitable for its programs.

Problems of Empirical Research

California has been unique, at least until recently, among all the states in creating highly competent research programs within its adult and juvenile correctional agencies. Staff in these programs operate independently of other agency personnel, and have published studies which are of value to the correctional field. Recent years have seen the beginning of similar research in other states largely through grants from foundation and federal sources. Every project funded by the Federal Department of Health, Education and Welfare is required by the terms of its grant to incorporate within it a research plan.[3]

All too often, however, treatment considerations take precedence over research requirements and, as a result, few useful findings have to date emerged.

The major obstacle to carrying out scientifically based research designs in the correctional field is the inability (and frequently the downright impossibility) of assigning equal numbers of persons to the experimental as opposed to the control group, on any consistently random — or matched — basis. This is especially true for those halfway houses which receive probationers directly from the court. Highfields, the New Jersey residential center, was geared to such a research effort when it first opened, but since it was up to each judge to determine whether a boy before him went to Highfields or to the Annandale reformatory, random assignment was impossible.[4] The research study attempted to find a control subject to match each Highfields boy by using several gross variables characteristic of those boys committed to the reformatory. But without completely random assignment to the two programs, a basic prerequisite of valid research was violated.

A similar experience was had at Pinehills in Provo, Utah and at Southfields in Louisville, Kentucky, — both programs based on the Highfields model. At Provo, the judge, whose concern for children had brought about its establishment in the first instance, simply would not follow the random selection plan, which called for his selecting one of three envelopes each containing one of three possible destinations — probation, reformatory, or halfway house.[5] At Southfields a political change removed the judge who had agreed to the random assignment plan and his successor could not be persuaded to cooperate with the necessary procedures.[6]

The original research design at the MacLaren Center in Portland, Oregon, called for three groups of boys to be drawn at random from a population pool. One group of boys was assigned to the halfway house. A second group was placed on parole in their own homes or in foster homes, but with equal access to the vocational services provided to the halfway house residents. The third group represented a typical parole caseload, to receive no training or employment benefits other than those customarily obtained for them by their parole agents. Staff at the training school objected to random assignment of boys for whom they believed other placement was preferable; parole agents for the third group wanted access for their boys to the same training and employment opportunities that were available to the other groups, with the result that:

While the research design specified random assignment to produce equivalency of the study groups, in practice we found this difficult to achieve . . . The research design, itself, simply did not allow for the multiplicity of factors that emerged to complicate the selection process.

This project emphasized for us the difficulty of establishing research within a social action setting.[7]

As research projects based on the principle of random assignment fail as a result of such complications as these, resort has been had to alternative procedures. One method matches its control group as closely as possible according to the variables of family history, delinquency record, school performance, ethnic background and socioeconomic level. One of the most recent of such undertakings involves three residential group centers in New Jersey: the nonresidential Essexfields center, the Annandale Reformatory and the Essex County Probation Department. Groups of boys were matched on the basis of the variables just listed as well as in subgroups from all six programs, in accordance with the pretreatment scores obtained on the Minnesota Multiphasic Personality Inventory.[8]

Another alternative research procedure, when attempts at random assignment have failed, is the follow-up study. When it was apparent that Highfields' experimental population was comprised of less serious offenders than the population which the judges committed to the reformatory, a second control group was selected. This consisted of boys sentenced to Annandale three years prior to Highfields' establishment from among those whose records indicated that they would have been considered as candidates for Highfields had it existed at that time. The later adjustment of these boys in the community was then contrasted with those boys who had later actually passed through the Highfields program. Results of this post hoc projection are open to criticism on at least several counts: validity of the matching procedures, time differences, changes in patterns of delinquency no less than in correctional programs.

The inability to furnish a sufficient number of subjects for both the experimental and the control groups is another hazard. The Provo research team could not turn up enough boys in each of the three programs they were studying — the halfway house, the state training school, and probation — to compose a statistically adequate population. Departing from their original design, therefore, the researchers then filled the training school control group with boys in institutions who had been committed from other counties but who seemingly resembled the Provo experimental subjects in other important particulars.[9]

In much the same way, Shaw Residence in Washington could not produce a sufficiently large number of men to form a control group, compelling the research team to select its controls from among men who either had no desire to be placed in Shaw Residence, or who were unaware of its existence.[10]

Another problem in conducting valid controlled research in this area arises from a conflict in aims:

The demands of research designs usually require that there be some interference with the normal decision-making and treatment process. . . In other words, in seeking to select boys randomly for placement, the judgment of the regular staff was bypassed. Perhaps it is asking too much of a staff member to continue to have responsibility for a boy and then let research endeavor make an important decision about the boy's program.[11]

On more than one occasion, a research staff may be found to hold itself aloof from those in charge of program. This results in resentment, deriving, if only partially, from the understandable curiosity of the latter to be kept informed of the progress of the study. The mere presence of a research team can have direct, though unmeasurable influence on the program.[12] At one California residence for offenders, administrators of the program requested information about the research results, but the study personnel, viewing their function as one of observation and analysis rather than of consultation, refused. Tension between the two staff groups grew to the point where necessary communication between them was substantially reduced.[13] To overcome this, the research staff had no choice but to play a role in developing the program, in addition to their responsibility to test and evaluate it. When treatment personnel introduced new elements into the program, the researchers in turn provided whatever feedback they could obtain, in recognition of the fact that they had to ". . . accept the fact that both the experimental and the control programs are bound to change and grow if they are to be effective; therefore, it will be hard to measure them in the rigorous ways of science."[14]

The effect of the introduction of a research effort upon an existing program can also be considerable. Prior to the establishment of Provo, the probation officers in this part of Utah claimed a success rate of 55% with what they termed their persistent offenders. When they realized that their results were being compared with those of the halfway house, they apparently felt compelled to exert themselves, for in a later evaluation their percentage rate of successful performance rose to seventy-three.[15] It is also conceivable that the probationers themselves, aware of their role in the experiment, may have wanted to perform better than they might have under ordinary circumstances.[16]

Difficulties of Comparison

Comparison of the effectiveness of the programs of a particular halfway house in one state with one in another area is not feasible because of the large numbers of variables (and the interaction between them): population, program, location, admission criteria, method of assignment, and the period of time selected for evaluating their relative effectiveness. Then, too, definitions of successful adjustment after release from treatment, differ. Experimental and control samples tend to be extremely small, in itself a potential source of statistical error, with the result that conclusions drawn from them are at best, tentative.

Another potential area for studying the results of treatment (other than postrelease recidivism), is available in a review of those who leave or are released before they should be. For obviously not all children assigned to a halfway house can — or will — complete the program. These "in-program terminations" include both runaways and those returned to court or institution by reason of a staff, or joint staff-resident, decision that they are unsuitable. Such reasons might include homosexual exploitation of another resident, physical attack, consistent refusal to perform the assigned tasks, verbal threat to maim or knife, use of narcotics, persistent late return, or failure to return from furlough.

The original Highfields study reported its rate of AWOL's and other in-program failures at 18.6% of all boys admitted.[17] A more recent research on guided group centers reports for three New Jersey residential centers for boys, an average in-program failure rate of 27%, with Essexfields (a nonresidential center) scoring 23%.[18] Few guided group centers in other parts of the country report such favorable results. Walton Village reported an in-program termination rate in 1967 of 19.5%.[19] This was not based on any research effort involving a control group. It is further significant that the sixteen boys who were terminated for unsatisfactory conduct, running away, or other reasons were not thereafter institutionalized, but permitted by the court to remain in the community.

Halfway houses which admit seriously delinquent adolescents and which also adhere to careful statistical procedures report a rate of in-program failure which is generally higher than that just cited. Southfields in Kentucky reporting in March, 1966 on its first four years of operation gave an in-program failure rate of 48%,[20] comparable to that of Silverlake, started in 1964 in Los Angeles.[21]

Of those who failed, 35% ran away and approximately 15% were returned by staff as unsuitable for open programs — for further court disposition. Southfields in its attempt to discover the reason for its high failure rate ascribes it to lack of competent staff, inadequate support from the local court, failure of halfway house and court staff to work together, incompetent administration, and poorly designed program.[22]

In-program failures occur within differing periods of time, some within the first weeks after arrival, others after several months. Those who ran away, or were returned to court as unsuitable for the Highfields program, were in residence there an average of three weeks or less.[23] A recent New Jersey study suggests that failure is more likely to come within the first twelve weeks.[24]

Characteristics of In-Program Failures

Efforts have also been made to discover the characteristics of those who fail to complete the halfway house program, in order to modify it in such a way as to reduce such failures. The original Highfields study found many of these to be small town boys, boys from disrupted family situations, whites more readily than blacks. In contrast, Southfields with blacks comprising approximately one-fourth of its population, reports precisely the opposite with respect to race. Those blacks who did not make it at Southfields were more likely to be returned to court for failure to adjust suitably in the program rather than for absconding.[25]

The Southfields research also found among their in-program failures a large number of boys with IQ's below 90, as well as those with five or more prior appearances before the juvenile court.[26] These findings as to intelligence are echoed in recent New Jersey findings that boys doing well in school were less likely to be program failures.[27] This was particularly true for the probation group.

The Minnesota Multiphasic Personality Inventory has been used to help in differentiating in-program successes from failures,[28] with significant differences also found in the probation group. Otherwise:

In these groups, there are practically no significant differences between program successes and failures as determined by the MMPI tests. However, failures in both programs generally score more negatively than do successes on most tests . . . Although many of the success-failure differences in the Essexfields and Group Centers programs are in the same direction as those found in Probation, they are milder and less able to distinguish between the criterion groups.[29]

At Southfields, younger boys, those with an IQ below 90, and those with histories of running away were found to be the most frequent absconders.[30] Most boys who ran from Highfields were readmitted; those only were not permitted to return "who kept running away every week for several weeks, each time taking with him an additional boy."[31] This lenient policy, applied in the beginning, became far more rigid as time went on, in both Southfields and Highfields.

During adolescence, an age difference of two or three years can have great significance in terms of sophistication, physical strength, coordination and emotional maturity, with the younger boys less able to tolerate demands made upon them by adults and by fellow group members. The high rate of association between age and in-program failure may to some extent be explained by the fact that younger boys are intimidated and exploited by their elders, and, as a result, have a stronger motivation for running away.[32]

Despite the contradictory nature of many of these findings in regard to success or failure within community-based programs, further studies of this type will and should be made. Certainly not every resident needs this form of supervision, and it is evident from at least one source that some types of boys may actually be harmed by a halfway house experience as, for example, those who find themselves completely unable to live harmoniously with others of their own age. The unauthorized departure from the program of such a boy may be the result of his own misery, rather than of any persistent delinquent drive, and probation or parole supervision would therefore seem preferable for him. By studying and recording the reactions of different types of boys to the various halfway house programs, correctional authorities should in time be able to individualize the process to make it increasingly effective. Such studies might also aid in determining the role which staff members play in the eventual success or failure of their efforts.

Success and Failure: In-Program and Post-Release

The usual measure for gauging the effectiveness of the halfway house program continues to be the recidivism rate of its graduates. The question then arises: should in-program terminations be counted as failures, or only those who have completed the program and fail after release to the community?[33]

The original Highfields study and the Provo experiment of a few years later appear to be the only careful research efforts which report success and failure in terms both of those who completed the program, and of those who entered but never finished. Using the Annandale reformatory for comparison, the Highfields research concludes that, when both groups are counted, the overall success rate for Highfields was 63%, as against 47% for Annandale.[34] Of 229 Highfields boys, 145 had not been committed to a correctional institution within a year following their release (63%). The Annandale control group contained only 116 boys, of whom 55 had similarly succeeded.

When the experimental group is studied according to its racial composition, the success and failure rates take on another significance. There was no statistical difference between the failure rates of white boys at Highfields or Annandale; only in the case of the black boys, who comprised a very small percentage of the Highfields population, was the difference between the two groups pronounced: "Thus the overall differences in the success rates were almost wholly due to the large discrepancy between the rate for Negroes sent to Highfields and that for Negroes sent to Annandale."[35]

The Provo experiment research followed the Highfields example by studying both the in-program failures and those who failed after leaving the program. Here the boys at the Utah Industrial School were used for comparison. When in-program and post-release failures were grouped together, Pinehills' success record surpassed the correctional institution, but equalled the results obtained by probation supervision.

A recent Walton Village report based its success-failure percentages both on in-program terminees and boys who completed the program. Several unusual features of this study make it difficult to relate its findings to others, in that no control group is available; no time period is specified for the duration of the follow-up period; its population contains boys who are officially designated as dependent rather than delinquent; and, finally, the criteria for failure include both commitment to a correctional institution, or consistently unsatisfactory adjustment in the community even if no conflict with the law is reported. With these considerations in mind, the report proceeds to find that 67.3% of all its graduates have been successful. The study conjectures that inasmuch as at least one-half of those now performing unsatisfactorily, but still not in difficulty with the law, will eventually improve their adjustment — this success rate "will increase to approximately eighty per cent or more when we include the successful borderline cases."[36]

Effectiveness of Guided Group Interaction

Research leaves the efficacy of guided group interaction still open to question. Some years after the original Highfields program was begun, two claims were made that its results were more successful than those of the reformatory, in the treatment of older youths.[37] These claims were based largely upon comparative violation rates of graduates of the two places, claims which have been criticized for their failure to utilize control and experimental groups.[38] For some years thereafter no further efforts seem to have been made to evaluate either these New Jersey centers or similar programs which appeared in other states. In 1967, a Rutgers University study of more than one thousand delinquents gave credence to the original Highfields claims.[39]

A number of factors appear to support the finding that guided group interaction programs do measurably improve the attitudes and behavior of adolescent offenders. No research effort based on recidivism studies alone can be conclusive, if only because a finding of recidivism — or of its absence — does not tell the whole story. If involvement in a guided group interaction program can, within a period of four to six months, reverse long-held antisocial standards, then later re-exposure to the delinquent culture outside can be expected with time, to undo — at least partially — these effects. Until aftercare programs are available which will offer reasonable continuity of treatment to persons who have undergone immersion in group processes in either residential or nonresidential situations, no assertion as to the effectiveness or ineffectiveness of such programs can be made with any validity or finality.

Using a variety of treatment approaches, including group programs, the research plan of the Community Treatment Project of the California Youth Authority has meticulously followed[40] the requirement of random assignment to experimental and contol groups.[41] Its findings lend far more credence to the value of community-based correctional programs than any others which have so far appeared in the literature. The project consists of two phases. The first — for children from Stockton and Sacramento — was completed in 1964; the second, which also involves children from San Francisco, is expected to continue into the 1970's.[42] Findings are presently available, therefore, only for Phase I.

Boys and girls from the Stockton and Sacramento areas are eligible for the project, as long as they represent first commitments to the California Youth Authority, and have not been adjudicated for a serious assault or other act which has aroused the community.[43] Such cases are placed in a common pool at the Authority's northern diagnostic center where they are randomly assigned either to the Community Treatment Project or to a state training school. Of the children received at the reception center, 90% of the girl first-timers and almost 75% of the boy first commitments have been eligible for the experiment: "By December, 1966, 270 experimental cases had entered the Phase I community program in Sacramento and Stockton, and 357 comparable control subjects had been assigned to the traditional Youth Authority Program."[44]

After five years of study, the research division of the Authority reports, for the community-based program, demonstrably greater success. Fifteen months after their return to the community only 28% of the experimental group had failed on parole, as contrasted with a failure rate of 52% for the controls.[45] This fifteen-month period began somewhat later for the control group than for the experimental group; for the latter, as soon as they left the reception center; for the controls, not until they had been released from the training school to which they had been assigned from the reception center.

The girls seem to have fared particularly well in the community-based program, only 13% of them failing on parole, as contrasted with 57% for girls in the control group. Success for boys in the experimental group was not as outstanding as for the girls: a 30% failure rate as compared with 51% for boys who had been routed through the training schools.[46] After they had been in the community for two years, 61% of the controls had been returned to institutions, as compared with only 38% of the experimentals.[47] No breakdown by sex is available for this twenty-four month period of observation.

The California Youth Authority has also been concerned with the effect of different forms of treatment on different types of offenders, based upon three levels of interpersonal maturity which includes nine subtypes as described earlier. Of these nine subtypes, the ninth — or the highest in respect to level of maturity — is the only one to show "a failure rate difference in favor of the control program."[48] This type of youth has been classified as the "cultural identifier (Ci)":

Ci's are viewed as "normal" youths who need to learn that crime does not pay. Project results suggest that perhaps the more efficient way of teaching this may be to deprive the Ci of something which is very important to him — his freedom — by a short stay in an institution.[49]

Without disparaging the excellent showing of the project, at least one observation may be warranted. The Youth Authority permits its agents to return certain of their wards to the institution for periods of temporary detention, which may range from a few days to a month. Such children are not deemed to be program failures, even though they may be placed in detention more than once, at the discretion of the parole staff. The research summarized above notes that the community treatment subjects have been placed in temporary detention more often than the control subjects.[50] Although the reason for such detention was often the commission of a minor offense such as "placement failure, poor home or school adjustment, truancy or runaway,"[51] it is also possible that some agents may have used "suspension of parole" on occasions which, strictly speaking, may have warranted revocation of parole.

A research report from the MacLaren Vocational Center in Portland, Oregon, a halfway house which functioned for a year and a half, sought to ascertain whether boys living in a group situation and exposed to intensive vocational training would perform better on parole than those paroled directly to their homes. Its results while interesting, are hardly encouraging:

The index of community adjustment was whether or not a boy failed to adjust in the community and had to be returned to MacLaren. This would normally involve persistent violation of parole regulations or the commitment of law violations. Forty-three per cent of the boys in the Vocational Center were returned to the campus, during the study period, as compared to thirty-one per cent of the control group.[52]

Group Home Research

The effectiveness of the foster group home program has also been assessed.[53] Three groups of boys were released from Wisconsin training schools to three types of aftercare: their own homes, boarding homes (either singly, or with one or two others), and group care homes. Each sample contained approximately 65 boys, released for the first time from institutions, between 1959 and 1963. Adjustment was evaluated six months after departure from the training schools.

All indications pointed to the fact that boys placed in the group care foster homes were more difficult and more disadvantaged than those released to their own homes. Of the group home boys 62% came from families broken by death, divorce or desertion, as compared to only 16% of boys returned to their own homes. Of the group home boys 51% came from lower-lower socioeconomic levels compared with 19% for the "own home" sample. Of the group boys 41% had been institutionalized more than eight months, as contrasted to only 13% of boys who went back to their parents.

Both the Wisconsin Juvenile Review Board and the training schools had expressed some hesitancy about the chances for success of the boys recommended for the group program, predicting a 52% failure rate for them as compared to 36% for boys about to return to their own homes.

Little difference in outcome between the boarding home and group home samples emerged, but the research did find that boys placed in group homes had a failure rate of only 30%, while those who returned to their own parents failed in 48% of the cases. The two samples virtually reversed the predictions made in advance by the institution staff.

Other signs of progress for the group home boys are also reported. Prior to commitment, only 3% of the group home boys were said to have adjusted well in public school, but six months after release, 25% of them won satisfactory school ratings for both adjustment and scholarship. One of the most surprising findings was that the group home boys were more likely to select nondelinquent companions than those in the "own home" sample. While at the time of commitment 23% of them were rejective of adults, only 4% still revealed this hostile attitude six months after placement in a group foster home: "Boys placed in group homes also had less disruptive use of alcohol and were less assaultive after release than the own home sample."[54] An Ohio study also supports the Wisconsin research results: ". . . institutional return is significantly lower for youth in foster care than for youth placed in their own homes."[55]

The Bureau of Prisons has published considerable data on its prerelease guidance centers both as to program effectiveness as measured by recidivism or other measures as well as on characteristics of its populations. One of its first studies disproved the criticism that transfer to a prerelease center entailed a longer period of confinement than would otherwise be the case.[56] Placement in a prerelease center permitted the prisoner to leave institution custody 90 to 120 days earlier, but if he failed during his stay and then had to be returned, he did serve on the average an additional year in custody.[57]

Recidivism rates as a measure of success or failure disclosed that of 145 men placed in the three prerelease centers in 1965, 109 were placed under parole supervision after several months at the centers, while 36 were returned to the institution — 14 for failure to adjust, 9 for escapes, and 13 for a new offense.[58] The 109 men released on parole were then studied after one year of supervision, recidivism being defined as "any offense leading to either a new commitment in a state or federal institution or suspension of parole."[59] A new misdemeanor resulting in a brief jail period but not in parole revocation was not considered to constitute a failure.

Based on these criteria, the failure rate was either 30.3% or 47.6%.[60] The former figure applied to men sent back to prison while still under center supervision who were not counted as parole failures; the higher figure applied to those so regarded. In either instance, the recidivism figures after one full year of prerelease center operation did not differ from the overall federal institution rate which ran between 30% and 40%.[61]

A more charitable view of performance holds that the young center residents were not representative of the general run of federal prisoners. Because they were persons sentenced under the Federal Youth Corrections Act or the Federal Juvenile Delinquency Act, they were an atypically young sample. The overall failure rate for other federal prisoners of the same age is not this 30% to 40% range, but 40% to 50%. "Furthermore, the Center residents had a higher proportion of urban and a smaller proportion of Southeast, South Central, and Northwest state residents than are found in a cross-section of federal prison releasees."[62]

Several additional explanations of the results obtained are that the three centers were still so new that many difficulties had not yet been resolved.[63] Center personnel may have needed more time to adjust to the novel community-based program. At the same time, the level of supervision the men received was far more rigorous than that of normal parolees being returned for transgressions which might very likely have remained undetected had they not been on parole.[64]

Factors usually associated with successful adjustment in other places and programs were not found to be operative with prerelease residents, nor were efforts to predict recidivism successful.[65] Many men who should have succeeded, failed, while many of the least likely appearing candidates were not returned to prison:

This failure to find factors associated with recidivism — extremely unusual for this type of study — suggests the possibility that the Centers have had a differential impact upon residents by which prisoners with normally poor chances of success upon release were considerably helped at the Centers while prisoners with normally good chances of success upon release may actually have been harmed by transfer to Centers.[66]

Results of a later study supported the earlier research hypothesis that prerelease guidance centers may have had differential impacts on various types of offenders.[67] Federal prisoners, totaling 285 released during 1964 from four centers were followed up after a minimum of two years' parole supervision. Definition of success and failure now differed somewhat: "failure" was defined as commitment to an institution of any kind for one or more days, or issuance of a parole violation warrant; "success" meant no arrests, as well as arrest without conviction and even conviction without commitment.

Using a 1961 Base Expectancy Study, in which the characteristics of prior commitments, offense, and number of codefendants were found to be related to rates of recidivism, research results reported that prerelease centers appeared to be helpful to young car thieves who had been previously committed, but might actually be harmful to men with no previous commitments, or those in prison for offenses other than car thefts.[68] Nor did this latter group with a potentially high success rate do so well upon leaving the center. Car thieves with previous records, on the other hand, did much better than their anticipated high failure rate would indicate.

Excluding the 54 men returned to institutions for "in-program" failure at the centers, 57.6% of the 231 men released to the free community on parole were judged "successes," while 42.4% were considered "failures." The anticipated overall failure rate for the groups had been estimated at 52.3%.[69] The difference between actual and expected failure rate according to the federal researchers was "an index of increased program effectiveness attributable to the prerelease guidance centers."[70]

Performance of prisoners in the community upon release from prerelease centers also involves their ability to survive the three to four month stay in the center. In the course of a little over a year and a half, of 456 men who had spent time in one of the four centers, 361 (80%) were released to the community; 41 (9%) were returned to institutions prior to parole; and 52 (11%) absconded.[71]

More of the young men in the "returned to institution prior to parole" group were sentenced under the Federal Juvenile Delinquency Act and had also been arrested at an earlier age. During their nine months in prison or reformatory prior to placement in the centers, they had received more disciplinary reports, were more likely to be nonwhite, and to score lower on IQ and achievement tests than men in the other categories. The absconders, in comparison with other groups, included more probation or parole violators, more auto thieves, and persons with a larger number of previous commitments.[72]

Of the 361 who completed the prerelease program and were released to parole supervision, both race and educational level showed a high correlation to the amount of money saved at the time of release. White boys with higher scholastic ratings not only participated more actively in the program, but were also rated most likely to succeed in parole. Conversely, black boys with less than a tenth grade education rated low on both of these counts.[73]

A final finding casts an interesting sidelight on the vocational training program in the federal correctional institutions which is admittedly superior to that of most state systems. The Bureau of Prisons also places great emphasis on locating employment for men in its prerelease centers. All this gives added point to the comment that: "Only twenty-six per cent of the total group had jobs at the time of release which were considered to be related to the vocational training received during the service of the current sentence."[74]

A British Comparison

A study by the Research Unit of the British Home Office affords an interesting comparison with the findings just cited.[75] A follow-up study on 327 releases from Dartmoor Prison in 1961 included some men who were placed in halfway houses, and some who were released directly into the community. Those in the first group were released from maximum custody some six months before those who composed the control groups.[76] This research discovered no major differences in the community adjustment of the two groups, or any great validity in staff prognoses regarding future behavior.

The tendency for community centers to relax their admission criteria is confirmed by the British study that ". . . selection boards tend to become more daring as the hostel scheme becomes more firmly established."[77] It likewise suggests that much of the public anxiety concerning the danger of admitting murderers and sex offenders to halfway houses is not well founded. "Men serving sentences for murder, manslaughter, homo- or hetero-sexual offenses and also fraud were less often reconvicted than were those convicted of the more common kinds of offense."[78] In fact, those most likely to fail in the community were the more typical offenders — men who had committed crimes of violence and larceny, with many previous convictions and prison experiences, who in their youth had also spent time in juvenile institutions.[79]

The research study compensated for the fact that the better risks were sent to halfway houses by means of the base expectancy score ratings which attempted to equate the halfway house populations more fairly with the prison populations, with the result that: ". . . even when allowance has been made for the hostel selection, there is still a very favorable outcome for the hostel group compared with the prison group."[80]

When Recidivism Is Most Likely to Occur

Both the studies of recidivism made in New Jersey during the 1950's and in the mid-1960's disclose a markedly similar finding: that the months immediately following release are the crucial ones, with from 56% to 75% getting into trouble before the end of their first year out. If not involved with the law during the first two years of life in the community, however, they were not likely to get into trouble thereafter.[81]

Do Attitudes Change with Treatment?

Since attitudes may be viewed as latent actions, it would be fair to assume that as attitudes improved during the course of treatment, so would behavior. When measures for predicting recidivism (the eight attitude scales, the Army Psychoneurotic Screening Adjunct, and the sentence completion test) were employed by the first Highfields research team to test this hypothesis, their conclusions were that:

There is very little evidence that Highfields boys, over the length of their treatment, change their attitudes toward family and toward law and order, and their outlook toward life . . .

From the measuring instruments used, there is no indication that, in general, Highfields boys change more in different directions than do Annandale boys.[82]

A rather different picture is presented by a book written by the originators of Highfields who, basing their findings on the same tests, found that:

The Highfields boys moved in the direction of frankness, expressiveness, and recognition of social values (not always acceptance, but at least awareness). The conventional reformatory boys in contrast became more guarded, covered their thoughts under cliches . . . and avoided coming to grips with issues of importance — social or personal . . . Whereas the conventional reformatory group developed quite uniformly a bleaker, darker and more depressed outlook, the Highfields group showed a generally positive and more varied, more realistic outlook.[83]

All in all they showed, that although there is no reason to conclude that "primary goals or basic drives of either groups were substantially changed," the Highfields boys gained in self-respect and made greater progress than did the Annandale boys in relating to authority.[84]

The results with regard to the boys' personality obtained by the extensive New Jersey study of 1967 found that although the changes revealed by the MMPI test were not great, "general improvement in attitudes and ego strength" was found in all programs except that of the reformatory.[85] In addition, boys in the three residential centers and in the nonresidential center were found to evidence less anxiety than those who had been in the reformatory. Although the pretest profiles of the boys on probation were the most favorable consistent with their less serious delinquent histories, their overall improvement was below that of the boys in the halfway houses:

The more marked changes in Essexfields and Group Center boys and the relative absence of change in Annandale boys . . . suggest that the nature of the treatment may have had some influence on the post-treatment MMPI's . . . If the posttests represent simply a replication of the pretests, conditioned by the more favorable circumstances under which the posttests were taken, the probation boys should have shown the most improvement.[86]

Personality changes have also been reported in the Silverlake research study based on a control group from a small (130 boys), private, correctional institution, where the lack of reliance on security and custody is at variance with most larger, state-operated training schools. Although scores on the Jesness Inventory were available for only 37 halfway house graduates and 21 institution releasees, the Silverlake research found that both groups had changed in a positive fashion during treatment, becoming more trusting and also less alienated from persons in authority. Their emotional control improved, as did their attitudes toward social conventions and rules. Post-treatment test results revealed that some lower class values had been discarded in favor of an ability to deal with the demands of the environment in more acceptable fashion.[87]

Despite the slight differences between the two groups in relation to the changes that had taken place in them, the institution controls appeared to be somewhat less alienated than the Silverlake boys. The research team ventured the opinion, as a result, that this difference might have been related to the fact that boys remain in treatment at the institution much longer than at Silverlake — an average of 16.5 months as compared to a stay of 6.5 months, respectively.[88]

The findings of the California Community Treatment Project research resemble to some extent the Silverlake data, using the same Jesness Inventory to test experimental and control groups both before and after treatment. Results showed that children in the community-based program and those committed to institutions "both were more likely to show a positive than a negative direction of change" at the time of the posttests. As at Silverlake, the institution controls here did rather well on the Jesness Inventory, showing a "more positive posttest score on two of the eight scales," while the experimentals had a more positive score on only one of the scales. Controls and experimentals were tied regarding "greater degree of positive change," with each group scoring well on two of the eight scales. In regard to those "more likely to change in a positive direction," the community treatment experimentals did well on four of the eight scales, and the controls on three.[89]

In addition to the Jesness Inventory, the California Psychological Inventory was also employed.[90] Here the experimental group did far better than the controls from the institutions. While community treatment children "showed significantly more positive posttest scores than the control wards on eight of the fourteen scales," the controls revealed no improvement: no positive change on any of the scales as against experimental group gains on three out of eight. The research concludes that children in the community-based experimental program demonstrated "more positive change, together with a higher level of personal and social adjustment at posttest," than did those who had been in institutions.[91]

Formal testing has not been the only measure of attitudinal change. At both Highfields and Southfields, for example, probation officers were asked their impressions of boys released from halfway house treatment. These reported that the majority of the Highfields graduates seemed to show improvement in all areas.[92] Although the least improvement was noted in the area of work, over one-half the boys were considered to have developed a more positive approach toward employment. Interestingly enough, the greatest positive change related to the boys self-image.[93]

The Ashley Weeks' account of the original Highfields experiment discloses that a composite picture was sought regarding each boy admitted to Highfields and the reformatory. Weeks writes:

During the second year of research, five persons who knew each boy intimately were interviewed at the time he was sent to one of the facilities and again after he was released. A comparison of the interviews concerning Highfields and Annandale boys shows that, in general, Highfields boys were considered to have improved.[94]

Summary

Many halfway houses, particularly those under private auspices make no attempt to measure the effectiveness of their programs. Even when funds are available, many research designs are unable to achieve truly random assignment to an experimental and to a control group. In others, population samples are too small to make valid any conclusions based on them. More than one instance has been reported of conflicts developing between research teams and staff. Changes in program which take place during an evaluative study make research results based on a previous program no longer completely comparable.

On the basis of available research results, no single halfway house program can be rated as superior or inferior to any other, not only because programs vary, but also because no group of residents is precisely comparable to any other. Intake criteria also differ widely. In some places commitment to a halfway house may be mandatory, in others voluntary. Definitions of later successful community adjustment also differ, and there is no agreement as to whether in-program failures should be included in any evaluative program. Periods of time in the community as a basis for follow-up studies range from a few months to several years. In short, "In human situations, knowledge is not necessarily exportable. What works one place may not apply elsewhere."[95]

With the exception of the data from California's Community Treatment Project, virtually all credible research has come from halfway houses which apply guided group interaction procedures. Findings from several studies as to their effectiveness are nevertheless contradictory. Black boys may be found to adapt easily to halfway house life in one program; another place may indicate precisely the opposite result. Efforts to predict recidivism have also led to contradictory results. Highfields research in the 1950's found that boys who committed property offenses, especially car theft, were prone to fail. Silverlake, however, discovered an association between low social status, number of runaways, and seriousness of past criminal behavior with later failure.

One conclusion which seems to have validity is that the residential halfway house is not necessarily an alternative to standard probation care. Where a delinquent child can possibly live at home under the supervision of a probation officer, there is no necessity for committing him to a residential center. In fact, some boys seem clearly unable to adjust to group situations, and are therefore better off under some other form of treatment. The rather high in-program failure rate of some halfway houses supports the finding of the California Community Treatment Project that different types of offenders benefit from a variety of treatment styles. The Silverlake research finding that boys with extensive delinquent histories can adjust satisfactorily to community-based programs is strengthened by the research result that: ". . . there is some indication that boys usually considered poor risks in general may be especially appropriate candidates for the guided group interaction programs."[96]

In addition to research programs aimed at evaluating treatment results on the basis of recidivism rate, attempts have also been made to assess attitudinal changes. One of the two original Highfields studies found no attitudinal differences during halfway house treatment, but a later study indicated that change had actually taken place. Southfields and Crofton House observed no real difference between pretreatment and posttreatment scores, while a study of Silverlake found improvement in both the experimental and control group attitudes.

The rather elaborate California Youth Authority research efforts and those from Rutgers University report improved attitudes as a result of community-based treatment. The former, using both the Jesness Inventory and the California Psychological Inventory, reported for the experimental (community-based) cases "more positive change than for the control cases, together with a higher level of personal and social adjustment.[97] The latter, employing the Minnesota Multiphasic Personality Inventory and claiming only "modest changes," found halfway house treatment ". . . somewhat successful in reducing the boys' anxieties, hostilities, and doubts, and in building their confidence and self-esteem. These programs are certainly more successful in these respects than Annandale (reformatory) and very probably probation as well."[98]

Despite the inherent difficulties in conducting valid research, the gravity and proportions of our national crime problem demand continued efforts to assess the value of different correctional programs. Sums appropriated for research purposes in the past have been infinitesimal in comparison to the millions of dollars which every year are appropriated to traditional forms of treatment. Annual compilations of statistics on prisoner populations are hardly research. Research necessitates a constant and statistically valid process of comparing the results of various programs. At the probation level, where the attitude of the court makes random assignment unlikely, subjects can still be matched on the Base Expectancy Scores which are drawn from variables associated with community adjustment.

Further research must also be pursued with respect to specific categories of offenders who are likely to adjust well to community-based programs, as well as those who are sent to institutions and later released to the community. Knowledge applicable to one situation cannot always be transferred satisfactorily to another, but exploration in greater depth of the variables associated with good and poor adjustment in various types of agencies under a wide variety of treatment programs must continue to be made.

The classic follow-up study of recidivism, *Five Hundred Criminal Careers,* although published almost forty years ago, still stands as the model for studies of the success of institutional treatment. Its reported failure rate of 88.2%, which shocked the penal field when first announced, brought denunciation both of its methods and of its definition of what precisely was meant by failure. Unfortunately, the failure of the treatment method which was revealed was never subjected to either the same criticism or degree of denunciation as the methods followed by the Gluecks to uncover it. Many of our large penitentiaries and reformatories are over one hundred years old. The methods they employ — and the attitudes expressed by program and all too often by staff — are equally outmoded. No approach to the handling of any other basic social problem (mental health, hospital care, welfare administration) which had so consistently proven itself to be such a failure would have so long been permitted to endure. The pressure upon government to protect society against the depredations of the lawless has forced it to fall back upon measures of restraint and repression in the name of "security" (or "law and order"), despite the obvious fact that almost every single person presently in confinement will some day again take part in the life of the community.

The conclusion should at this point be obvious: if society continues to permit institutions to contain people in accordance with programs which every evaluative study has shown to be productive of a rate of failure of one-half to two-thirds of its graduates, then the halfway house facility, whether residential or nonresidential, should not be held to a higher standard of critical self-examination. First it must be permitted to extend its efforts to help influence the behavior of offenders either instead of, or after, a period of institution custody. This is not to argue that the halfway house should not continue to attempt to evaluate its results with all the care and accuracy that it can muster. It asks only that other considerations be borne in mind while it is being given the chance to prove itself one way or another as alternate weapon in the armamentarium of crime control.

These considerations are two. The first is that costs — in the way of buildings, staff and money — are appreciably lower in the halfway house than in prison or training school. The second is that, granted a success rate which is not demonstrably higher than that of these traditional places, dedication to an atmosphere and program which aims to be truly and consistently rehabilitative, is productive of a correctional way of life for offenders which is demonstrably more civilized, more humane, and less destructive. In the process, the values of the larger society in which it makes its contribution, through its influence on those committed to its care, are sure to be enhanced, however difficult it may be to measure that influence with precision.

13 In Prospect . . .

As the materials for this book were being drawn together for publication, a most significant overview of the problem of crime in American society today, the Report of the President's Commission on Law Enforcement and Administration of Justice,[1] appeared. This report makes it very clear that there is no panacea for this national problem, that a close interdependence exists between every step and every program in the correctional continuum from apprehension through court process, institution and on through parole. Therefore, any advocacy of the significance of the halfway house movement in the United States should, by rights, indicate how its facilities fit into this total system.

The visible display of force and controls exercised by society to keep the committed adult criminal or the juvenile delinquent in line inevitably result in an awareness on his part that he is being stigmatized not only as an enemy of society but as an outcast from it as well. When shut off, away from other citizens, in the constant companionship of other antisocial individuals, animus toward authority is heightened, and rehabilitation, in any basic sense, becomes well-nigh impossible. Huge complexes with many hundreds or even thousands of persons in confinement must resort to the lowest common denominator of societal control: security, routine, the threat of further punishment and an overall impersonalness. When the enlightened administrator attempts to establish some rapport between inmates and staff, the gulf between them can only in the rarest instances be bridged, with the result of reinforcing the inmate subculture in which the individual finds confirmation of his view of himself as a criminal.[2]

What Is Treatment?

The claim that the young offender in confinement is usually better off than his adult counterpart is difficult to uphold. For even children as young as nine or ten are today found to be housed in overlarge institutions, whose inadequate resources, poorly qualified personnel and need to maintain an orderly regime, hamper any genuine efforts at treatment:

. . . the rehabilitative ideal has been debased in practice and . . . the consequences resulting from this debasement are serious, and, at times, dangerous. This proposition may be supported, first, by the observation that, under the dominance of the rehabilitative ideal, the language of therapy is frequently employed, wittingly or unwittingly to disguise the true state of affairs that prevails in our custodial institutions and at other points in the correctional process.[3]

Absence of any desire to provide a truly therapeutic milieu is compounded by lack of knowledge as to how treatment may be applied. The correctional field has in the past been largely avoided by competent clinicians, while many of those who do enter it ultimately fall back on the single, ancient reliance of custodial care.[4]

It is indeed questionable whether a large professional staff and a high per capita cost can successfully make any one specific correctional program more effective. In such seemingly more desirable places the child is often transferred to a diagnostic center for observation, tests and interviews. During this period, the lack of program or activity may often result in unalloyed antagonism and an introduction to homosexual behavior. Once the recommendation with regard to him has been made, the young person is then transferred to still another institution which may or may not be prepared — in attitudes, facilities or staff — to follow out the recommendations made at the diagnostic center.[5]

What happens when we remove a child from his home community? Is the present state of knowledge in the behavioral sciences sufficiently advanced to justify confinement of children in institutions for indefinite periods? Can such placement damage more than it helps? In short,

It should be pointed out, first, that the values in individual liberty may be imperiled by claims to knowledge and therapeutic technique that we, in fact, do not possess, and by our failure to concede candidly what we do not know.[6]

Fostering Delinquency

Yet many such inept correctional programs are only part of a total system. Its young people may have already been handled by parents, teachers, police, detention personnel, and court officials in a manner which has profoundly influenced their basic concepts of self. In terms of the self-fulfilling prophecy, such children cannot help but see themselves as different, even deviant from their fellows. What began as trouble in school may end with the student at war with all adult authority. The teenage boy who runs away from home because his father does not think he can do anything on his own may shortly thereafter find himself lodged in jail or in a detention facility, where his bitterness can only be increased by the fact that his father's estimate of him has suddenly taken a fatefully accurate, prophetic turn.

Recent Supreme Court decisions have sharply revealed that many programs originally created to assist young people have fallen abysmally short of the hopes of their sponsors. The *Kent* decision, for one, underscored a long existing skepticism with regard to the role of the juvenile court as the all-wise and protective state-parent:

There is evidence, in fact, there may be grounds for concern that the child receives the worst of both worlds: that he gets neither the protections accorded to adults nor the solicitous care and regenerative treatment postulated for children.[7]

In 1967, the Supreme Court went further when in its *Gault* decision it ruled that basic constitutional rights cannot be denied to children before the juvenile court. As a result, no child may be adjudicated a delinquent on the basis solely of a probation officer's brief report, based largely on hearsay evidence. From here on out, the young accused has the right to know the charges against him, to confront his accusers, to crossexamine witnesses, and to have access to a written record. Most important, he now has the right to be represented by counsel.

Despite this increased protection of the child in court, many inadequacies still persist. For example, many of our most competent jurists prefer to avoid assignment to the juvenile bench, while those who do preside often discover that no real resources exist with which to assist children in difficulty. Both before and after sentencing, young persons are all too frequently held for days or weeks in company with adult criminals. One of the reasons for the creation of the juvenile court seventy years ago was to prevent the commingling of child offenders with adult. Yet still, today, 93% of juvenile court jurisdictions have no place to detain children other than the common jail. Full diagnostic services are not available; adequate funds are not appropriated for foster homes or other substitute care; probation caseloads are often so large that personal contact between officer and child is infrequent and superficial.

A Systems Approach — As Related to Corrections

Community resources must interrelate with the various steps and agencies in the correctional process if children are to be truly helped.[8] Many actions which today bring children before the juvenile court: school problems, family conflicts, minor offenses can be handled rather by noncourt agencies. Inept police work can compound a minor problem by the frequently unnecessary formalizing of the matter at the police station.

Diversity of Treatment Needed

A variety of treatment programs are needed to serve the wide range of children who get into trouble. The young joyrider in a stolen automobile may well merit a different program from the gang member who shoots a bus driver. Differentiation of offenders must mean really significant differentiation in treatment. Most simply put, our training schools and reformatories are too large, too regimented and too dependent on security and the threat of punishment. The rapid expansion of the halfway house and community center movement is a direct outgrowth of the growing awareness in this country that isolation and mass treatment in huge institutions may actually conduce to further criminality in our young.

Probation

If adequate supervision is provided at the probation level, many offenders can avoid further involvement in the court-correctional process. This means small caseloads to permit frequent contact and help to the probationer in dealing with problems of home, school, and job. Probation departments can enhance their effectiveness by using imaginative programs which provide challenge and interest. Effective probation is, of course, by far the least expensive of all correctional measures. Despite their recent rapid growth, halfway houses for young people still at the court level should not be considered as a substitute for probation, because many young people can continue to live in their own homes, and benefit from regular and intensive supervision from competent probation officers.

Probation Halfway Houses

If one accepts the premise that children should, wherever possible, be treated in their home communities, then the halfway house or community center offers an excellent alternative to incarceration. Whether residential or nonresidential, it offers a structured program of value to those children who, having failed probation, now face the prospect of removal to a training school or reformatory. Located in the home community, the halfway house can encourage parental participation as well as serve to remind people in the neighborhood that they, too, have an obligation to children in trouble and a part to play in the prevention of delinquent conduct as well.

The group care foster home offers considerable promise, when foster parents are carefully recruited, adequately paid and provided with helpful guidance. Many delinquent children, who are unable to live at home, unwilling to accept single placement in a foster home, and not needing the confinement of an institution, do very well in such homes. From a financial point of view, this is the least expensive of all residential correctional programs.

Agency-operated halfway houses for probationers also show promise. They preclude removal of children from their home areas, avoid the humiliation and stigma entailed in placement in a state training school, and offer opportunity for genuine change in attitudes and behavior. These group centers, whether residential or for day-care, permit close interaction between staff and children and are small enough to avoid the authoritarian approach which is characteristic of the large institution. Since the care of offenders in halfway houses is more intensive, movement through them is usually faster than through the training schools and reformatories, thereby reducing costs.

"Halfway-in" houses which utilize guided group interaction, appear to deal effectively with many teen-age probationers. Their use of peer groups to confront participants with the need for change appears to be both helpful — and noncostly. By demanding an honest appraisal of one's life situations, and forcing the participants to assume responsibility both for themselves and for others in their group, a culture is created which is apparently successful in influencing norms and behavior.

Delinquent offenders, especially those of very young years or with deep emotional problems may derive greater benefit from group counseling. Still others may respond more readily to unusual adventure programs such as are found in forestry camps or in the Outward Bound program.[9]

Institutions

Institutions will remain an integral part of the American correctional scene for years to come, for the development of community-based programs cannot possibly proceed swiftly enough to replace all of them. In addition, large and vocal elements of the public will continue to demand, fearfully, that all wrongdoers be removed from their midst. Nor is the present state of knowledge, or art, in the behavioral field sufficiently advanced to permit the treatment of every young offender in a community-based open program. There will always be an irreducible core of offenders who are simply too dangerous to allow outside maximum security conditions. The expansion of community-based programs must also await the development of sufficient numbers of staff members who are trained and capable of dealing with offenders on a nonsecurity basis. To date the number of leaders skilled in group work and counseling is too small to meet anywhere near the demand — or the need — for their services.

Even the best of existing institutions — and there are some few good ones — can be reduced in size, at the same time that a moratorium is called on the construction of more mammoth complexes for delinquents such as have been bequeathed to us from the past.

Much can be done within institutions to introduce guided group interaction as well as to improve existing academic and vocational programs. The use of programmed learning holds promise for delinquent children, many of whom are so inured to failure that they seem defeated before they have opened the book. Programmed instruction permits children to make gains surprising to themselves in a field previously associated only with discouragement and repeated failure.

Vocational instructional programs now being developed in some federal institutions offer considerable improvement over much that passes for training at the state correctional level. In place of maintenance jobs which exist chiefly to benefit the institution, these new approaches provide inmates with job skills which they will find useful and remunerative when they are released, because they are carefully geared to the current demands of industry.

Parole

Parole, or aftercare, presumably completes the correctional cycle. Some states still release young people from institutions with no follow-up or supervision. Other state parole systems have been unable to keep up with the large number of young people whom they released. Caseloads of seventy or more do not allow parole agents to give their children very much in the way of individual or personal attention.

Group care foster homes and halfway houses can help to ease the transition from the correctional setting to the community for many parolees in need of such placement. Providing security during the difficult first months in the community, they offer more than a roof and three meals a day: assistance in finding employment or the proper academic niche, friendly counsel, help with money matters, and assistance in solving other problems which arise in the course of the gradual advance toward independent living. For a young person who is doing poorly under regular parole supervision, the halfway house can provide an interim short-term refuge where he can be encouraged to make one more new effort.

The traditional lack of continuity in the correctional process is nowhere more clearly marked than at the state level, where the program of the institution is all-too-often unrelated to the system of parole and aftercare supervision. Recommendations made at the training school are ignored when the child is released, and even where continuity of interest is shown, resources are seldom available to carry out the recommendations made. Attempts to introduce new programs are often negated by the failure of the various parts of the system to work together, so that:

In the scattering of innovations . . . one common factor stands out. This is the lack of integration. A good institutional treatment program loses effectiveness because of floundering support in field services. An imaginative field program suffers from a separation from supporting institutional services under which mutual support is hampered.[10]

For example, some residential halfway houses have impressed a number of observers with their apparent ability to alter delinquent attitudes and behavior on the part of some of their residents, whose later performance on parole proves disappointing. How much of the blame should fall on the halfway house itself and how much on the inadequacy of the aftercare system, can only be determined by careful research.[11]

Despite its many shortcomings, correctional research has helped to call attention to inadequacies — and even fallacies — in traditional methods of handling offenders. Few can any longer contend, for example, that the great majority of prisoners need maximum security now that research into the federal pre-release guidance center program has revealed not only that many men adjust well to community-based programs, but even that some of the poorer parole risks may turn out to profit most.[12]

Staff

The growing number of community-based facilities emphasizes the desirability of considering the use of nonprofessionals to help staff them. Several states report outstanding success in the recruitment of ordinary citizens to serve as foster parents, while volunteers in all parts of the country have displayed skill and dedication in their work with persons in difficulty. Many older retired persons have intelligence and talents for helping others, and only await the opportunity and the call. Former offenders are other likely persons who although without formal training in the social sciences, may have much to offer. Current emphasis on group sessions and self-help programs attests to the practicality of turning some staff functions over to men who have themselves successfully moved through the halfway house program: "Enormous pools of talent exist in penitentiaries and among ex-convicts. Many bright, aggressive Negro youths, for example, end in prison. Greater use should be made of such individuals as subprofessionals."[13]

Bernard Shaw has said that the true public attitude toward any group in a society may be judged by the rates currently paid for work with that group: stockbrokers who deal with investors, for example, as compared with guards who deal with prisoners. Certainly the apathy and indifference of the general public is directly reflected in the penuriousness of state legislatures and the consequent grossly inadequate salaries paid to personnel in the correctional field, to professionals no less than to guards and to cottage parents.

In a field where the shortage of staff with advanced degrees is perennially acute, efforts to elevate the efficiency of lower echelon personnel in a state correctional service suggest a division of staff in-training and development. Its director should be a top person in the correctional administration. It would then be his responsibility — and opportunity — clearly to voice the administration's treatment philosophy and to provide interstaff communication at all levels. Through instruction sessions designed to attract and hold the interest of those in attendance, the director can help to upgrade all levels of staff performance. When professional staff help to guide and instruct cottage parent and work supervisors, they become, in the process, better informed and more clearly aware of the problems confronting the live employee.

Community Involvement

Total community involvement is essential if the problem of juvenile crime is not to remain the sole province of those who deal with it professionally:

The underlying problems are ones that the criminal justice system can do little about. The unruliness of young people, widespread drug addiction, the existence of much poverty in a wealthy society, the pursuit of the dollar by any available means are phenomena which the police, the courts, and the correctional apparatus . . . cannot confront directly. They are strands that can be disentangled from the fabric of American life only by the concerted action of all society. They concern the Commission deeply, for unless society does take concerted action to change the general conditions and attitudes that are associated with crime, no improvement in law enforcement and administration of justice . . . will be of much avail.[14]

The inertia and disinterest of the general public are directly reflected in the lack of basic community services for children. Where such services do exist, they often function independently, sometimes even in a sense of rivalry with one another. No one experienced in this field is surprised when a dependent child who first appeared in court at age eight or nine reappears there a few years later, charged with the commission of a serious offense.

In dealing with individuals or with groups, effective solutions are those which attack causes rather than symptoms. Cracking heads with police billies cures neither urban riot nor juvenile depredation. The upheavals in our major cities in recent summers, the unrest of the young on university campuses are as sure an indicant of social pathology in their totality as the violent act is of the disturbance of an individual delinquent.

"Delinquency and crime will be considerably reduced only when and as those persons who are presently alienated and shut off from the mainstream of American life are fully enabled to enjoy equal participation within it."[15] "We are in error when we speak about 'rehabilitation.' How can someone be rehabilitated, when he never belonged in the first place?"[16] If crime is largely the result of social factors interacting with a variety of individual factors, then the major effort must first be made to end racial discrimination, replace our slum housing, improve our systems of education and raise some millions up from actual starvation and 27 million of our population above the present poverty line.

A major onslaught on these social problems will cost initially more billions of dollars than crime itself now costs. Nor can it be expected that in the process crime will be abolished completely: all that can be promised is that eradication of social inequities will not be as expensive as the sums presently spent to send satellites probing into space, or to wage wars of "containment." One year's national defense budget would replace all the substandard housing in all the ghettos of America. As with individuals,

The manner in which a nation allocates its scarce resources, the manner in which it spends its public treasure, is the most revealing index of its values and priorities — the clearest reflection of the relative importance it attaches to the things in which it believes."[17]

14 In Conclusion

The first few months represent the most difficult time in the life of the released offender. Yet he is sent out into the world with many unreal expectations as to the possibility of subsequent adjustment, given the problems he brought with him to the institution, and the sizable residuum still unresolved when he leaves. Adjustment to any social situation requires a natural endowment, a set of skills and above all an attitude. For the returning inmate, this adjustment is rendered all the more difficult when it is realized that in preparation for his return to society, he has, in the process, been shut up away from it.

It may be asking too much of the residential center program that it should not attempt to be therapeutic per se, but that it should deal rather with the problems of here and now. The length of stay is usually too brief to permit an attempt to be made to get at deep-seated emotional disorders. The residence must act on the presumption that these problems have been solved — or at least mitigated — at the institution. If they have not been, it then devolves upon the center to call the attention of the referring institution to that which is lacking in its program and facilities which may need bolstering or expansion. This is but one of the many ways in which the community-based center can make an important contribution to the correctional field by highlighting the deficiencies in the institutions from which its residents come.

Pertinent examples can be found in the relationship between vocational training programs in the institution and the job opportunities available in the world outside. One such institution teaches the craft of upholstering. This is not the best-paid of occupations, or one in which there has ever been a notable shortage of trained workers. Yet year after year this same institution turns out persons trained in this not-too-highly skilled craft, without regard for their chances of finding employment in it. In another instance, young men from an institution which had an excellent program of airplane repair found, when they went to look for jobs in their field, that there was no shortage of mechanics for piston engines but a great demand for jet repair specialists. A long-term offender, who had developed great skill in the dry-cleaning shop at the institution, found on his first day out, that the machines he had trained on were at least twenty years behind the times.

The community center can make another valuable contribution to the training or treatment institution by providing opportunities for its personnel to spend some time observing their ex-charges in a community setting, and in appraising the effects of the institution treatment program. Staff members can bring back to the institution, after such a period of internship, a new approach which may be found to influence their dealing with others still in confinement.

The residence idea also has implications for the institution field in respect to length of stay. If three or four months of intensive and individualized program within a residential center can be the equivalent of at least twice that amount of time spent within a treatment-training institution, then perhaps it may not be unrealistic to look forward to a shortening of the institution stay. There is concern and interest in this prospect, because of the rapidly spiralling costs of institution custody and the need to reduce their drain on public budgets. This need is not limited to the United States; indeed what has been described here as a limited national experience is in reality part of a worldwide development in correctional treatment.

Of all the fields of social endeavor which are starting now to feel the effect of the new winds which are blowing away old concepts and outmoded ways of treatment, only in the field of corrections has the fixed institution continued to be the major tool. Happily this bastion is finally being breached. As in so many other areas, it is the emphasis on the young which may well be responsible for bringing about a change in attitude. It is perhaps easier to justify treatment rather than retribution where young persons are involved. The greater flexibility in laws pertaining to children reflects the greater emphasis on treatment, too. The correctional process is bound to profit from this new emphasis, and more than just incidentally, society at large may also benefit by reason of this re-examination and reorientation of its historic attitudes toward the offender.

The residence movement has helped to break down the separation which has traditionally existed between the institution and the community. Already in those communities where such stations have been operating for some time, the period of time spent in the community residence is coming to be regarded as just another step in the treatment-training process, another stop on the way to complete release from correctional control. The question is being asked – should all committed offenders who are technically eligible go first to a residence before release, if only for appraisal?

At the moment, the entire correctional field seems to be more responsive to new ideas than it has been in a very long time. It may well be that it is at the edge of a major breakthrough. Given a willingness to listen to the novel and to experiment with the untried, together with some degree of patience, formulas for tomorrow's dealing by society with its antisocial members may be devised which will bring a greater measure of success than what has been seen in the past. It is with this hope that a final word of forebearance is inserted – that these new devices within the community not be permitted to become fixed before their full potential has been tried and their worth proved.

In view of the hope which the community residential center represents in the correctional process, it is with regret that such a final word of caution should have to be inserted. Americans tend in many ways to be a nation of faddists — as much in their institutions as in matters of everyday living. The idea of the halfway house — its very name — has become a catchword. Certainly it is not the intent here to discourage any group which is both impatient of the current state of the correctional art and desirous of trying new devices. But it would be a matter of keen regret if residential centers were to proliferate faster than present research and evaluation have to date justified. Too rapid a development, and the outstripping of resources in personnel, proven methods and solid acceptance might in the long run do the cause as much — or greater — harm than good.

One basic fact in the correctional process justifies continued work by other than institutional means. This is that offenders who had had difficulties in adjusting to society before commitment can hardly be expected to resolve them by being isolated from society. From this it follows that unless somewhere within the training-treatment experience the offender is helped to develop a positive social experience and to identify with the aims of his society, the custodial experience is very likely to continue to result in failure.

Of all adult offenders sentenced to confinement, upwards of 98% are ultimately released. It has been fairly clearly established that an inmate's desire and resolution not to return to the institution is at its height at the point of release. There is a motivation here and at this time which may not soon come again. It would appear to be an act of prudence to seize this moment to help bring into the life of the now liberated inmate a program of support and help which can well prove to be the turning point in the process.

It is in the light of these simple postulates that the role of the residential center holds great promise. For it aims at the rehabilitation of persons whom society hopes may one day once again make their home within the larger community of responsible and self-controlled individuals.

The idea of the community treatment station has been greeted with more enthusiasm than any other idea in the correctional field for a very long time. It is nevertheless still too new to give ready answers to the questions being asked today about the effectiveness of traditional modes of treatment of offenders. There are not enough adequately trained survey persons in this field to do the requisite research, even if its importance were universally recognized, which it is not. There are many places which still depend upon the inspiration and devotion of a founding figure whose spirit and example have fired all around him to come to the support of his cause.

Yet it may well be unnecessary to wait fifty years to say: this is the most important breakthrough in the correctional field in the past fifty years. The idea is here, the need is now; the application of what is known to areas where it is needed, should not tarry. At the same time every possible evaluative technique is required to discover where are the strengths and weaknesses of this new service, what are its implications for the entire correctional field, and how it can be deepened and extended to cope with an ever larger share of the burden of crime which today lies so heavily upon every community in our nation.

Notes

Notes

Notes to CHAPTER 1

1. Charles Dickens, *American Notes* (London: Thomas Nelson and Sons, 1904), p. 59.
2. Christopher Hibbert, *The Roots of Evil* (London: Weidenfeld and Nicolson, 1963), p. 26.
3. Harry Elmer Barnes and Negley K. Teeters, *New Horizons in Criminology* (3d ed.; Englewood Cliffs: Prentice-Hall, Inc., 1960), p. 324.
4. Hibbert, *op. cit.*, p. 56.
5. Barnes and Teeters, *op. cit.*, p. 336.
6. *Ibid.*, p. 339.
7. Dickens, *op. cit.*, p. 58.
8. Negley K. Teeters and John Otto Reinemann, *The Challenge of Delinquency* (Englewood Cliffs: Prentice-Hall, Inc., 1950), p. 44.
9. *Ibid.*, p. 431.
10. *Ibid.*, p. 396.
11. National Conference of Charities and Corrections, *Proceedings of Twelth Annual Session* (Washington, D.C., 1886), p. 131.
12. *Ibid.*, p. 523.
13. *Ibid.*, p. 475.
14. U.S. President's Commission on Law Enforcement and Administration of Justice, *The Challenge of Crime in a Free Society* (Washington: U.S. Government Printing Office, 1967), p. 160.
15. Clifford R. Shaw, *The Natural History of a Delinquent Career* (Chicago: University of Chicago Press, 1931), pp. 151-154.
16. Erving Goffman, *Asylums* (Garden City, N.Y.: Anchor Books, Doubleday and Company, Inc., 1961), p. 14.
17. Daniel Glaser, *The Effectiveness of a Prison and Parole System* (Indianapolis: Bobbs-Merrill Co., 1964), p. 226.
18. Barnes and Teeters, *op. cit.*, p. 964.
19. Roul Tunley, *Kids, Crime and Chaos* (New York: Harper and Brothers, 1962), p. 159.
20. Hibbert, *op. cit.*, p. 46.
21. Goffman, *op. cit.*, p. 13.
22. Teeters and Reinemann, *op. cit.*, p. 47.
23. John Conrad, *Crime and Its Correction* (Berkeley: University of California Press, 1965), p. 275.
24. Gilbert Geis, *The East Los Angeles Halfway House for Narcotic Addicts*, Report of a Program Conducted under a Grant from the National Institute of Mental Health (MH-808) (Sacramento: The Institute for the Study of Crime and Delinquency, 1966), pp. 40-43.

25. Edwin Powers, "Halfway Houses: An Historical Perspective," *American Journal of Correction*, XXI (July-August, 1959), p. 35.

26. Letter from Doris S. Whitney, Executive Director, The Women's Prison Association and the Isaac T. Hopper Home, New York, March 14, 1966.

27. *75th Year Report, The Home of Industry for Discharged Prisoners* (Camp Hill, Pa.: State Correctional Institution Print Shop, 1965).

28. Susan F. Welty, *Look Up and Hope* (New York: Thomas Nelson and Sons, 1961), p. 141.

29. *Ibid.*, p. 186.

30. *Ibid.*, p. 226.

31. Teeters and Reinemann, *op. cit.*, p. 78.

32. Nat Auerbach *et al.*, "A Concept Explication: The Halfway House in Corrections" (unpublished Master's dissertation, school of Social Work, Syracuse University, 1966), p. 25.

33. William Krasner, "Hoodlum Priest and Respectable Convicts," *Harper's*, CCXXXII (February, 1961), pp. 57-62; Robert Cromie, "A Chance to Go Straight," *Saturday Evening Post*, CCXXXIII (April 30, 1960), pp. 26ff; and Robert G. Crosswhite and Maurice A. Breslin, "A Report on 308 West Residence," *Proceedings of the Ninetieth Annual Congress on Corrections of the American Correctional Association* (Denver, Colo., 1960), pp. 381-401.

34. U.S., Bureau of Prisons, *Trends in the Administration of Justice and Correctional Programs in the United States*, A Report Prepared for the Third United Nations Congress on the Prevention of Crime and Treatment of Offenders (Washington: U. S. Government Printing Office, 1965), p. 34.

Notes to CHAPTER 2

1. U.S., Bureau of Prisons, *Trends in the Administration of Justice and Correctional Programs in the United States*, A Report Prepared for the Third United Nations Congress on the Prevention of Crime and Treatment of Offenders (Washington: U.S. Government Printing Office, 1965), p. 34.

2. William D. Dawson, "Half-Way Houses," Paper read before the Eleventh Annual Midwest Correctional Conference, Iowa State University, Ames, Iowa, April 14-16, 1964.

3. Nat Auerbach *et al.*, "A Concept Explication: The Halfway House in Corrections" (unpublished Master's dissertation, Graduate School of Social Work, Syracuse University, 1966), p. 73.

4. U.S., Bureau of Prisons, *op. cit.*, p. 39.

5. *Ibid.*, p. 35.

Notes to CHAPTER 3

1. Nat Auerbach *et al.*, "A Concept Explication: The Halfway House in Corrections" (unpublished Master's dissertation, Graduate School of Social Work, Syracuse University, 1966), p. 73.

2. *Ibid.*, p. 72.

3. Letter from Harry Vorrath, while Superintendent, Woodsbend State Boys' Camp, West Liberty, Ky., Jan. 5, 1966.

4. Letter from Richard Rachin, Resident Director, J. Stanley Sheppard Youth Center, New York, May 16, 1967.

5. "Partway is a Better Way," San Francisco, Mission Neighborhood Centers, Inc., 1967, p. 4.

6. Letter from Edward C. Boyle, Casework Director, Family Service Department, Salvation Army, Los Angeles, July 17, 1967.

7. Interview with Richard Rachin, Resident Director, J. Stanley Sheppard Youth Center, New York, Feb. 7, 1966.

8. Letter from Harry Vorrath, while Superintendent, Woodsbend State Boys' Camp, West Liberty, Ky., March 15, 1966.

9. Auerbach *et al.*, *op. cit.*, p. 58.

10. *Ibid.*, p. 59.

11. Marvin Hersko, "Community Therapy in an Institution for Delinquent Girls," *Federal Probation*, XXVIII (June, 1964), p. 41.

12. "Individual Counseling Held Ineffective," *NCCD News*, XLIV (May-June, 1965), p. 3.

13. Daniel Glaser, *The Effectiveness of a Prison and Parole System* (Indianapolis: Bobbs-Merrill Company, Inc., 1964), p. 191.

14. *Ibid.*, p. 186.

15. *Ibid.*

16. Correspondence from Daniel Glaser, Chairman, Sociology Department, University of Illinois, Champaign, May 17, 1967.

17. Interview with Charles Leonard, Director, Highmeadows Child Study and Treatment Home, Hamden, Conn., July 11, 1966.

18. Correspondence from Glaser, May 17, 1967.

19. William C. Menninger, "The Therapy of Friendship," An address before the Eighth Annual Meeting of the Big Brothers of America, St. Louis, 1956.

20. Interview with John Wall, Director, Southfields, Anchorage, Ky., Dec. 6, 1965.

21. Gisela Konopka, "Social Group Work: A Social Work Method," *Social Work*, V (October, 1960), p. 58.

22. *Ibid.*

23. Letter from Rachin, May 16, 1967.

24. Konopka, *loc. cit.*

25. Sethard Fisher, "The Rehabilitative Effectiveness of a Community Correctional Residence for Narcotic Users," *Journal of Criminal Law, Criminology, and Police Science*, LVI (June, 1965), p. 191.

26. Interview with Patrick Deehy, Research Associate, Robert Bruce House, Newark, N.J., during the Third Annual Conference of the International Halfway House Association, Windsor, Ontario, Apr. 24, 1966.

27. Glaser, *op. cit.*, p. 151.

28. Fisher, *loc. cit.*, p. 194.

29. *Ibid.*, p. 193.

30. John J. Galvin (ed.), *Treating Youth Offenders in the Community*, A Report on Four Years Experience with Pre-Release Guidance Centers (Washington, D.C.: Correctional Research Associates, under a grant by the Ford Foundation, June, 1966), p. 118.

31. Letter from Rachin, May 16, 1967.

32. Interview with Albert Axelrod, Resident Director, Highfields Residential Group Center, Hopewell, N.J., Jan. 12, 1966.

33. See Chapter Seven.

34. Auerbach *et al.*, *op. cit.*, p. 59.

35. Letter from Rachin, May 16, 1967.

36. Norman Fenton, *An Introduction to Group Counseling in State Correctional Service* (Sacramento, Calif.: Department of Corrections, 1957), p. 2.

37. Calvin S. Hall and Gardner Lindzey, *Theories of Personality* (New York: John Wiley and Sons, Inc., 1957), p. 153.

38. Lloyd W. McCorkle, Albert Elias, and F. Lovell Bixby, *The Highfields Story* (New York: Henry Holt and Co., 1958), p. 74.

39. Walter C. Reckless, "The Small Residential Treatment Institution in Perspective," *Youthful Offenders at Highfields*, ed. H. Ashley Weeks (Ann Arbor: University of Michigan Press, 1958), p. 158.

40. S. R. Slavson, *A Textbook in Analytic Group Psychotherapy* (New York: International Universities Press, Inc., 1964), p. 37.

41. *Ibid.*, p. 27.

42. McCorkle, Elias, and Bixby, *op. cit.*, p. 79.

43. Slavson, *op. cit.*, p. 65.

44. *Ibid.*, p. 127.

45. *Ibid.*, p. 414.

46. Aaron Stein, "Training of the Group Psychotherapist," *Group Psychotherapy and Group Function*, ed. Max Rosenbaum and Milton Berger (New York: Basic Books, 1963), pp. 558-576.

47. Konopka, *loc. cit.*, p. 58.

48. Slavson, *op. cit.*, pp. 99-106.

49. *Ibid.*, p. 117.

50. C. Wright Mills, *Power, Politics, and People* (New York: Ballantine Books, 1963), p. 450.

51. *Ibid.*, pp. 446, 448.

52. William Glasser, *Reality Therapy: A New Approach to Psychiatry* (New York: Harper and Row, 1965).

53. Helen E. Durkin, *The Group in Depth* (New York: International Universities Press, Inc., 1964), p. ix.

54. Letter from Rachin, May 16, 1967.

55. Albert K. Cohen, *Delinquent Boys, The Culture of the Gang* (Glencoe, Ill.: The Free Press, 1955), pp. 157-159.

56. Ruth Shonle Cavan, *Juvenile Delinquency* (Philadelphia: J. B. Lippincott Co., 1962), pp. 123-124.

57. William C. Kvaraceus and Walter B. Miller, *Delinquent Behavior, Culture and the Individual* (Washington, D.C.: National Education Association of the United States, 1959), pp. 99, 100.

58. *Ibid.*, p. 100.

59. Bruno Bettelheim, "The Problem of Generations," *Youth: Change and Challenge*, ed., Erik H. Erikson (New York: Basic Books, Inc., 1963), p. 66.

60. *A Report of the Juvenile Institutions Project* (New York: The Osborne Association and the National Council on Crime and Delinquency, September, 1966), pp. 196, 198. (Unedited draft prior to publication.) Cited hereafter as "Juvenile Institutions Project."

61. Interview with Harry Vorrath, Group Consultant, District of Columbia Department of Public Welfare and United Planning Organization, Washington, D.C., June 1, 1967.

62. Interview with Caroline Winters, Director, GUIDE, Richmond, Calif., March 3, 1966.

63. *Juvenile Institutions Project*, p. 221.

64. Interview with John Wall, Director, Southfields, Anchorage, Ky., Dec. 5, 1965.

65. *Juvenile Institutions Project*, p. 214.

66. Interview with Anthony Monacchio, Director, Silverlake, Los Angeles, Feb. 28, 1966.

67. Interview with William Dickerson, Director, Marshall Program, Southern Reception Center, California Youth Authority, Los Angeles, March 1, 1966.

Notes to CHAPTER 4

1. LaMar T. Empey and Jerome Rabow, "The Provo Experiment in Delinquency Rehabilitation," *American Sociological Review*, XXVI (October, 1961), p. 681.

2. Charles H. Cooley, "The Social Self," *Theories of Society*, Vol. II, ed. Talcott Parsons, Edward Shils, Kasper D. Naegele, and Jesse R. Pitts (New York: The Free Press of Glencoe, Inc., 1961), p. 824.

3. Charles H. Cooley, "Primary Groups," *Ibid.*, Vol. I, p. 315.

4. George C. Homans, *The Human Group* (New York: Harcourt, Brace and Co., 1950), p. 313.

5. George H. Mead, *Mind, Self and Society*, ed. Charles Morris (Chicago: University of Chicago Press, 1934), p. 135.

6. *Ibid.*, p. 155.

7. Tamotsu Shibutani, "Reference Groups and Social Control," *Human Behavior and Social Process — An Interactionist Approach*, ed. Arnold M. Rose (Boston: Houghton Mifflin Co., 1962), p. 129.

8. Muzafer Sherif, "Group Influences Upon the Formation of Norms and Attitudes," *Readings in Social Psychology*, ed. Eleanor E. Maccoby, Theodore

M. Newcomb, and Eugene L. Hartley; Prepared for the Committee on the Teaching of Social Psychology of the Society for the Psychological Study of Social Issues (New York: Holt, Rinehart, and Winston, Inc., 1958), pp. 219-232.

9. S. E. Asch, "Effects of Group Pressure upon the Modification and Distortion of Judgments," *Ibid.*, pp. 174-183.

10. Fredric M. Thrasher, *The Gang* (Chicago: Phoenix Books, University of Chicago Press, 1963), p. 200.

11. William F. Whyte, *Street Corner Society* (Chicago: University of Chicago Press, 1943), pp. 255, 256.

12. Morton A. Lieberman, "The Therapist Versus the Group," Paper read before the meeting of the Tri-State Group Psychotherapy Society, Cincinnati, Ohio, Oct. 7, 1966.

13. Thrasher, *op. cit.*, p. 229.

14. Emile Durkheim, "The Solidarity of Occupational Groups," *Theories of Society*, Vol. I, p. 357. See also Michael Olmstead, *The Small Group* (New York: Random House, 1959), p. 21.

15. Empey and Rabow, *loc. cit.*, p. 682.

16. James F. Short, Jr. and Fred L. Strodtbeck, *Group Process and Gang Delinquency* (Chicago: University of Chicago Press, 1965), p. 271.

17. Howard S. Becker, "Marijuana Use and Social Control," *Human Behavior and Social Process*, (Boston: Houghton Mifflin, 1962), p. 606.

18. Robert K. Merton, *Social Theory and Social Structure* (2nd ed. rev.; Glencoe, Ill.: The Free Press, 1957), p. 139.

19. Albert K. Cohen, *Delinquent Boys, The Culture of the Gang* (Glencoe, Ill.: The Free Press, 1955), pp. 121-179.

20. Olmstead, *op. cit.*, p. 79.

21. Homans, *op. cit.*, p. xix.

22. *Ibid.*, p. 1.

23. Cooley, *loc. cit.*

24. Homans, *op. cit.*, p. 87.

25. *Ibid.*, pp. 88-90.

26. *Ibid.*, p. 91.

27. *Ibid.*, pp. 95-97, 126-130.

28. *Ibid.*, p. 109.

29. *Ibid.*

30. *Ibid.*, p. 113.

31. Olmstead, *op. cit.*, p. 29.

32. Homans, *op. cit.*, p. 117.

33. *Ibid.*, p. 88.

34. Shibutani, *loc. cit.*, p. 135.

35. Lloyd W. McCorkle, Albert Elias, and F. Lovell Bixby, *The Highfields Story* (New York: Henry Holt and Co., 1958), pp. 3-8.

36. Olmstead, *op. cit.*, p. 27.

37. Homans, *op. cit.*, pp. 360-362.

38. Walter C. Reckless, Simon Dinitz, and Barbara Kay, "The Self-Component in Potential Delinquency and Potential Non-Delinquency," *American Sociological Review*, XX (October, 1957), p. 568.

39. Frank R. Scarpitti, Ellen Murray, Simon Dinitz, and Walter C. Reckless, "The 'Good' Boy in a High Delinquency Area: Four Years Later," *American Sociological Review*, XXV (August, 1960), pp. 555, 556.

40. *Ibid.*, p. 556.

41. *Ibid.*, p. 557.

42. *Ibid.*, p. 558.

43. Simon Dinitz, Frank R. Scarpitti, and Walter C. Reckless, "Delinquency Vulnerability," *American Sociological Review*, XXVII (August, 1962), p. 515.

44. *Ibid.*, p. 516.

45. *Ibid.*, p. 517.

46. Michael Schwartz and Sandra S. Tangri, "A Note on Self-Concept as an Insulator Against Delinquency," *American Sociological Review*, XXX (December, 1965), p. 924.

47. Cooley, *loc. cit.*, Vol. II.

48. Empey and Rabow, *loc. cit.*, p. 681.

49. Erving Goffman, *Asylums* (Garden City, N.Y.: Anchor Books, Doubleday and Co., Inc., 1961), pp. 151-152.

50. Gresham M. Sykes and David Matza, "Techniques of Neutralization," *American Sociological Review*, XXII (December, 1957), pp. 664-670.

51. Goffman, *op. cit.*, p. 162.

52. Arnold M. Rose, "A Social-Psychological Theory of Neurosis," *Human Behavior and Social Process*, p. 548.

53. Shibutani, *loc. cit.*, p. 141.

54. R. P. Noel Mailloux, "Un Symptome de Desocialisation: l'Incapacité de Communiquer avec Autrui," *Annales Internationales de Criminologie*, 5 Annees de Société Internationale de Criminologie 1ᵉʳ Semestre (Paris: Societe Generale, 1966), pp. 23-32.

55. Albert Elias, "The Highfields Program for Juvenile Delinquents" (Bordentown, N.J.: New Jersey Reformatory, 1963), pp. 9-10 (mimeographed); and Vincent J. Regan, "Ocean Residential Group Center 1966-67 Budget Request" (Forked River, N.J.: Ocean Center, 1966), pp. 3, 4 (mimeographed).

56. LaMar T. Empey, George E. Newland, and Stephen G. Lubeck, *The Silverlake Experiment: A Community Study in Delinquency Rehabilitation, Progress Report No. 2* (Los Angeles: Youth Studies Center, University of Southern California, 1965), p. 25.

57. Olmstead, *op. cit.*, p. 71.

Notes to CHAPTER 5

1. Lloyd W. McCorkle, Albert Elias, and F. Lovell Bixby, *The Highfields Story* (New York: Henry Holt and Co., 1958), p. vi.

2. *Ibid.*, p. 8.

3. LaMar T. Empey and Jerome Rabow, "The Provo Experiment in Delinquency Rehabilitation," *American Sociological Review*, XXVI (October, 1961), p. 683.

4. *Ibid.*

5. LaMar T. Empey, George E. Newland, and Stephen G. Lubeck, *The Silverlake Experiment: A Community Study in Delinquency Rehabilitation, Progress Report No. 2* (Los Angeles: Youth Studies Center, University of Southern California, 1965), p. 11.

6. Paul Keve, *Imaginative Programming in Probation and Parole* (Minneapolis: University of Minnesota Press, 1967), p. 148.

7. Interview with William Dickerson, Unit Administrator, James Marshall Program, Southern Reception Center-Clinic, California Youth Authority, Los Angeles, Aug. 9, 1967.

8. McCorkle, Elias, and Bixby, *op. cit.*, p. 78.

9. *Ibid.*

10. Interview with John Wall, Director, Southfields, Anchorage, Ky., Dec. 6, 1965.

11. Interview with Harry Vorrath, while Superintendent, Woodsbend State Boys' Camp, West Liberty, Ky., Dec. 8, 1965.

12. Interview with Vincent Regan, Superintendent, Ocean Residential Group Center, Forked River, N.J., Feb. 9, 1965.

13. McCorkle, Elias, and Bixby, *op. cit.*, p. 28.

14. Tamotsu Shibutani, "Reference Groups and Social Control," *Human Behavior and Social Process — An Interactionist Approach,* ed. Arnold M. Rose (Boston: Houghton Mifflin Co., 1962), p. 141.

15. George C. Homans, *The Human Group* (New York: Harcourt, Brace and Co., 1950), p. 247.

16. *Ibid.*, p. 440.

17. McCorkle, Elias, and Bixby, *op. cit.*, p. 1.

18. Interview with Dickerson, Aug. 9, 1967.

19. Interview with Vorrath, Dec. 8, 1965.

20. Interview with Eugene Montone, Director, Walton Village, Central YMCA, Philadelphia, during third annual International Halfway House Association conference, Windsor, Ontario, Apr. 23, 1966.

21. Interview with John Wall, Director, Southfields, Anchorage, Ky., Dec. 7, 1965.

22. McCorkle, Elias, and Bixby, *op. cit.*, p. 45.

23. Empey and Rabow, *loc. cit.*, p. 686.

24. McCorkle, Elias, and Bixby, *op. cit.*, p. 76.

25. Interview with Vincent Regan, Superintendent, Ocean Residential Group Center, Forked River, N.J., Feb. 10, 1966.

26. Keve, *op. cit.*, p. 144.

27. McCorkle, Elias, and Bixby, *op. cit.*, pp. 76-79.

28. Interview with Vincent Regan, Superintendent, Ocean Residential Group Center, Forked River, N.J., Feb. 9, 1966.

29. McCorkle, Elias, and Bixby, *op. cit.*, p. 42.

30. Interview with Wall, Dec. 6, 1965.

31. McCorkle, Elias, and Bixby, *op. cit.*, p. 77.

32. Interview with boy, Silverlake, Los Angeles, Feb. 28, 1966

33. Keve, *op. cit.*, p. 142.

34. R. P. Noel Mailloux, "Un Symptome de Desocialization: l'Incapacité de Communiquer Avec Autrui," *Annales Internationales de Criminologie*, 5 Annees de Société Internationale de Criminologie 1er Semestre (Paris: Société Generale, 1966), p. 29.

35. Interview with Albert Axelrod, Superintendent, Highfields Residential Group Center, Hopewell, N.J., Jan. 11, 1966.

36. Correspondence from Harry Vorrath, Group Consultant, District of Columbia Department of Public Welfare and United Planning Organization, Washington, D.C., May 10, 1967.

37. Interview with John Wall, Director, Southfields, Anchorage, Ky., Dec. 5, 1965.

38. Interview with Harry Vorrath, while Superintendent, Woodsbend State Boys' Camp, West Liberty, Ky., Dec. 9, 1965.

39. McCorkle, Elias, and Bixby, *op. cit.*, p. 28.

40. Mailloux, *loc. cit.*, p. 28.

41. Interview with Vorrath, Dec. 9, 1965.

42. *Ibid.*

43. McCorkle, Elias, and Bixby, *op. cit.*, p. 66.

44. Interview with Lee Pollard, Assistant Director, Southfields, Anchorage, Ky., Dec. 6, 1965.

45. Mailloux, *loc. cit.*, pp. 26-31.

46. Albert Elias, "The Highfields Program for Juvenile Delinquents" (Bordentown, N.J.: New Jersey Reformatory, 1963), p. 9 (mimeographed); and Vincent Regan, "Ocean Residential Group Center 1966-67 Budget Request" (Forked River, N.J.: Ocean Center, 1966), pp. 3, 4 (mimeographed).

47. Elias, *op. cit.*

48. *Ibid.*

49. Interview with Albert Elias, Superintendent, New Jersey Reformatory for Males, Bordentown, N.J., Jan. 12, 1966.

50. *Ibid.*

51. Interview with Vorrath, Dec. 9, 1965.

52. *Ibid.*

53. Keve, *op. cit.*, p. 158.

54. Daniel Glaser, *The Effectiveness of a Prison and Parole System* (Indianapolis: Bobbs-Merrill Company, Inc., 1964), p. 151.

55. Lewis Yablonsky, *The Tunnel Back: Synanon* (New York: Macmillan Co., 1965), p. 138.

56. Keve, *op. cit.*, p. 140.

57. Mailloux, *loc. cit.*, p. 30.

58. Interview with boy, Southfields, Anchorage, Ky., Dec. 6, 1965.

59. Interview with boy, Essexfields, Newark, N.J., Jan. 13, 1966.

60. Interview with Vorrath, Dec. 8, 1965.

61. Interview with Wall, Dec. 7, 1965.

62. Interview with George Lattimore, Director, Essexfields, Newark, N.J., Jan. 13, 1966.

63. LaMar T. Empey, *Peer Group Influences in Correctional Programs*, A Report to the President's Commission on Law Enforcement and Administration of Justice (Los Angeles: Youth Studies Center, University of Southern California, 1967), pp. 42-45.

64. William Glasser, *Reality Therapy: A New Approach to Psychiatry* (New York: Harper and Row, 1965).

65. Keve, *op. cit.*, p. 139.

66. McCorkle, Elias, and Bixby, *op. cit.*, p. 106.

67. Empey and Rabow, *loc. cit.*, p. 681.

68. Interview with Vincent Regan, Superintendent, Ocean Residential Group Center, Forked River, N.J., Jan. 11, 1966.

69. Interview with Charles Tarr, Superintendent, Dugan START Center, Auburn, N.Y., Feb. 8, 1966.

70. Interview with Ian Cox, Superintendent, "Turana" Center, State of Victoria, Australia, July 11, 1966.

71. *Ibid*.

72. Interview with William Skiff, Director, Brace Youth Camp, Masonville, N.Y., Feb. 9, 1966.

73. McCorkle, Elias, and Bixby, *op. cit.*, p. 42.

74. Interview with Regan, Jan. 11, 1966.

75. Yablonsky, *op. cit.*, p. viii.

76. Letter from Alexander Bassin, Director, Research and Education, Supreme Court of the State of New York, Brooklyn, N.Y., Oct. 25, 1966.

77. Interview with Charles Tarr, Superintendent, Dugan START Center, Auburn, N.Y., Feb. 7, 1966.

78. Interview with Vincent Regan, Superintendent, Ocean Residential Group Center, Forked River, N.J., Jan. 12, 1966.

79. Interview with Wall, Dec. 6, 1965.

80. Interview with Anthony Monacchio, Director, Silverlake, Los Angeles, Feb. 28, 1966.

81. Yablonsky, *op. cit.*, p. 41.

82. Interview with boy, Kentucky Village, Lexington, Ky., Dec. 9, 1966.

83. Empey and Rabow, *loc. cit.*, p. 693.

84. Interview with Albert Axelrod, Superintendent, Highfields Residential Group Center, Hopewell, N.J., Jan. 12, 1966.

85. LaMar T. Empey, Maynard L. Erickson, and Max L. Scott, "The Provo Experiment in Delinquency Rehabilitation, Fifth Annual Progress Report, 1963-64" (Provo, Utah: Brigham Young Univ.), pp. 20-23 (mimeographed).

86. McCorkle, Elias, and Bixby, *op. cit.*, p. 155.

87. Interview with Wall, Dec. 7, 1965.

88. Interview with Vincent Regan, Superintendent, Ocean Residential Group Center, Forked River, N.J., Jan. 10, 1966.

89. Interview with Milton Luger, Director, New York Division for Youth, in Chicago, Ill., Apr. 7, 1966.

90. Interview with Vorrath, Dec. 9, 1965.

91. Interview with Albert Wagner, Director, Division of Correction and Parole, Trenton, N.J., Jan. 10, 1966.

92. Interview with Robert W. Chandler, Program Associate, Public Affairs, Ford Foundation, in Chicago, Sept. 7, 1966.

93. Empey and Rabow, *loc. cit.*, p. 686.

94. *Ibid.*, p. 692.

95. Interview with Rosemary McGrath, Superintendent, Turrell Residential Group Center, Allaire, N.J., Jan. 12, 1966.

96. "The Ex-Offender as a Staff Member," *Robert Bruce House Journal*, III (June 30, 1967), p. 1. (Mimeographed by Robert Bruce House, Newark, N.J.)

97. Keve, *op. cit.*, p. 166.

98. "Statement of Accomplishments and Goals," Ocean Residential Group Center (in 1969-70 Budget Request) pp. 5-7. Forked River, New Jersey.

99. Correspondence from Robert W. Chandler, Program Associate, Public Affairs, Ford Foundation, New York City, Sept. 5, 1966.

100. *Ibid.*

Notes to CHAPTER 6

1. Interview with Sanger Powers, Director, Division of Corrections, Department of Public Welfare, Madison, Wis., Nov. 8, 1965.

2. Interview with Amos E. Reed, Superintendent, MacLaren School for Boys, Woodburn, Ore., Aug. 4, 1967.

3. *The Status of Current Research, Annual Report* (Sacramento, Calif.: Department of the Youth Authority, July, 1967), pp. 29-32.

4. Letter from Ruth M. Davis, Supervisor, Special Services, Division of Children and Youth, Denver, Colo., Jan. 17, 1966.

5. Interview with Andrew Basinas, Administrator, Foster Home Unit, Probation and Parole Services, Division of Corrections, Department of Public Welfare, Madison, Wis., July 12, 1967.

6. "Foster Homes Report" (Madison, Wis.: Division of Corrections, Department of Public Welfare, Dec. 1, 1966). (Xeroxed.) Cited hereafter as "Foster Homes, Wisconsin."

7. Interview with Alan L. Christensen, Chief, Community Services, Division of Corrections, Board of Control of State Institutions, Des Moines, Iowa, Aug. 4, 1967.

8. "Foster Homes, Wisconsin."

9. "Fact Sheet on Group Home Position Statement" (Minneapolis: Citizens Council on Delinquency and Crime, Dec. 15, 1964). (Mimeographed.)

10. Interview with Allen C. Hubanks, Executive Director, Correctional Services of Minnesota, Minneapolis, May 23, 1967.

11. Interview with Joseph L. Kleine, Supervisor of Program Development, Department of the Youth Authority, Los Angeles, June 14, 1967.

12. Interview with Reed, Aug. 4, 1967.

13. Interview with John E. Miller, Aftercare Coordinator, Department of Social Welfare, Lansing, Mich., Apr. 22, 1966.

14. Letter from Andrew Basinas, Administrator, Foster Home Unit, Probation and Parole Services, Division of Corrections, Department of Public Welfare, Madison, Wis., Apr. 14, 1967.

15. "Living Together, A Guide to Foster Home Care" (Madison, Wis.: Division of Corrections, Department of Public Welfare, n.d.), (final page; pages unnumbered). (Xeroxed); and Interview with Milton Olson, while Group Home Supervisor, Department of Corrections, St. Paul, Minn., Nov. 10, 1965.

16. Interview with Christensen, Aug. 4, 1967.

17. Interview with Joseph L. White, Acting Commissioner, Community Services, Ohio Youth Commission, Columbus, O., Dec. 6, 1966.

18. Interview with Archie Gingold, Judge of District Court, Juvenile Division, St. Paul, Minn., Nov. 10, 1965.

19. "Group Homes" (St. Paul, Minn.: Division of Youth Conservation, Department of Corrections, Aug. 30, 1965), p. 2. (Mimeographed.)

20. *Ibid.*

21. Memorandum from John E. Miller, Aftercare Coordinator, to Lewis Knaggs, Supervisor of Technical Services Unit, Department of Social Services, Lansing, Mich., Nov. 22, 1965, p. 3.

22. *Ibid.*

23. Letter from Alan L. Christensen, while Chief of Field Services, Iowa Division of Corrections, to Lynn Wilson, Bureau of Juvenile Placement, Cleveland, Ohio, Oct. 5, 1965.

24. Interview with White, Dec. 6, 1966.

25. Interview with John E. Raffel, while Administrator, Foster Home Unit, Probation and Parole Services, Division of Corrections, Department of Public Welfare, Madison, Wis., Nov. 9, 1965.

26. Letter from Davis, Jan. 17, 1966.

27. Interview with Raffel, Nov. 9, 1965.

28. Interview with John E. Miller, Aftercare Coordinator, Department of Social Services, Lansing, Mich., Jan. 24, 1967.

29. Interview with Joseph R. Rowan, while Deputy Director, Division of Youth Conservation, Department of Corrections, St. Paul, Minn., Sept. 14, 1966.

30. Interview with Reed, Aug. 4, 1967.

31. "Foster Homes, Wisconsin."

32. Interview with Archie Gingold, Judge of District Court, Juvenile Division, St. Paul, Minn., May 23, 1967.

33. *Ibid.*

34. Letter from John E. Raffel, Administrator, Liaison and Special Benefits Unit, Division of Corrections, Dept. of Public Welfare, Madison, Wis., Feb. 27, 1967.

35. Memorandum on Group Homes from Milton S. Olson, while Supervisor of Group Homes, St. Paul, Minn., to DYC Supervisors, Agents, Institutions, and County Probation Officers, Aug. 30, 1965, p. 2.

36. Frederic L. Faust, "Determinants in the Use of Foster Care as a Re-Socialization Resource for Youth on Aftercare Status" (Columbus, O.: Ohio Youth Commission, Bureau of Probation Development, n.d.) (Xeroxed).

37. Letter from Raffel, Feb. 27, 1967.

38. Interview with Raffel, Nov. 9, 1965.

39. Interview with Milton S. Olson, while Supervisor of Group Homes, Department of Corrections, St. Paul, Minn., Nov. 11, 1965.

40. Interview with Raffel, Nov. 9, 1965.

41. Interview with Gingold, May 23, 1967.

42. Interview with Raffel, Nov. 9, 1965.

43. Letter from Andrew Basinas, Administrator, Foster Home Unit, Probation and Parole Services, Division of Corrections, Department of Public Welfare, Madison, Wis., Aug. 9, 1967.

44. Interviews with Gingold and Olson, Nov. 10, 1965.

Notes to CHAPTER 7

1. National Conference on Prevention and Control of Juvenile Delinquency, *Report on Institutional Treatment of Delinquent Juveniles*, (Washington, D.C., U. S. Government Printing Office), 1946, p. 47.

2. Interview with Frank Loveland, Director, American Foundation, Philadelphia, Pa., covering period when he had been Assistant Director, Bureau of Prisons, Washington, D.C., May, 1966.

3. *Ibid.*

4. *Ibid.*

5. *Ibid.*

6. Interview with John Kilkeary, Director, Pre-Release Guidance Center, Chicago, Aug. 22, 1967.

7. The President's Commission on Law Enforcement and Administration of Justice, *Task Force Report: Corrections* (Washington: D. C.: U. S. Government Printing Office, 1967), p. 105.

8. Interview with Kilkeary, Aug. 22, 1967.

9. Interview with Myrl Alexander, Director, U.S. Bureau of Prisons, Washington, D.C., March 17, 1966.

10. Interview with Kilkeary, Aug. 22, 1967.

11. Donald T. Dickson, "Post-Institutional Treatment for Young Offenders: The Residential Half-Way House" (unpublished independent research project for Prof. Francis A. Allen, Law School, University of Chicago, 1964), pp. 34ff.

12. U.S. Congress, *An Act to Provide a System for the Treatment and Rehabilitation of Youth Offenders, to Improve the Administration of Criminal Justice, and for Other Purposes*, Public Law 865, 81st Cong., 2d Sess., 1950, p. 1085; and U.S. Congress, *An Act to Provide for the Care and Treatment of Juvenile Delinquents*, Public Law 666, 75th Cong., 3d Sess., 1938, p. 764.

13. Interview with Robert Nicholas, Director, Pre-Release Guidance Centers, United States Bureau of Prisons, Washington, D.C., Dec. 6, 1966.

14. *Ibid.*

15. Dickson, *op. cit.*, p. 23.

16. Larry Karacki, *Youthful Auto Theft Offender Study*, A Comparative Study of 632 YCA Auto Theft Offenders with 369 YCA Other Offenders (Washington, D.C.: Research and Editorial Branch, Division of Management, Bureau of Prisons, Jan. 1, 1966).

17. Reis H. Hall, Mildred Milazzo, and Judy Posner, *A Descriptive and Comparative Study of Recidivism in Pre-Release Guidance Center Releasees* (Washington, D.C.: U.S. Department of Justice, Bureau of Prisons, Dec. 28, 1966), pp. 4,9.

18. John J. Galvin (ed.), *Treating Youth Offenders in the Community*, A Report on Four Years' Experience with Pre-Release Guidance Centers (Washington, D.C.: Correctional Research Associates, under a grant by the Ford Foundation, June, 1966), p. 94.

19. *Ibid.*, p. 82.

20. *Ibid.*, p. 73.

21. Letter from Frank C. Eldridge, Director, Springfield College Guidance Center, New York City, Feb. 28, 1966.

22. Interview with Kenneth A. McDannell, Director, Pre-Release Guidance Center, Oakland, Calif., June 13, 1967.

23. Memorandum from William S. Garmon, Director, Ex-Prisoner Rehabilitation Study, Home Mission Board, Southern Baptist Convention, Chicago, Feb. 8, 1966.

24. Interview with Frank C. Eldridge, Director, Springfield College Guidance Center, New York City, June 10, 1966.

25. A. Richard Taft, "The Chicago Federal Pre-Release Guidance Center: A Study of a Half-Way House" (unpublished paper for Prof. Francis A. Allen, Law School, University of Chicago, 1965), p. 1.

26. Letter from Reis H. Hall, Chief, Research, Statistics, and Development, United States Department of Justice, Washington, D.C., June 22, 1967.

27. Interview with John Kilkeary, Director, Pre-Release Guidance Center, Chicago, Jan. 19, 1967.

28. Letter from Hall, June 22, 1967.

29. Interview with Kilkeary, Jan. 19, 1967.

30. Correspondence from W. R. Nelson, Assistant Director, District of Columbia Department of Corrections, Washington, D.C., Dec. 15, 1965.

31. "Guidance Center Procedures: Quantification and Appraisal," A research proposal for the Pre-Release Guidance Center, Kansas City, Mo., Oct., 1966. (Xeroxed.)

32. Correspondence from Daniel Glaser, Chairman, Sociology Department, University of Illinois, Champaign, Ill., May 17, 1967.

33. Interview with Gerald Collins, while he was Director, Pre-Release Guidance Center, Kansas City, Mo., Nov. 5, 1966.

34. Interview with Kilkeary, Jan. 19, 1967.

35. *Ibid.*

36. Interview with Clarence Guienze, Director, Pre-Release Guidance Center, Washington, D.C., March 17, 1966.

37. Interview with McDannell, June 13, 1967.

38. Interview with Nicholas, Dec. 6, 1966.

39. Interview with Collins, Nov. 5, 1966.

40. Memorandum from Garmon, Feb. 8, 1966.

41. Interview with Collins, Nov. 5, 1966.

42. "Project Design, Pre-Release Guidance Centers" (Washington, D.C.: Bureau of Prisons, July 15, 1961; rev. Sept., 1965), p. 1 (mimeographed). Cited hereafter as "Project Design."

43. "Project Design," p. 4.

44. Galvin, *op. cit.*, p. 60.

45. "Project Design," p. 4.

46. Interview with Nicholas, Dec. 6, 1966.

47. *Ibid.*

48. "Project Design," p. 9.

49. Interview with Eldridge, June 10, 1966.

50. *Ibid.*

51. Interview with Kilkeary, Aug. 22, 1967.

52. Interview with Edward M. McDermott, Employment Placement Specialist, Pre-Release Guidance Center, Chicago, Ill., Aug. 28, 1967.

Notes to CHAPTER 8

1. President's Commission on Law Enforcement and Administration of Justice, *Task Force Report: Corrections* (Washington: U.S. Government Printing Office, 1967), p. 143.

2. John E. Miller, "Use of Group Homes in Overall Department Delinquency Program" (Lansing, Mich.: Department of Social Services, March 16, 1966) (mimeographed).

3. Edgar Z. Friedenberg, *The Vanishing Adolescent* (New York: Dell Publishing Co., 1962), pp. 175-201.

4. Letter from E. Kent Hayes, Chief Probation Officer, Juvenile Court of Shawnee County, Topeka, Kan., March 11, 1966.

5. Letter from Benedict Alper, Lecturer in Criminology, Boston College, Newton, Mass., Oct. 12, 1966.

6. "Michael Nicolson *et al.* versus The Connecticut Halfway House, Inc.," *Connecticut Law Journal*, XXVII (March 29, 1966), p. 7.

7. LaMar T. Empey, George E. Newland, and Stephen G. Lubeck, *The Silverlake Experiment: A Community Study in Delinquency Rehabilitation, Progress Report No. 3* (Los Angeles: Youth Studies Center, University of Southern California, 1966), p. 116.

8. "Suit Against Halfway House Dismissed," *NCCD News*, XLIV (September-October, 1965), p. 7.

9. Interview with Edward C. Boyle, Casework Director, Salvation Army's Family Service Department, Los Angeles, Calif., June 14, 1967.

10. *Ibid.*

11. *Ibid.*

12. *Ibid.*

13. William Glasser, *Reality Therapy: A New Approach to Psychiatry* (New York: Harper and Row, 1965).

14. Interview with Boyle, June 14, 1967.

15. Empey, Newland, and Lubeck, *op. cit.*, p. 130.

16. Interview with John E. Riggs, Treatment Supervisor, Guided Group Interaction Unit, San Francisco, Calif., March 28, 1967.

17. *The Status of Current Research, Annual Report* (Sacramento, Calif.: Department of the Youth Authority, July, 1967), pp. 21, 22. Cited hereafter as "Current Research."

18. Marguerita Q. Warren, "The Community Treatment Project: An Integration of Theories of Causation and Correctional Practice," Paper presented at the Annual Conference of the Illinois Academy of Criminology, Chicago, May 14, 1965. (Available from California Youth Authority, Sacramento, Calif.)

19. *The Community Treatment Project After Five Years* (Sacramento, Calif.: Department of the Youth Authority, n.d.), p. 3. Cited hereafter as "Community Treatment After Five Years."

20. *Ibid.*

21. *Community Treatment Project, Progress Report* (Sacramento, Calif.: Department of the Youth Authority, Dec., 1965), pp. 11, 12.

22. *Community Treatment After Five Years*, p. 1.

23. *Current Research*, p. 22.

24. *Community Treatment After Five Years*, pp. 10, 11.

25. *A Report of the Juvenile Institutions Project* (New York: The Osborne Association and the National Council on Crime and Delinquency, September, 1966), p. 190. (Unedited draft prior to publication.)

26. *Community Treatment After Five Years*, pp. 10, 11.

Notes to CHAPTER 9

1. Letter from Edward C. Boyle, President, International Halfway House Association, Los Angeles, July 17, 1967.

2. Letter from Richard Rachin, Resident Director, J. Stanley Sheppard Youth Center, New York City, May 16, 1967.

3. *Ibid.*

4. *Ibid.*

5. *Ibid.*

6. *Ibid.*

7. *International Review of Criminal Policy, Nos. 7, 8* (New York: United Nations, January-July, 1955), p. 70.

8. Letter from Paul H. Hahn, Director, Court of Common Pleas, Juvenile Division, Cincinnati, Ohio, Oct. 3, 1966.

9. Charles S. Prigmore, "Corrections Blueprint for National Action on Manpower and Training," *Federal Probation*, XXVIII (September, 1964), p. 26.

l0. Alexander Sutherland Neill, *Summerhill: A Radical Approach to Child Rearing* (New York: Hart Publishing Co., 1960).

11. Interview with William Dickerson, Director, James Marshall Treatment Program, Southern California Reception Center-Clinic, Los Angeles, March 1, 1966.

12. Interview with Albert C. Wagner, Director, Division of Correction and Parole, Trenton, N.J., Jan. 10, 1966.

13. Interview with Ruby Violette, Supervisor, Halfway House, Women's Correctional Institution, Skowhegan, Maine, July 28, 1967.

14. J. Douglas Grant, "The Offender as Participant, Not Recipient, in the Correctional Process," Paper presented at the "Recent Developments in Criminology and Corrections," Lectures sponsored by the Centre of Criminology, University of Toronto, Toronto, Can., Feb. 7, 1966.

15. Bertram M. Beck, "Milestones in the National Effort to Prevent and Control Juvenile Delinquency," Paper presented at the National Conference on Juvenile Delinquency, sponsored by the U.S. Department of Health, Education, and Welfare, Washington, D.C., June 1, 1967.

16. Larry Dye, "New Careers," Paper presented at the National Conference on Juvenile Delinquency, sponsored by the U.S. Department of Health, Education, and Welfare, Washington, D.C., June 1, 1967.

17. Judith G. Benjamin, Marcia K. Freedman, and Edith F. Lynton, *Pros and Cons: New Roles for Non-Professionals in Corrections* (New York: National Committee on Employment of Youth, 1965), p. 91.

18. Letter from Rachin, May 16, 1967.

Notes to CHAPTER 10

1. Interview with Andrew Gillin, University of Chicago Law School student, regarding employment during summer of 1966, at the Brondbyhus Probation Hostel in Chicago.

2. Interview with Patrick T. Deehy, Research Associate, Robert Bruce House, during International Halfway House Association's third annual convention, Windsor, Ont., Apr. 24, 1966.

3. *Walton Village, A Residential Group Center for Dependent Teen-Age Boys* (Philadelphia: YMCA, 1967), pp. 23-24.

4. Interview with John E. Miller, Aftercare Coordinator, Department of Social Services, Lansing, Mich., Apr. 22, 1966.

5. Interview with Edward C. Boyle, Casework Director, Manhattan Project, Salvation Army, during International Halfway House Association's third annual convention, Windsor, Ont., Apr. 23, 1966.

6. Interview with Harry Vorrath, while Director, Woodsbend Camp, West Liberty, Ky., Dec. 8, 1965.

7. Lloyd W. McCorkle, Albert Elias, and F. Lovell Bixby, *The Highfields Story* (New York: Henry Holt and Co., 1958), p. 169.

8. Interview with John Wall, Director, Southfields, Anchorage, Ky., Dec. 6, 1965.

9. Interview with Gerald Collins, while he was Director, Federal Pre-Release Guidance Center, Kansas City, Mo., Nov. 5, 1966.

10. Walton Village, *op. cit.*

Notes to CHAPTER 11

1. Letter from E. Kent Hayes, Chief Probation Officer, Juvenile Court of Shawnee County, Topeka, Kan., March 11, 1966.

2. Interview with Milton Luger, Director, New York Division for Youth, New York City, Dec. 12, 1966.

3. Interview with Albert C. Wagner, Director, Division of Correction and Parole, Department of Institutions and Agencies, Trenton, N.J., Jan. 3, 1966.

4. Lloyd W. McCorkle, Albert Elias, and F. Lovell Bixby, *The Highfields Story* (New York: Henry Holt and Co., 1958), p. 166.

5. *Ibid.*, p. 165.

6. Interview with Thomas G. Stevens, Planning Director, Metropolitan Youth Commission, St. Louis, Mo., Nov. 4, 1966.

7. Interview with Robert Emmons, Director, Youth Farm, Peoria, Ill., Apr. 20, 1967.

8. Interview with Gerald Collins, while he was Director, Federal Pre-Release Guidance Center, Kansas City, Mo., Nov. 5, 1966.

9. Letter from Benedict Alper, Research Associate, Center for Studies in Criminal Justice, Law School, University of Chicago, June 5, 1966.

10. Interview with Dave Moore, Head Resident, Gateway Club, Chicago, Ill., Feb. 14, 1967.

11. Memorandum from William S. Garmon, Director, Ex-Prisoner Rehabilitation Study, Home Mission Board, Southern Baptist Convention, Chicago, Ill., Feb. 8, 1966.

12. Letter from Jack Dalton, Executive Director, In As Much, Inc., Seattle, Wash., Sept. 20, 1966.

Notes to CHAPTER 12

1. *Youth Commission Biennial Report, 1959-1960* (Springfield, Ill.: Illinois Youth Commission, 1961), p. 9.

2. "Residential Training Program a Success," *NCCD News*, XLIII (November-December, 1964), p. 5.

3. Interview with Virginia Burns, Chief, Training Section, U.S. Department of Health, Education, and Welfare, Washington, D.C., March 18, 1966.

4. Lloyd W. McCorkle, Albert Elias, and F. Lovell Bixby, *The Highfields Story* (New York: Henry Holt and Co., 1958), p. 136.

5. LaMar T. Empey, Maynard L. Erickson, and Max L. Scott, "The Provo Experiment in Delinquency Rehabilitation, Fifth Annual Progress Report, 1963-64" (Provo, Utah: Brigham Young Univ.). (mimeographed). p. 8

6. Interview with John Wall, Director, Southfields, Anchorage, Ky., Dec. 6, 1965.

7. "The MacLaren Vocational Center," Report on a special demonstration project conducted by the MacLaren School for Boys, Woodburn, Oregon in conjunction with the Youth Opportunity Center, Portland, Ore., July, 1967, p. 17. Cited hereafter as "MacLaren Vocational Center."

8. Richard M. Stephenson and Frank R. Scarpitti, *The Rehabilitation of Delinquent Boys*, A Final Report Submitted to the Ford Foundation (New Brunswick, N.J.: Rutgers — The State University, 1967), p. 23.

9. LaMar T. Empey, "The Provo Experiment: A Brief Review" (Los Angeles: Youth Studies Center, University of Southern California), p. 33 (mimeographed).

10. Interview with George Wolfe, Research Director, Shaw Residence, Washington, D.C., Feb. 23, 1966.

11. "MacLaren Vocational Center," p. 18.

12. Gilbert Geis, *The East Los Angeles Halfway House for Narcotics Addicts*, Report of a program conducted under a grant from the National Institute of Mental Health (MH-808) (Sacramento, Calif.: Institute for the Study of Crime and Delinquency, June, 1966), p. 98.

13. *Crofton House, A Community Oriented Halfway House for Local Offenders, Progress Report* (San Diego: San Diego State College, September 1, 1966), p. 78.

14. *Ibid.*, p. 79.

15. Empey, Erickson, and Scott, *op. cit.*, p. 23.

16. F. J. Roethlisberger and William J. Dickson, *Management and the Worker* (Cambridge, Mass.: Harvard University Press, 1947).

17. McCorkle, Elias, and Bixby, *op. cit.*, p. 100.

18. Stephenson and Scarpitti, *op. cit.*, p. 48.

19. *Walton Village, Residential Treatment Center, Interim Report, June 1, 1965-January 1, 1967* (Philadelphia: YMCA, 1967), p. 1. Cited hereafter as "Walton Village."

20. *Southfields Residential Group Center, A Four Year Report* (Anchorage, Ky.: Southfields, March, 1966), p. 31. Cited hereafter as "Southfields Report."

21. LaMar T. Empey, George E. Newland, and Stephen G. Lubeck, *The Silverlake Experiment: A Community Study in Delinquency Rehabilitation, Progress Report No. 3* (Los Angeles: Youth Studies Center, University of Southern California, 1966), p. 121.

22. *Southfields Report*, p. 31.

23. McCorkle, Elias, and Bixby, *op. cit.*, p. 102.

24. Stephenson and Scarpitti, *op. cit.*, p. 50.

25. *Southfields Report*, p. 24.

26. *Ibid.*, p. 6.

27. Stephenson and Scarpitti, *op. cit.*, p. 52.

28. S. R. Hathaway and J. C. McKinley, *Minnesota Multiphasic Personality Inventory* (rev.; New York: The Psychological Corporation, 1951).

29. Stephenson and Scarpitti, *op. cit.*, p. 55.

30. *Southfields Report*, p. 24.

31. McCorkle, Elias, and Bixby, *op. cit.*, p. 171.

32. Howard W. Polsky, *Cottage Six* (New York: John Wiley and Sons, Inc., 1962).

33. Edward M. Brooks and Larry Karacki, "Federal Pre-Release Guidance Centers," Preliminary study of the effectiveness of three centers during first full year of operation (Washington: Bureau of Prisons, June 8, 1964), pp. 2-4 (xeroxed).

34. H. Ashley Weeks, *Youthful Offenders at Highfields* (Ann Arbor: University of Michigan Press, 1958), p. 42.

35. *Ibid.*

36. *Walton Village*, p. 3.

37. McCorkle, Elias, and Bixby, *op. cit.*; and Weeks, *op. cit.*

38. See Chapter 9.

39. Stephenson and Scarpitti, *op. cit.*

40. *The Community Treatment Project After Five Years* (Sacramento, Calif.: Department of The Youth Authority, n.d.), p. 1. Cited hereafter as "Community Treatment After Five Years."

41. *The Status of Current Research, Annual Report* (Sacramento, Calif.: Department of the Youth Authority, July, 1967), p. 24. Cited hereafter as "Current Research."

42. *Community Treatment After Five Years*, p. 1.

43. *Ibid.*

44. *Ibid.*, pp. 5-6.

45. *Ibid.*

46. *Ibid.*, p. 6.

47. *Ibid.*, p. 7.

48. *Ibid.*, p. 12.

49. *Ibid.*, p. 6.

50. *Ibid.*

51. "MacLaren Vocational Center," p. 20.

52. "Analysis of Wisconsin's Foster and Group Home Program for Delinquent Juvenile Males on Aftercare," Research Project Summary, Project No. 66 (Madison, Wis.: Division of Corrections, October, 1965) (xeroxed).

53. *Ibid.*

54. Frederic L. Faust, "Determinants in the Use of Foster Care as a ReSocialization Resource for Youth on Aftercare Status" (Columbus, Ohio:

Ohio Youth Commission, Bureau of Probation Development, n.d.) (xeroxed).

55. Brooks and Karacki, *op. cit.*, p. 6.

56. *Ibid.*, p. 7.

57. *Ibid.*, p. 3.

58. *Ibid.*, p. 8.

59. *Ibid.*

60. *Ibid.*

61. Correspondence from Daniel Glaser, Chairman, Sociology Department, University of Illinois, Champaign, Ill., May 17, 1967.

62. Brooks and Karacki, *op. cit.*, p. 8.

63. *Ibid.*

64. *Ibid.*, p. 10.

65. *Ibid.* (summary page).

66. Reis H. Hall, Mildred Milazzo, and Judy Posner, *A Descriptive and Comparative Study of Recidivism in Pre-Release Guidance Center Releasees* (Washington, D.C.: U.S. Department of Justice, Bureau of Prisons, December 28, 1966), p. 9.

67. *Ibid.*

68. *Ibid.*, p. 3.

69. *Ibid.*, pp. 7-9.

70. *Pre-Release Guidance Center Study* (Washington D.C.: Bureau of Prisons, November 1, 1965), p. 2.

71. *Ibid.*, pp. 5, 6.

72. *Ibid.*, p. 6.

73. *Ibid.*, pp. 9, 10.

74. *Ibid.*, p. 7.

75. W. H. Hammond, C. P. Nuttall, J. M. Atkinson, "A Note on Dartmoor Releasees, 1961-62, with Particular Reference to the Problems of Parole for Long-term Ordinary Prisoners" (London: Home Office Research Unit, March, 1967) (mimeographed). Cited hereafter as "Dartmoor Releases."

76. *Ibid.*, p. 2.

77. *Ibid.*, p. 5.

78. *Ibid.*, p. 6.

79. *Ibid.*, pp. 5-7.

80. *Ibid.*, p. 11.

81. Weeks, *op. cit.*, pp. 122, 125.

82. McCorkle, Elias, and Bixby, *op. cit.*, p. 125.

83. *Ibid.*, p. 126.

84. Stephenson and Scarpitti, *op. cit.*, p. 66.

85. *Ibid.*, p. 108.

86. Empey, Newland, and Lubeck, *op. cit.*, p. 154.

87. *Ibid.*, p. 156.

88. *Current Research*, p. 25.

89. Harrison Gough, *CPI, California Psychological Inventory* (Palo Alto, Calif.: Consulting Psychologists Press, Inc., 1957).

90. *Community Treatment After Five Years*, p. 7.

91. McCorkle, Elias, and Bixby, *op. cit.*, p. 120.

92. *Ibid.*, pp. 119, 120.

93. Remarks by Leslie T. Wilkins, Professor, School of Criminology, University of California, before 14th National Institute on Crime and Delinquency, Anaheim, Calif., June 13, 1967.

94. Weeks, *op. cit.*, p. 62.

95. Stephenson and Scarpitti, *op. cit.*, p. 106.

96. *Community Treatment After Five Years*, p. 7.

97. Stephenson and Scarpitti, *op. cit.*, p. 107.

98. *Ibid.*, p. 109.

Notes to CHAPTER 13

1. President's Commission on Law Enforcement and Administration of Justice, *The Challenge of Crime in a Free Society* (Washington: U.S. Government Printing Office, 1967).

2. Harry Elmer Barnes and Negley K. Teeters, *New Horizons in Criminology* (3d ed.; Englewood Cliffs, N.J.: Prentice-Hall, Inc., 1959), pp. 361-63.

3. Francis A. Allen, *The Borderland of Criminal Justice* (Chicago: University of Chicago Press, 1964), p. 33.

4. *Ibid.*, p. 34.

5. *Ibid.*, p. 58.

6. *Ibid.*, p. 37.

7. President's Commission, *op. cit.*, p. 85.

8. John Conrad, *Crime and Its Correction* (Berkeley, Cal.: University of California Press, 1965), p. 281.

9. "Metamorphosis of a Marshmallow," *The Healthy Life*, ed. Norman P. Ross and Richard L. Williams (New York: Time Inc., 1966), pp. 58-63.

10. Conrad, *loc. cit.*

11. *Ibid.*, p. 269.

12. Edward M. Brooks and Larry Karacki, "Federal Pre-Release Guidance Centers," Preliminary study of the effectiveness of three centers during first full year of operation (Washington: Bureau of Prisons, June 8, 1964), p. 11 (xeroxed).

13. *Ibid.*, p. 12.

14. President's Commission, *op. cit.*, p. 55.

15. Allen, *op. cit.*, p. 60.

16. Remarks by Edward C. Boyle, President, International Halfway House Association, before 14th National Institute on Crime and Delinquency, June 13, 1967.

17. Walter Adams and Adrian Jaffe, "Government, the Universities and International Affairs: A Crisis in Identity," 90th Congress, 1st Session, House Doc. No. 120, 1967, pp. 14 & 15.

Index

Index

About the Authors

Oliver J. Keller, Jr. is presently Director of the Florida Division of Youth Services. He brings to this post a varied experience in youth work extending back twenty years, at which time he worked as a disc jockey on a Springfield, Illinois radio station, after his war service as a Navy navigator. His appeal to young people as a result of his unusual broadcast programs, his service as President of the Springfield Board of Education, and his experience as a civic leader in children's work, led to the creation of Boys' Farm, a private institution for delinquents and dependents in Sangamon County. Appointed by the governor to the Illinois Youth Commission, he served here for three years, one year as chairman. He holds an MA degree in Sociology from Northern Illinois University. After completing the course work for his Doctorate at the University of Chicago, during which time he conducted a national survey of half-way houses, he was appointed by Governor Claude Kirk to his present post in 1967. Professional affiliations include the Vice-Presidency both of the National Association of State Juvenile Delinquency Administrators and of the National Association of Training Schools and Juvenile Agencies. He is a member of the Professional Council of the National Council on Crime and Delinquency.

Benedict S. Alper is Visiting Lecturer in Criminology at Boston College, Chestnut Hill, Massachusetts. He has also taught at the Rutgers Law School in Newark, and the New School for Social Research in New York City. His initial apprenticeship in the field was as probation officer in the Boston Juvenile Court and as correctional officer in the Massachusetts State Prison. Professional experience includes posts at the state, national and international level: as research director of a New York Legislative Committee, Field Secretary of the American Parole Association, chief statistician and special assistant to the Director, Federal Bureau of Prisons, first Chief of the Section of Social Defense at the United Nations. In the United States Army, at the end of World War II, he administered five prisons in Trieste. He has served as consultant to the American Foundation of Philadelphia and as Research Associate to the Center of Studies in Criminal Justice, University of Chicago Law School. He participated in the Third United Nations Crime Congress in Stockholm in 1965, and as Consultant to the United Nations Consultative Group on Crime in Geneva in 1968. Most recently he was invited to confer with the Judges of the Indian Courts on the Navajo Reservation in New Mexico on problems related to the juvenile court and probation. He is the author of several books and numerous articles in professional journals.